Jesus' Directions for the Future

A Source and Redaction-History Study
of the Use of the Eschatological Traditions
in Paul and in the Synoptic Accounts
of Jesus' Last Eschatological Discourse

NEW GOSPEL STUDIES 9

Jesus' Directions for the Future

A Source and Redaction-History Study
of the Use of the Eschatological Traditions
in Paul and in the Synoptic Accounts
of Jesus' Last Eschatological Discourse

by
Allan J. McNicol

MERCER

ISBN 0-86554-497-2   MUP/H390

BS
2575.2
.M34
1996

Jesus' Directions for the Future
Copyright ©1996
Mercer University Press, Macon, Georgia USA
All rights reserved
Printed in the United States of America
First printing November 1996

The paper used in this publication meets the minimum requirements
of American National Standard for Information Sciences—
Permanence of Paper for Printed Library Materials,
ANSI Z39.48-1984.

Library of Congress Cataloging-in-Publication Data

McNicol, Allan J. (Allan James), 1939–   .
Jesus' directions for the future : a source and redaction-history study
of the use of the eschatological traditions in Paul
and in the synoptic accounts of Jesus' last eschatological discourse
/ by Allan J. McNicol.
xiv+210pp.—(New Gospel Studies ; 9)
Includes bibliographical references and indexes.
ISBN 0-86554-497-2 (alk. paper).
1. Bible. N.T. Matthew xxiv—Criticism, interpretation, etc.
2. Bible. N.T. Luke xxi—Criticism, interpretation, etc.
3. Bible. N.T. Mark xiii—Criticism, interpretation, etc.
4. Bible. N.T. Thessalonians—Criticism, interpretation, etc.
5. Griesbach hypothesis (Synoptics criticism).
6. Eschatology—Biblical teaching.
7. Jesus Christ—Teachings. I. Title. II. Series.
BS2575.2.M34   1996
225.6'6—dc20   96-5041

CIP

Table of Contents

Foreword

Professor Allan McNicol's monograph is especially significant for three reasons. First, it is a landmark work in source criticism. The theory that the synoptic gospels were composed in the sequence Matthew–Luke–Mark, known as the Two-Gospel Hypothesis, has established itself as the major alternative to the still widely accepted Two-Source Theory. Compositional work assuming the sequence Matthew–Luke–Mark has been under way for some time. But with McNicol's book we now have a major treatment of an extensive set of synoptic texts, far more detailed than anything heretofore available. McNicol's work can serve the source critic as a significant test of the exegetical usefulness of the Two-Gospel Hypothesis.

Second, McNicol offers his readers a comprehensive analysis of the eschatological tradition beginning with the important texts in Paul's Thessalonian correspondence. Readers are now in a position to see what difference it makes in understanding Jesus' directions for the future when one begins with Paul and then traces the development of the tradition through Matthew, Luke, and Mark. McNicol's conclusions are credible and important for the church.

Third, this monograph is destined to play an important role in the question of establishing a reliable historical basis for dating the gospels. At least for those who are willing to learn from synoptic research assuming the Two-Gospel Hypothesis, McNicol offers good reasons for dating Matthew's Gospel in the period just prior to the fall of the temple. On this basis, there is no reason for dating Luke and Mark long thereafter, not more than a decade or so.

William R. Farmer

Introduction and Acknowledgments

This project had its beginnings in Jerusalem in April 1984, at the Symposium on the Interrelations among the Gospels. During the symposium I presented a paper on behalf of a research team of scholars defending the Neo-Griesbach or Two-Gospel Hypothesis. The title of the paper was "The Composition of the Synoptic Eschatological Discourse."[1] After the paper had received searching responses from Christopher Tuckett,[2] and M.-É. Boismard,[3] Professor Peter Stuhlmacher suggested that this material should be expanded extensively into a monograph. The subject matter of the paper in Jerusalem was confined to an explanation of the composition of Luke 12:35-48, 17:20-37, and 21:5-36, on the assumption that Luke utilized Matthew 24:1-51 as a major source; and of the composition of Mark 13:1-37, on the presupposition that Mark had access to the texts of Matthew and Luke. Stuhlmacher observed that he had noticed that the closest echoes between Paul and the Synoptics on eschatological matters usually came in Matthew. He suggested that further investigation into why this was so could be helpful to the case the Griesbach team was making concerning the source and redaction history of the Synoptic accounts of Jesus' Last Eschatological Discourse. This monograph is an attempt to follow up these suggestions.

In essence, in this work the task is to explain how a number of eschatological sayings attributed to Jesus were utilized both by Paul and the Synoptic writers to give direction on certain issues concerning the future within the earliest Christian messianic communities. Although we can determine only in incoherent form the nature of the collections of these sayings and interpretations of biblical texts on eschatological matters, there is some evidence that very early they functioned to form a basic *Gestalt*, namely, that the people of God were living in perilous times, needed to brace for a coming crisis, and that only after they had

---

[1]The full proceedings of the Symposium have been published as *The Interrelations of the Gospels*, BETL 95, ed. David L. Dungan (Leuven: Leuven University Press/Peeters, 1990). The Two-Gospel Hypothesis or revised Griesbach Hypothesis argues that Matthew was the first Gospel written, that Luke used Matthew as a major source; and that Mark blended these first two Gospels in a special Sitz im Leben to create a third Gospel with its own peculiar theological agenda. At the Jerusalem symposium advocates of the Two-Gospel Hypothesis discussed their views on the source question vis-à-vis other positions with advocates of the popular Two-Source Theory and the Multi-Stage Hypothesis.

[2]Ibid., 63-76.

[3]Ibid., 265-288.

survived a time of martyrdom and apostasy would the faithful be vindicated with the appearance of a new world. Here I will show how this common theological framework, to which these sayings contributed, was deepened and expanded by Paul and the Synoptics into an organized picture of reality concerning the future.

Indeed, as Richard Bauckham's recent study on *The Conversion of the Nations* has shown, the author of Revelation later develops this focus. At the end-time, the praise of God, already apparent in the early Christian messianic communities, will be broadened so that it will be offered by all the nations.[4] Thus the writings of the prophet John function to complete the canonical treatment of this theological vision of the future triumph of the Lordship of Christ which already had emerged in the earliest Christian communities, taken shape in an inchoate form in Paul, and developed a more definite configuration in the Synoptic Eschatological Discourses.

This study will not deal with the book of Revelation. We will be content to undertake the slightly less ambitious task of observing how both Paul in the Thessalonian letters and the Synoptic authors in Matthew 24, Luke 21, and Mark 13, shaped and articulated, for their own theological purposes, certain fragmentary traditions about Jesus' teachings on the future which they had received. Since the writings of Paul and the Synoptic Gospels became part of the canon of the church, and since these compositions had great influence in providing the basis for subsequent discussions in Christian theology about the future, it is defensible to confine this discussion within these boundaries.

At the outset, let me point out two important features of this study. First, beginning with a discussion about the origin of the collections of verbal sayings attributed to Jesus that were used in early Christian catechesis, I will attempt to trace the process of how these eschatological traditions were formed into what became known as the Synoptic accounts of Jesus' Last Eschatological Discourse. Most contemporary treatments of the subject focus on only one version of the Discourse—usually Mark's; I will attempt to account for the composition of each particular version of the Last Eschatological Discourse in all three of the Synoptic Gospels. Thus, this work is much more diachronic in scope. However, in order to accomplish this task, I have found it impossible to engage fully the voluminous secondary literature on each version of the Last Eschatological Discourse in the gospels. Instead, I have had to settle for entering into dialogue with some major representatives of alternative positions.

The closest recent work in the secondary literature that approximates this approach is that of David Wenham.[5] From his monograph and several related

---

[4]Richard Bauckham, *The Climax of Prophecy: Studies on the Book of Revelation* (Edinburgh: T.&T. Clark, 1993) 238-337.

[5]David Wenham, *The Rediscovery of Jesus' Eschatological Discourse.* Gospel Per-

articles I have learned much. Wenham has also noted the close literary relationships between Paul and Matthew on eschatological matters. But methodologically
my work moves in a very different direction from the claim that each one of the
Synoptic writers had access to an extensive pre-Synoptics version of Jesus' Last
Discourse.[6] Instead, I take the position that the author of Matthew played the
critical role of being the composer of the earliest version of Jesus' Last Eschatological Discourse; the later accounts of this Discourse, both in the Synoptics and
in early Christian literature, were heavily dependent upon the Matthean account.

Second, as I have already noted, this work proceeds on the basis of the Neo-
Griesbach or Two-Gospel Source Hypothesis.[7] For some time critics have called
for examples of how this source hypothesis, in the arena of Redaction Criticism,
actually works with the text. The detailed textual analysis of a number of gospel
texts in this study furnishes an answer to that question. The textual analysis is
supplemented by a number of original synopses. Both the synopses and textual
analyses are designed to help the reader see how the use of our source theory
accounts for these texts in their present forms. The Greek text herein is based on
Nestle-Aland, *Novum Testamentum Graece*, 26. Auflage (Stuttgart: Deutsche
Bibelstiftung, 1981). Where my choice of text differs from Nestle-Aland, this is
indicated by brackets in the synopses; and usually there is a brief discussion on
the matter.

It is important to note that this study does not attempt to furnish an argument
to prove that the Griesbach Hypothesis is true, nor that its major rival, the Two-
Source Theory, is wrong. Rather, similar to the adherents of other source hypoth-
eses, I assume the source theory with which I am working has validity. What I
am attempting to do is to show that historical insight and advances in understanding the origins and development of the early Christian doctrine about the
future can be made through use of this methodology.

Thus, procedurally, in the first chapter, I state the case for the existence of
collections of verbal tradition on eschatological matters attributed to Jesus that
were transmitted regularly among the earliest Christian communities. In the
second and third chapters I give evidence for the existence of these traditions
from 1 and 2 Thessalonians and show how Paul utilized them to address critical
issues about the future faced by the mission communities he founded. Then, in
the last section of the book, in chapters 4, 5, and 6, I discuss how Matthew,

---

spectives 4 (Sheffield: JSOT Press, 1984).
    [6]Ibid., 365.
    [7]The reader is directed to the entry of David L. Dungan, "Two-Gospel Hypothesis,"
Anchor Bible Dictionary 6 (New York: Doubleday, 1992) 671-679. Dungan furnished a
thorough bibliography of the secondary literature that provides the theoretical basis for
the Neo-Griesbach Hypothesis.

Luke, and Mark composed their respective versions of the Last Eschatological Discourse, and how they shaped their versions of the Discourse according to their theological concerns. A brief epilogue will summarize the results.

This project could never have come to completion without the encouragement of many people. I am particularly thankful to Lamar Cope, David Dungan, David Peabody, and Philip Shuler, longtime members of the Two-Gospel Research team, who have encouraged me throughout this project. Professor Earl Ellis of Southwestern Baptist Theological Seminary read carefully the first three chapters and made a number of suggestions that have, in my estimation, improved the final product. Professor William Farmer of the University of Dallas, and editor of the series *New Gospel Studies*, has been a source of great encouragement throughout the project. Of course, the final product is totally my work; none of these colleagues should be held responsible for any infelicities in the argumentation that may emerge.

I am deeply grateful to the Institute for Christian Studies for a research leave in the spring of 1994 that enabled me to almost finish the project. Special thanks are also due to Jackie Hays, Julie Chamberlain, and Linden Penland for their yeoman task in helping with word-processing duties; and also to my family who were and remain fully supportive of both this writing project and my work in gospel studies.

Finally, I am deeply indebted to my deceased parents Alice and Donald McNicol who raised me in the Christian faith and instilled in me a deep love for the gospels. This work, which is dedicated to them, is but a small token of my appreciation.

—Allan J. McNicol

Abbreviations

AB	The Anchor Bible
AnBib	Analecta Biblica
ASNU	Acta seminarii neotestamentici upsaliensis
BBB	Bonner Biblische Beiträge
BETL	Bibliotheca ephemeridum theologicarum lovaniensium
BZNW	Beihefte zur *Zeitschrift für die neutestamentliche Wissenschaft*
ConBNT	Coniectanea biblica, New Testament series
ConNT	Coniectanea neotestamentica
EKKNT	Evangelisch-Katholischer Kommentar zum Neuen Testament
ETS	Erfurter theologische Studien
FRLANT	Forschungen zur Religion und Literatur des Alten und Neuen Testaments
HNTC	Harper's New Testament Commentaries
HUT	Hermeneutische Untersuchungen zur Theologie
JSNTSSup	*Journal for the Study of the New Testament* supplement series
JSOT	*Journal for the Study of the Old Testament*
LEC	Library of Early Christianity
NCB	New Century Bible
NGS	New Gospel Studies
NIGTC	The New International Greek Testament Commentary
NovTSup	*Novum Testamentum*, supplements
SBLDS	Society of Biblical Literature Dissertation Series
SBLMS	SBL Monograph Series
SBLSP	SBL Seminar Papers
SHT	Studies in Historical Theology
SNTSMS	Society for New Testament Studies Monograph Series
WBC	Word Biblical Commentary
WUNT	Wissenschaftliche Untersuchungen zum Neuen Testament

I

Sayings of Jesus
Common to the Synoptic
Eschatological Discourse
and the Thessalonian Correspondence

1.
The Formation of the Gospel Tradition
A Discussion of Procedure

To what extent does certain material in the last eschatological discourse of Jesus (Matt 24:1-51; Mk 13:1-37; Lk 21:5-36), which has echoes in Paul's letters to the Thessalonians, indicate that there is a direct literary relationship between Thessalonians and the Synoptic Gospels?[1] Or does the literary evidence indicate that it is more likely that both the Synoptic authors and Paul are dependent on a common tradition of the sayings of Jesus? And if there were such a tradition, what was its origin and earliest history? Before we proceed to take up these issues by looking at the texts, a brief review of some of the research and a discussion of a few of the methodological problems encountered in the modern discussion is in order. That will be the focus of this opening chapter.

Discussion of this issue was stimulated by a bold proposal, in 1938, of Bernard Orchard.[2] Assuming a traditional position on the dating of the Thessalonian correspondence (50–51 CE), Orchard argued that the verbal parallels between Matthew and Thessalonians were so striking, and the order of the wording, phraseology, and ideas of the two was so similar, one must infer direct literary dependence between them. Orchard concluded it was Paul who was dependent upon Matthew.

Aside from a question arising from Orchard's view of both Matthean priority and its assumed very early dating (before Thessalonians), the essay was not argued form critically. Thus, at the time, Orchard's conclusions were disregarded on the grounds of both his presuppositions and methodology.

Nevertheless, the article did fulfill a valuable function. It succeeded in isolating several passages in the eschatological discourses of Matthew and Luke on

---

[1]Numerous commentators have drawn attention to an apparent configuration of literary relationships between the Pauline Thessalonian correspondence and the Synoptic eschatological material. B. Rigaux, *Saint Paul: Les Èpitres aux Thessaloniciens* (Paris: J. Gabalda, 1956) 95-105, presents the entire literary evidence in parallel columns as well as an accompanying commentary on the history of the discussion. It is evident that some of Rigaux's work is heavily dependent upon G. R. Beasley-Murray, *Jesus and the Future: An Examination of the Criticism of the Eschatological Discourse, Mark 13, with Special Reference to the Little Apocalypse Theory* (London: Macmillan, 1954) esp. 232-34.

[2]J. B. Orchard, "Thessalonians and the Synoptic Gospels," *Biblica* 19 (1938) 19-42.

the one hand and in Thessalonians on the other that did appear to have definite literary connections.[3] We thus learned that any *adequate* assessment of the composition of the Synoptic eschatological discourses must take into consideration that, at the very least, echoes of the use of similar material are found in Paul.

At the end of World War II C. H. Dodd also found significant parallels between Matthew and Paul.[4] Dodd argued that there were strong thematic connections between the respective eschatological scenarios in Paul and the gospel of Matthew as a whole. This could be seen in the way that both writers distinguished between the kingdom of Christ and the kingdom of God; both referred to the anticipated return of Christ by using the word παρουσία and both asserted that after the παρουσία comes the τέλος (1 Cor 15:24/ Matt 24:6, 13, 14).[5] Dodd also detected important similarities in intra-Jewish polemic as carried on by both Paul and Matthew (1 Thess 2:15-16; Matt 23:34-36).[6] His conclusion was that it was impossible that Paul had read Matthew; rather both Paul and Matthew had made use of common early sayings of Jesus tradition (διδαχή).[7] However, this did not entail that there was either a direct literary connection between the two or that they derived these common ideas from the same literary source; only that both Matthew and Paul made use of similar tradition.

In a later article Dodd argued that Paul, in the process of founding mission churches, and in association with a presentation of the Kerygma, habitually utilized a pattern of catechetical teaching (τύπος διδαχῆς) among his converts.[8] This catechesis typically concluded with a list of motives for obeying the teaching. These motives were cast in the form of eschatological catechesis and were used for hortatory purposes. He supposed that the catechesis itself was derived from early Christian eschatological formulations which had their origin in the Jesus tradition (cf. 1 Thess 5:3 ‖ Lk 21:34-36). Dodd formulated the thesis that the same eschatological catechesis that appears in parenetical sections of the Pauline epistles was edited into the composition of the Synoptic eschatological discourses.[9] This explained why the Synoptic eschatological discourses ended

---

[3]A sample of texts that attracted the attention of Orchard can be listed as follows: 1 Thess 2:14-16 ‖ Matt 23:29-38 ‖ Lk 11:47-51; 1 Thess 4:16-17 ‖ Matt 24:30-31; 1 Thess 5:1-2 ‖ Matt 24:42-43; 1 Thess 5:3 ‖ Lk 21:34-36; 2 Thess 2:1-10 ‖ Matt 24:4, 6, 11-13, 24, 27, 31 ‖ Mk 13:5, 7, 22, 27 ‖ Lk 21:8.

[4]C. H. Dodd, "Matthew and Paul," *Expository Times* 58 (1946–1947) 293-98.

[5]Ibid., 293.

[6]Ibid., 296-97.

[7]Ibid., 293, 297.

[8]Cf. Rom 6:17. C. H. Dodd, "The Primitive Catechism and the Sayings of Jesus," *More New Testament Studies* (Grand Rapids: Eerdmans, 1968) 12-13.

[9]Ibid., 16.

with direct eschatological exhortation and a similar feature was found in the pare-netical sections toward the end of the Pauline letters (Matt 24:36-51; Mk 13:33-37; Lk 21:34-36; cf. 1 Thess 4:13-5:11). According to Dodd, these eschatological parenetical appeals had a similar *Sitz im Leben*: the catechesis that took place within the earliest Christian communities.[10]

On this basis a way was put forward to account for the verbal parallels in Thessalonians and the Synoptic eschatological discourses. Both Paul and the gospel writers utilized the common terminology that they found in very early Christian eschatological catechesis. This catechesis was not direct source material for the Jesus tradition but may have been derived from it.

G. R. Beasley-Murray has expounded a version of this thesis in his recent works.[11] He argued that not only the endings of Jesus' last discourse, but the foundational materials for the entire speech have been drawn from disparate eschatological sayings of Jesus.[12] The gospel writers found these sayings em-bedded in the catechesis of the earliest Christian communities and thus these say-ings were not derived from an earlier apocalypse. (The latter view, in some form or other, has been a popular explanation for the earliest form of the Synoptic Eschatological Discourse.)[13] In this view, Paul knew some of these sayings through his knowledge of the earliest catechesis which he received and trans-

---

[10]Ibid., 16-20. Dodd, in *The Apostolic Preaching and its Developments: Three Lectures with an Appendix on Eschatology and History* (repr. New York: Harper & Bros. 1964 = 1936) 37-38 did vary from this pattern by saying that 2 Thess 1:7-10 and 2:3-10 were derived from a Jewish or Jewish Christian apocalypse which had possibly come into being when Caligula (37–41 CE) attempted to bring the Roman standards into the temple precincts.

[11]G. R. Beasley-Murray, "Second Thoughts on the Composition of Mark 13," *New Testament Studies* 29 (1983): 414-20; also Beasley-Murray's *Jesus and the Kingdom of God* (Grand Rapids: Eerdmans, 1986) 323; "The Vision on the Mount: The Eschatological Discourse of Mark 13," *Ex Auditu* 6 (1990): 39, 42; and the revision of his earlier work on *Jesus and the Future* (1954), now entitled *Jesus and the Last Days: The Interpretation of the Olivet Discourse* (Peabody MA: Hendrickson, 1993) 350-65.

[12]Beasley-Murray, "Vision on the Mount," 42, argues that the core of this eschatologi-cal catechesis in Jesus' last Discourse is found in Mark 13. There it centers on four groups of sayings: (1) Sayings on the Distress of Israel (13:14, 19); (2) Sayings on the Distress of the Church (13:9, 11); (3) Sayings on Pseudo-Messiahs and the True Messiah (13:21, 24-26); (4) Sayings on the Parousia and Watchfulness (13:26-27) and the parable of the Doorkeeper behind 13:34-36.

[13]The idea that the Last Eschatological Discourse is an expansion of an earlier Jewish or Christian apocalypse has a long history in critical discussion. See G. R. Beasley-Murray, "Jesus and the Future," 33-80. An influential, fairly recent major analysis of Mark 13 which argues on behalf of a version of this position is R. Pesch, *Naherwartung-en: Tradition und Redaktion in Mk 13* (Düsseldorf: Patmos, 1968) 215-23. However, in later writings Pesch gave up this view.

mitted. Thus, as with Dodd, a case can be made for the view that the common parallels and echoes in Jesus' sayings on eschatological matters in the Synoptics and Paul came from a common origin: eschatological teaching material.

However, both the work of Dodd and Beasley-Murray assume these sayings of Jesus were structured in an early stage of the development of the gospel tradition, and embedded in certain versions of eschatological catechesis used in the church. This presupposition about the formation of the gospel tradition was part and parcel of the whole form critical enterprise which supplied the basic raison d'être for so much of the study of the gospels during the past generation. But should an alternative model for the development of the Jesus tradition be considered: namely, that units of Jesus tradition were collected at the earliest stages of the Jesus movement and that these collections, handed down by traditioners in the church, were used by Paul in his teaching, alluded to in his letters, and incorporated at a later time into the composition of the Synoptic gospels? A strong case can be made for the latter perspective.

Problems Encountered by the Form-Critical Model

For classical form criticism, the sayings in the gospels attributed to Jesus are basically deposits of early Christian material which derived primarily from the oral mission preaching, catechesis, communal life, and controversies of the post-Easter community.[14] But conclusions about the formation of the gospel tradition, based on this model of viewing the development of tradition, can no longer be accepted at face value.[15] E. Earle Ellis, working closely with Peter Stuhlmacher,

---

[14]Martin Dibelius, *From Tradition to Gospel*, trans. from the rev. 2nd ed. (1933) of *Die Formgeschichte des Evangeliums* (New York: Charles Scribners, 1934) 233-65; for a modern restatement of this position that owes much to Dibelius, see W. Kelber, *The Oral and the Written Gospel: The Hermeneutics of Speaking and Writing in the Synoptic Tradition, Mark, Paul, and Q.* (Philadelphia: Fortress, 1983) 15-16, 24-26, 28-29, 34-36. Although this may not be the intention of a good number of the form critics with respect to the eschatological material attributed to Jesus, this position has given birth to an interesting loophole. If certain esoteric expectations such as the appearance of the Son of Man on the clouds, the anticipation of the sound of the last trumpet, etc., can be moved into the slot of the "post-Easter community," Jesus would no longer be held accountable for this language with its assumed attendant worldview of a radical end to the current space-time in history. Such material was the product of a few fanatics in the early church. Since it did not come from Jesus, the gospels can be saved for theological purposes. Thus, through the use of literary-critical methodology, a potential offense can be removed from taking the teaching of the earthly Jesus seriously. Such a bias especially pervaded the work of J. A. T. Robinson, *Jesus and His Coming* (Philadelphia: Westminster, 1979), and must be taken into serious consideration in evaluating the scientific validity of his and similar other works.

[15]R. Riesner, "Der Ursprung der Jesus-Uberlieferung," *Theologische Zeitschrift* 38

has noted that this model is open to very serious question because it is built on dubious assumptions about the formation of the gospel tradition.[16] These major assumptions bear noting.

1. The (written) gospel tradition only began to cohere after the vivid expectation of the near end of the age began to fade in the church.

2. The gospel accounts were composed both from certain *remembrances* of Jesus' teachings and deeds and oral material generated in the life of the post-Easter church. These materials were freely edited by the gospel writers. The possibility that there were pre-Easter (oral or written) collections of Jesus material was not considered seriously.[17]

3. The compositional framework of the gospels, including geographical references and the chronological scheme of the writing, was almost entirely the editorial creation of the gospel writers.

4. Words of the heavenly Christ received by the prophets in their post-Easter assemblies were intermingled in the gospel tradition with remembered sayings of the earthly Jesus.

5. The gospel tradition gradually developed over time, growing from small units to ever-increasing larger ones.

6. The history of development of the Jesus in the gospels may be traced most accurately on the basis of the Two-Source Hypothesis.

These assumptions, which have served as essential presuppositions for much of the work done by the form critics, have been exposed, one by one, as highly questionable as to their validity.[18] Put together, they can no longer serve without qualification as the methodological basis for a coherent model to reconstruct the earliest history of the gospel tradition.

Essentially, the impression is left that these presuppositions, which under-girded the major form-critical studies, turned the gospel tradition into a massive eerie abstraction. The basic problem is that these literary theories were not informed by concrete studies as to how traditions deriving from a teacher on sacred matters were transmitted and remembered in the first century of our era in Palestine and adjacent areas of the Greco-Roman world. Instead, as is well known, gospel form criticism gained its basic models from studies in the oral folklore of vastly different cultures at other times. It is highly questionable that

---

(1982): 493-94; P. Stuhlmacher, "The Theme: The Gospel and the Gospels," in *The Gospel and the Gospels*, ed. Stuhlmacher (Grand Rapids: Eerdmans, 1991) 1-25. This volume was originally published in 1983 as *Das Evangelium und die Evangelien. Vörtrage vom Tübinger Symposium 1982*, in which see also E. Earle Ellis, "Gospels Criticism: A Perspective on the State of the Art," 26-54.

[16]Ellis, "Gospels Criticism," 38; Stuhlmacher, "Gospel and the Gospels," 2-4.

[17]Cf. Riesner, "Jesus-Uberlieferung," 494.

[18]Ellis, "Gospels Criticism," 38-43.

these studies are appropriate to serve as models for a literate culture such as we find among the Jews and godfearers in the Eastern Mediterranean cities of the first century. Thus, it is very doubtful such a model of the formation of the gospel tradition can allow us to account for and understand the connections between similar sayings of Jesus echoed in Paul's letters and the Synoptic accounts. Specifically, the theory that the eschatological sayings, attributed to Jesus in the Synoptics, were formulated in early Christian preaching, parenesis, and catechesis, and then through a process of radical editing found their way into the gospel tradition, is implausible.

With this in mind, it would seem important for our purposes to give attention to those recent studies that have focused on the origin of the collections of Jesus' sayings within the wider context of a study of the process of the transmission of all early Christian tradition. Then, and only then, can we be in a position to focus on the issue of what Paul and the gospel writers knew about the Jesus tradition and how they utilized it.

An Alternative Model to Account for
the Transmission of the Sayings of Jesus

It is in this context that the constructive contributions of Birger Gerhardsson should be reevaluated.[19] Following the lead of his teacher Harold Riesenfeld,[20] Gerhardsson drew a strong distinction between the sayings attributed to Jesus that were frequently quoted in early Christian kerygmatic preaching and catechesis, on the one hand, and the formulation of the parenesis and catechesis that was addressed to Christian converts in letters such as the epistles of Paul and James. Gerhardsson argued that it was the former that provides the substrata for what would later become the gospel tradition, and not the latter, as many of the form critics appeared to presuppose.[21] The origin of the collection of the Jesus tradition was to be found in Jesus' conscious teaching process of handing on his message to the disciples; and ultimately the same process continued among the teachers in the post-Easter community.[22]

---

[19]B. Gerhardsson, *Memory and Manuscript: Oral Tradition and Written Transmission in Rabbinic Judaism and Early Christianity* ASNU 22 (Lund: C. W. K. Gleerup, 1961); *Tradition and Transmission in Early Christianity* ConNT 20 (Lund: C. W. K. Gleerup, 1964); *The Origins of the Gospel Traditions* (Philadelphia: Fortress, 1979).

[20]H. Riesenfeld, "The Gospel Tradition and its Beginnings," in *The Gospel Tradition: Essays* (Philadelphia: Fortress, 1970) 1-29. (This article first appeared in 1957.)

[21]Gerhardsson, *Origins of the Gospel Traditions*, 38-40.

[22]Ibid. Procedurally, the process may be described in the following way. Early Christian believers in Jerusalem, Galilee, Transjordan, and places like Antioch received credible accounts and reports about Jesus and his mission from various people (primarily the twelve, other apostles, disciples, partisans, and sympathetic families) who were

This process of transmission of the sayings of Jesus must be clearly distinguished from the occurrence of parenesis which we find in the epistles. The latter alludes to and reinforces the message of the earlier transmitted verbal tradition of Jesus. This is why the Sermon on the Mount (a collection[s] of verbal tradition derived from the transmission of material from a first-century Jewish teacher [Jesus], which was remembered and nourished within the earliest Palestinian Christian communities), is quite different in form and structure from the epistle of James; the latter is a letter that purports to come from Jesus' brother and is a second level of parenetic exhortation to the churches based on the assumption that they already, on a primary level, had knowledge of the Jesus tradition.[23] In keeping with this view of the transmission of the Jesus tradition, the gospel eschatological discourses would then be an example of the culmination of the process of collecting verbal tradition rather than a collection of parenetic exhortations to appropriate conduct in view of the approaching end which we find in the epistles. Thus, when we understand this distinction we have the answer as to why there are so few direct quotes from the Jesus tradition in Paul and other epistles. This tradition, in at least summary form, is presupposed as already being taught to converts when they received the Christian story.

Gerhardsson has argued that this model of how the verbal Jesus tradition arose and was transmitted in the earliest Christian communities is fully congruent with our knowledge of how tradition was transmitted within the multilayered Judaism of that era.[24] Although some of the presuppositions he held concerning the procedures for oral transmission of tradition in Judaism have been strongly disputed, Gerhardsson's mature positions on how the first-century Jewish teachers

---

knowledgeable of the earthly mission of Jesus. The term for the reception of this information was παραλαμβάνειν (1 Cor 11:23; 15:3; Gal 1:9). In turn, this information was handed over (παραδίδοναι) to converts in the churches (cf. 1 Cor 11:23). Paul's story would be typical. He spent his early Christian years in the churches of the Transjordan and Antioch. There he had access to those who would have received this information, and he certainly transmitted it to others. This body of verbal information stemming from Jesus, and those influenced by his impact, was called the tradition (παράδοσις) (1 Cor 11:2; 2 Thess 2:15; 3:6). Gentile believers were also taught this tradition and were exhorted to hold fast to it (1 Cor 11:2; 15:1; cf. 2 Thess 3:6).

[23]Dale C. Allison, Jr. "The Pauline Epistles and the Synoptic Gospels: The Pattern of the Parallels," *New Testament Studies* 28 (1982): 22, has come to recognize this point in connection with the study of Paul's epistles. However, although recognizing that the epistles were not written to initiate one into the tradition but to discuss issues in the church subsequent to the reception of the tradition, he overstates the matter when he says "the substance of Paul's (Jesus) tradition and the mechanics of its transmission are forever hid from our eyes."

[24]B. Gerhardsson, "The Gospel Tradition," in *The Interrelations of the Gospels*, BETL 95, ed. David Dungan (Leuven: Leuven University Press/Peeters; Macon GA: Mercer University Press, 1990) 499-502.

passed on their interpretations of Torah to successors with considerable care and clarity appear to be methodologically sound.

In essence, Gerhardsson claims that primarily in the Palestinian Jewish community of the first century of our era there were authoritative teachers on Torah. These teachers programmatically passed on their knowledge of Torah to others, both orally through memorization and in written form by the distribution of private memoranda and notes on points they found in the oral tradition.[25]

For Gerhardsson this process of transmitting the tradition was the outer manifestation of a vital living inner center of understanding within Judaism of the nature of the claim of God. With the emergence of the ministry of Jesus the inner center had a different focus for his followers. But in many formal ways the process of the transmission of the outer verbal tradition of Jesus in the earliest Christian communities remained much the same as in the various versions of Judaism of the era.[26]

W. D. Davies is surely right when he says that for the Palestinian Judaism in which Jesus was raised the focus of the living inner center was on the God of the Exodus who had ineluctably linked himself to Sinai and the revelation of himself in the Torah. This accounts for the emphasis on concentration of the study of the written text and showing one's faithfulness to God by keeping Torah.[27] On the other hand, it would be hard to deny that the living center of the early Christian movement shifted the focus from the action of God at Sinai to the renewed activity of God in the eschatological preaching, death, and exaltation of Jesus.[28] Here the emphasis comes on the call to be faithful in discipleship to the risen and exalted Lord; and this surely not only involved the spotlight focusing on the drama of his salvific death and resurrection but also put increased emphasis on the importance of recalling and continuing to collect and transmit Jesus'

---

[25]Gerhardsson, "Origins of the Gospel Tradition," 19-24.

[26]For a cautious analysis and restatement of this view of the transmission of the outer verbal tradition see F. F. Bruce, *Tradition Old and New* (Grand Rapids: Zondervan, 1970) 68-71.

[27]W. D. Davies, "Reflections on a Scandanavian Approach to the Gospel Tradition," in *Neotestamentica et Patristica: Eine Freundesgabe, Oscar Cullmann*, ed. W. C. Van Unnik (Leiden: Brill, 1962) 14-34. More recently E. P. Sanders's theory of covenantal nomism seems to reflect some continuity with this approach.

[28]Gerhardsson, "The Gospel Tradition," 509-10, places the emphasis especially on the preaching of Jesus. Jesus proclaimed to his people that God will soon take power over the world in a new dramatic way. They will soon see what it means for God to be truly the one Lord and God. With this reality in view Jesus preaches his summons to repentance and calls for the people to love God with all their own heart and soul. We tend to center the focus more on the death and resurrection, but it cannot be separated from certain critical events in the life of the earthly Jesus.

sayings and deeds which provided the setting for his death.[29] Thus the collection and transmission of the sayings and deeds of Jesus begins with his ministry and becomes intensified when he is exalted after his death.

This conclusion has been substantiated by Riesner. He has shown that a considerable amount of the verbal sayings attributed to Jesus in the Synoptic gospels reflect a deliberate rhetorical structure that appears to be designed to facilitate memorization for purposes of transmission.[30] Just as among their neighboring Jewish communities in Greater Syria, the earliest Christian communities relied on authoritative teachers (e.g. the apostles) for the transmission of the verbal traditions about Jesus.

Therefore, it is not unreasonable to accept the hypothesis that Paul, shortly after his call, was taught a version of the Jesus tradition, perhaps in the messianic communities of the Transjordan, but certainly in Jerusalem (Gal 1:18).[31] Later, Paul the missionary also served as a traditioner and taught this same tradition to the small mission churches he founded among the Gentiles. Thessalonica and Corinth were among these churches. Ultimately, much of this same tradition that he transmitted orally would also be used as source material for the composition of the gospels.[32]

What is the evidence in Paul's letters for this hypothesis, especially in the letters to Corinth and Thessalonica?

The Corinthian letters give a clear indication that Paul was a traditioner of the kerygma (1 Cor 15:3-5). They give evidence that Paul knew and transmitted a liturgical usage of the words of Jesus (1 Cor 11:23-25; cf. Lk 22:19-20), or formulated rules for his community based on them (1 Cor 7:10-11; 9:14). There is also evidence that Paul served as a traditioner of church practice (1 Cor 11:2,

---

[29]N. Dahl, "Anamnesis: Memory and Commemoration in Early Christianity," in *Jesus in the Memory of the Early Church* (Minneapolis: Augsburg, 1976) 27.

[30]Rainer Riesner, *Jesus als Lehrer: Eine Untersuchung zum Ursprung der Evangelien-Überlieferung*, WUNT 2/7 (Tübingen: J. C. B. Mohr [Paul Siebeck], 1984) 353-498.

[31]W. R. Farmer, "Peter and Paul and the Tradition concerning the Lord's Supper in 1 Cor 11:23-26," *Criswell Theological Review* 2/1 (1987): 121-28, argues exhaustively that ἱστορῆσαι Πέτρον (the textual reading of Gal 1:18 he accepts) means "to get information from Peter." Likewise, J. D. G. Dunn, "The Relationship between Paul and Jerusalem according to Galatians 1 and 2," *New Testament Studies* 28 (1982): 461. This position seems to represent an emerging consensus among significant scholars despite the vigorous rejoinder of O. Hofius, "Gal 1:18: ἱστορῆσαι Κηφᾶν," *Zeitschrift für die neutestamentliche Wissenschaft* 78 (1984): 73-85.

[32]Thus Paul would have known a considerable amount of the Jesus tradition. This is a far different conclusion from that arrived at by V. P. Furnish, "The Jesus-Paul Debate: From Baur to Bultmann," *Bulletin of the John Rylands Library* 47 (1965): 342-81. It is more in keeping with the general direction of David Wenham, *Paul: Follower of Jesus or Founder of Christianity?* (Grand Rapids: Eerdmans, 1995).

16). Likewise, the same is true with the Thessalonians. It is enlightening to find how many things Paul knew he had in common with the Thessalonians as he shared remembrance of a memorable common past that could only have lasted several months. Frequently in his first letter Paul used the formula [καθὼς] οἴδατε to remind them of a shared memory (1 Thess 1:5: 2:1, 11; 3:3, 4; 4:1-2; 5:2). And this may not only refer to a mutual remembrance of shared experiences together (1 Thess 2:1-12) but the joint knowledge of a common early Christian tradition on how to live the Christian life (1 Thess 4:1-2; 6, 9, 12; 5:11). Especially by his conscious use of the technical term in early Christianity for the transmission of tradition (1 Thess 3:6; 4:1), we claim that there is enough evidence to substantiate the view that, while he was with them, Paul transmitted to the Thessalonians authoritative tradition on how to live the Christian life.

Thus, there are good reasons to claim that when Paul gave parenesis to the Thessalonians, it was given not only on the basis of common past associations,[33] but also on the grounds that they shared a common knowledge of early Christian tradition (at least in summary form), which, after all, was their only real basis for fellowship; and it may well have been that this tradition included collections of the words and deeds of Jesus. These collections would have been transmitted orally; but this does not preclude that some were written down by this time.

If this model of the formation of the gospel tradition is plausible, then the possibility exists (assuming the conventional view that 1 Thessalonians preceded the Synoptics) that Paul had knowledge of a number of sayings of Jesus, in some sort of organized arrangement, that preceded the use of these sayings in the composition of the gospels. Therefore, hypothetically, if we could determine that Paul knew of a body of eschatological sayings attributed to Jesus, and what they were, this would be important information for our understanding of the derivation and composition of the Synoptic Eschatological Discourse.

Of course, this hypothesis is not the only possible explanation of the verbal parallels between the Synoptic Eschatological Discourse and Thessalonians. There is always the possibility that the Synoptic writers utilized Paul's own letters directly as a source for their compositions.[34] Or, one can claim that the parallels are largely a chimera and that, in fact, there is hardly any clear relationship between the Thessalonian correspondence and the Synoptic Eschatological Discourse.[35]

---

[33]Abraham J. Malherbe, *Paul and the Thessalonians. The Philosophic Tradition of Pastoral Care* (Philadelphia: Fortress Press, 1987) 73.

[34]As claimed by M. D. Goulder, *Midrash and Lection in Matthew* (London: SPCK, 1974) 146-54.

[35]C. M. Tuckett, "Synoptic Tradition in 1 Thessalonians?" in *The Thessalonian Correspondence*, BETL 87, ed. R. F. Collins (Leuven: Leuven University Press/Peeters, 1990) 182.

In order to contribute to the clarification of this issue, which is a necessary prelude to any comprehensive study of the formation of the Synoptic Discourse, we will now attempt to determine the precise connections between certain eschatological traditions of Jesus that seem to have close parallels in the Thessalonian correspondence and in the Synoptic Eschatological Discourse. We turn then to a discussion of 1 Thessalonians.

2.
Jesus Tradition in 1 Thessalonians
and in the Synoptic Eschatological Discourse

The Structure of 1 Thessalonians

In an informative article on the structure of 1 Thessalonians as a letter, Helmut Koester has made the observation that 1 Thessalonians utilized both formal features of the private letter of the Greco-Roman world and the terminology drawn from the proclamation of the gospel in early Christian mission.[1] Like putting new wine into old wineskins, the outstanding feature of Paul's compositional method in his letter was that he took comparable topoi and rhetorical patterns operative within Greco-Roman literature, combined them with distinctive Christian themes, and produced a new literary creation.[2] This new literary creation broke old molds and produced the model for the genre of the epistle in subsequent early Christian literature. Thus, as examples of the use of Greco-Roman rhetorical patterns, Koester notes that Paul uses the topoi of the self-description of the pagan philosopher (1 Thess 2:1-12),[3] and the catalogues of virtues and vices (4:1-11; 5:12-22), frequently found in Hellenistic Jewish writings, to promote moral instruction.[4]

Significantly, when he comes to examine the eschatological section of 4:13–5:11 Koester finds no analogies for this unit among the topoi in use in the non-Christian literature of the Greco-Roman world. In this instance, he says that eschatological teaching is simply given because the eschatological orientation is so dominant and fundamental in Paul's gospel. He concludes that the appearance of eschatology is the most significant new feature of what, in essence, is the creation of a new genre: the Christian epistle.[5]

---

[1]H. Koester, "1 Thessalonians—Experiment in Christian Writing," in *Continuity and Discontinuity in Church History: Essays presented to G. H. Williams*, SHT 19, ed. F. F. Church and T. George (Leiden: E. J. Brill, 1979) 35.

[2]Ibid., 36-39.

[3]Here, Koester is echoing the work of Abraham Malherbe, " 'Gentle as a Nurse': The Cynic Background to 1 Thess 2," *Novum Testamentum* 12 (1970): 203-17.

[4]Koester, "1 Thessalonians—Experiment," 36-39.

[5]Ibid.

Debate continues to rage as to the precise description of the kind of epistle used by Paul in 1 Thessalonians. Boers[6] and Malherbe,[7] who are good representatives of mainstream scholarship, view it as essentially parenetic exhortation. Here, the absent Paul exhorts his readers, as if present with them, in order that they may continue to maintain the Christian life. On the other hand, Karl Donfried views 1 Thessalonians as a letter designed to console the Thessalonians and to assure them that he has not lost interest in them as a result of the persecution which the struggling community encountered.[8]

The debate is technical and it is not necessary for our purposes to make a definitive determination of the specific kind of Greco-Roman epistle that the rhetorical features of this particular letter most closely approximated. It is important that we see that, although Paul composed using certain phrases and themes that were characteristic of the formal letter of the Greco-Roman world, his appeals in 1 Thessalonians 4:13–5:11 to an authoritative tradition does break with old molds, and constitutes a fresh approach for giving parenetic advice. In a letter of exhortation in the Greco-Roman culture of this era, certain themes such as minimizing death as a sleep, calling for grief to cease, and taking comfort in the notion that the fate of the dead ones was now in the hands of the gods may constitute part of the general compositional stock-in-trade of giving advice.[9] But what is significant is that Paul does not stop with these standard phrases and cliches. His argument, as always, is informed by his commitment to the Christian gospel. Thus, such general statements that the dead will find rest and the loved ones will be blessed in the hereafter is not enough. His arguments are made on the basis of the reality of the death and resurrection of Jesus (4:14). Based on that reality, and both what he claims to be a word of the Lord (4:15) and a common remembrance of past tradition (5:2), Paul gives specific instructions on eschatological matters that must be heeded. It is in the linking of his advice and

---

[6]H. Boers, "The Form Critical Study of Paul's Letters: 1 Thessalonians as a Case Study," *New Testament Studies* 22 (1976): 158, views the structure of the letter along the lines of epistolary analysis (1:1-10, greeting and thanksgiving; 2:1-12, apostolic apology; 2:13-16, a later addition; 2:17-3:13, the apostolic parousia; 4:1–5:22, exhortation). A handy comprehensive table of views of various commentators on the rhetorical structure of 1 Thessalonians is furnished by Robert Jewett, *The Thessalonian Correspondence: Pauline Rhetoric and Millenarian Piety* (Philadelphia: Fortress, 1986) 216-21.

[7]A. Malherbe, "Exhortation in First Thessalonians," *Novum Testamentum* 25 (1983): 239; also "Paul and the Thessalonians," 65-78. Malherbe divides the letter into two parts. First, in 1:2–3:13 the letter is mainly autobiographical. The sympathetic wording functions as a substitute for Paul's real presence with the Thessalonians; in 4:1-5:22 the parenesis moves from autobiographical example to direct exhortation and advice.

[8]Karl Donfried, "The Cults of Thessalonica and the Thessalonian Correspondence," *New Testament Studies* 31 (1985): 351.

[9]As noted by Malherbe, "Exhortation," 255.

exhortation with the basic gospel tradition that the fresh new thrust of Paul's parenesis in 4:13–5:11 can be found.

First Thessalonians 4:13–5:11 in the Structure of 1 Thessalonians

In 1 Thessalonians 4:13, as part of his general exhortation to the congregation, Paul is in the process of taking up and addressing a series of topics. The various topics are introduced by the phrase περί with the genitive ("concerning this"; cf. 4:9, 13; 5:1). This is the same construction used in a later letter where Paul takes up topics that were brought to his attention by a delegation of supporters in a church which he had previously founded (1 Cor 7:1, 25; 8:1; 12:1 16:1,12). There seems to be no reason to doubt, that just as on this later occasion Paul addressed particular problems which had come to his attention as a result of personal contacts, he is doing the same with the Thessalonians. Timothy had recently returned from Thessalonica, and Paul was concerned to address certain issues in the church based on the report he had received from him.[10] 1 Thessalonians 4:1-12 is bracketed by a general exhortatory appeal (4:1-2; 10b-12). In 4:3-8 the topic of personal holiness is discussed. And, likewise, the matter of brotherly love is addressed in 4:9-10a.

After discussing the topics of personal holiness and brotherly love, Paul prepares to give parenesis on the situation of the believers who had died (4:13-18). This is followed by his discussion of the "times and seasons" in 5:1-11. The unit on parenesis then continues in 5:12-22 with various pieces of advice directed specifically toward the community.

Both 1 Thessalonians 4:13-18 and 5:1-11 are linked by the common theme of concern for eschatological matters. In 4:13-18 the delay of the parousia and subsequent death of some of the believers had caused a problem. In 5:1-11 additional issues surrounding the parousia (cf. 1 Thess 5:1) come under discussion. This commonality of theme is also indicated in the structure of 4:13-5:11.

Both units (4:13, 5:1) open with the περὶ δέ formula identifying the particular topos under discussion. Both 4:18 and 5:11 (the conclusion of the respective units) end with the imperative phrase παρακαλεῖτε ἀλλήλους ("exhort one another"). In turn, this phrase echoes similar language in 4:1, 10. Also, it is noticeable that before the concluding hortatory statements in 4:18 and 5:11 Paul uses the improper preposition ἅμα ("together") with a σύν ("with") formula in the dative (4:17; 5:10). In both units Paul holds tenaciously to the promise that believers ultimately will be united with the Lord. Thus 1 Thessalonians 4:13-18 and 5:1-11 are woven together very carefully in a pattern of

---

[10]Malherbe, "Paul and Thessalonians," 62-68, has an excellent discussion on the relationship between Timothy and the Thessalonians.

parenesis which features calls to maintain faith based on certain convictions about what will happen in the future.

The outline of the *topos* in 4:13-17 falls into four discernible parts that have a basic common structure.

1. Identification of the *topos* and its purpose (4:13)[11]
2. Recollection of the implications of the fundamental confession on the resurrection of Jesus (4:14)
3. Recollection of the implications of the Word of the Lord about the future resurrection of believers (4:15-17)
4. Closing Exhortation (4:18)

The outline of the topos in 5:1-11 also falls into four discernible parts.

1. Identification of the *topos* and its purpose (5:1)
2. Affirmation that the Day of the Lord will come suddenly (5:2-3)
3. Exhortation and *Aitia* to live as children of the day rather than as children of darkness (5:4-10)
4. Closing Exhortation (5:11)

Thus we conclude that thematically and structurally, 1 Thessalonians 4:13-5:11 is a basic unit on eschatological matters, constructed between two bodies of general ethical exhortation (4:1-12; 5:12-22) which forms the basic theological thrust of the Pauline parenesis in 1 Thessalonians 4-5.

Paul's Use of Jesus Tradition in 1 Thessalonians 4:13-5:11

There are two places in this text where Paul appears to draw upon Jesus tradition. First, in 4:15, Paul states that his argument is grounded on a word of the Lord (ἐν λόγῳ κυρίου). Second, in 5:2 Paul appeals to a common recollection of shared remembrances that he had with the Thessalonians αὐτοὶ γὰρ ἀκριβῶς οἴδατε ("for you know very well"). In both cases (4:16, 5:2) Paul's phraseology is followed by a recitative ὅτι ("that")[12] and wording that has been identified as echoing Jesus tradition found elsewhere in early Christian literature.

We will now give careful attention to both of these passages in order to determine precisely, to what extent, Paul reflected knowledge of a body of eschatological sayings attributed to Jesus. For procedural purposes we will discuss 1 Thessalonians 5:2-3 first.

---

[11]We follow fairly closely the outline of the unit proposed by R. F. Collins, *Studies on the First Letter to the Thessalonians*, BETL 66 (Leuven: Leuven University Press/ Peeters, 1984) 157.

[12]Collins, *Studies on the First Letter*, 160, notes that the ὅτι of 1 Thess 4:15 is exegetical while, 4:16, is recitative. We concur.

First Thessalonians 5:2 and Matthew 24:42-43a

There is a close sequential parallel between 1 Thessalonians 5:2 and Matthew 24:42-43a that should be noted closely:

1 Thessalonians 5:2	Matthew 24:42-43a
οἴδατε ὅτι	ὅτι οὐκ οἴδατε
ἡμέρα κυρίου	ποίᾳ ἡμέρᾳ ὁ κύριος ὑμῶν
ὡς κλέπτης ἐν νυκτὶ	
οὕτως ἔρχεται.	ἔρχεται.
	[43]ἐκεῖνο δὲ γινώσκετε ὅτι εἰ
	ᾔδει ὁ οἰκοδεσπότης ποίᾳ
	φυλακῇ ὁ κλέπτης ἔρχεται,
	ἐγρηγόρησεν ἂν καὶ οὐκ ἂν
	εἴασεν διορυχθῆναι τὴν οἰκίαν
	αὐτοῦ.

As the display indicates, there is a close link between the two units with respect to the coming of the Day of the Lord being compared to the appearance of a thief at night. In Paul the point is straightforward. The Day of the Lord will come suddenly and unexpectedly; just as a thief at night (cf. 1 Thess 5:3,5).

These basic features are also highlighted in the more expansive Matthean version (Matt 24:42-43). Linguistically, we see in the two units a common use of οἴδατε, ἡμέρα in association with κυρίος, κλέπτης, and ἔρχεται. Especially striking is the common idea between the two units that the coming of the thief will be at night.[13]

The point of Matthew 24:42-43 is also remarkably similar to 1 Thessalonians 5:2. The end (Day of the Lord in Thessalonians/ Lord's coming in Matthew) will come suddenly and without warning.[14]

On the basis of these common verbal and thematic similarities one could either be inclined to consider that direct literary dependence exists between the two works, or this is an instance of independent use of a common tradition by Matthew and Paul. If we go with the former view, on normal dating, accepted by most scholars, this would mean that Matthew has used Paul as a source for

---

[13]This has even led Michael Goulder to think that Matthew used Paul as a source for his composition of 24:42-43. He sets forth his arguments in *Midrash and Lection*, 146-47. However, we consider this to be a case of pushing the literary evidence too far.

[14]In the parallel in Lk 12:39 the householder does not know in ποίᾳ ὥρᾳ (ποίᾳ φυλακῇ in Matt 24:43) the thief will come. Luke's less explicit statement may be dependent upon the summary statement of Matt 24:44. In any case, the Matthean φυλακῇ (cf. Lk 12:38), alluding to the watches of the night, is very close to 1 Thess 5:2.

the basic metaphor of the thief, and has expanded it into a parable. Conversely, if Paul used Matthew, he would be viewed as alluding to the basic parable found in Matthew.

However, there is a strong reason why the position of direct literary dependence between Matthew and Paul is unacceptable. One needs to have evidence of copying elsewhere between two literary works to make plausible the claim of literary dependence in a particular instance - especially when it is disputed. It is a sound methodological rule to claim, that the degree and nature of verbatim agreement between two parallel texts must be of such a character as to make it unlikely to have been caused in any other way before one can say this constitutes evidence for direct copying. However, sufficient literary evidence constituting a number of parallels does not exist to cause this investigator to hypothecate that there is copying between Paul and the Synoptics.

For this reason, we put forward a hypothesis that Matthew and Paul used *common* source tradition on the comparison between the Day of the Lord and the thief at night for their respective compositions of 1 Thessalonians 5:2 and Matthew 24:42-43.

Such an explanation, combined with an understanding of the formation of the gospel tradition along lines congruent with the Griesbach Hypothesis that Matthew was the first Synoptic Gospel, will adequately account for the verbatim agreements in the parallels.

With regard to Paul, the additional echoes of the parable of the Thief at Night in 1 Thessalonians 5:3-11 may be explained as further Pauline exhortation given with the understanding that both the apostle and his audience shared a common knowledge of this parable. Specifically, when Paul uses "to watch" (γρηγορεῖν) in 1 Thess 5:6, 10, we presume that he was echoing the parable of the Thief as it appeared in the common tradition rather than drawing this term from the text of Matthew. As Paul gave his exhortation to Gentile converts in the Hellenistic world in 1 Thessalonians 5:4-10, his basic point was to contrast the stance of a believer as a person who "watches" (γρηγορεῖν) to maintain faith throughout the day as opposed to the unbeliever who lives a life of dissipation which is characteristic of a person of the night. Our argument is enhanced by the observation that in his exhortation, Paul radically shifted the use of γρηγορεῖν from its strong eschatological use in the common tradition of staying alert through the night to an ethical emphasis where the person of light (day) watches against the forces of darkness (night).[15] Such a shift is a perfectly understandable

---

[15]The basic comparison of the Day of the Lord coming as a thief in the night has been viewed by Jeremias as a genuine saying of Jesus. Joachim Jeremias, *The Parables of Jesus*, 2nd rev. ed., trans. S. H. Hooke (New York: Scribner's, 1972) 49. In support of this view we note that no parallel has been found in Jewish literature connecting the

procedure for someone giving exhortation based on common knowledge of a tradition.[16]

First Thessalonians 5:2 and Luke 12:39

In addition to the parallels between 1 Thessalonians 5:2 and Matthew 24:42-43 there is an additional parallel between 1 Thessalonians 5:2 and Luke 12:39 which should be considered.

1 Thessalonians 5:2	Matthew 24:42-44	Luke 12:35-40
		[35]Ἔστωσαν ὑμῶν αἱ ὀσφύες περιεζωσμέναι καὶ οἱ λύχνοι καιόμενοι· [36]καὶ ὑμεῖς ὅμοιοι ἀνθρώποις προσδεχομένοις τὸν κύριον ἑαυτῶν πότε ἀναλύσῃ ἐκ τῶν γάμων, ἵνα ἐλθόντος καὶ κρούσαντος εὐθέως ἀνοίξωσιν αὐτῷ. [37]μακάριοι οἱ δοῦλοι ἐκεῖνοι, οὓς ἐλθὼν ὁ κύριος εὑρήσει γρηγοροῦντας· ἀμὴν λέγω ὑμῖν ὅτι περιζώσεται καὶ ἀνακλινεῖ αὐτοὺς καὶ παρελθὼν διακονήσει αὐτοῖς. [38]κἂν ἐν τῇ δευτέρᾳ κἂν ἐν τῇ τρίτῃ φυλακῇ ἔλθῃ καὶ εὕρῃ οὕτως, μακάριοί εἰσιν ἐκεῖνοι.
αὐτοὶ γὰρ ἀκριβῶς οἴδατε ὅτι ἡμέρα κυρίου	[42]γρηγορεῖτε οὖν, ὅτι οὐκ οἴδατε ποίᾳ ἡμέρᾳ ὁ κύριος ὑμῶν ἔρχεται.	
ὡς κλέπτης ἐν νυκτὶ οὕτως ἔρχεται.	[43]ἐκεῖνο δὲ γινώσκετε ὅτι εἰ ᾔδει ὁ οἰκοδεσπότης ποίᾳ φυλακῇ ὁ κλέπτης· ἔρχεται, ἐγρηγόρησεν ἂν καὶ οὐκ ἂν εἴασεν διορυχθῆναι τὴν οἰκίαν αὐτοῦ.	[39]τοῦτο δὲ γινώσκετε ὅτι εἰ ᾔδει ὁ οἰκοδεσπότης ποίᾳ ὥρᾳ ὁ κλέπτης ἔρχεται, (ἐγρηγόρησεν ἂν καὶ) οὐκ ἂν ἀφῆκεν διορυχθῆναι τὸν οἶκον αὐτοῦ.

Day of the Lord with the coming of a thief. It is only in Christian literature where this connection is made (cf. 2 Pet 3:10 and echoes in Rev 3:3, 16:15; Did 16:1; and Gosp Thom 2).

[16]Cf. C. M. Tuckett, "Synoptic Tradition in 1 Thessalonians?" 170-71.

⁴⁴διὰ τοῦτο καὶ ὑμεῖς
γίνεσθε ἕτοιμοι, ὅτι ᾗ οὐ
δοκεῖτε ὥρᾳ ὁ υἱὸς
τοῦ ἀνθρώπου ἔρχεται.

⁴⁰καὶ ὑμεῖς γίνεσθε
ἕτοιμοι, ὅτι ᾗ ὥρᾳ οὐ
δοκεῖτε ὁ υἱὸς τοῦ
ἀνθρώπου ἔρχεται.

Luke uses the parable of the Thief in a body of composition (Luke 12:35-48) which has as its overall theme the need to be spiritually prepared for the coming of the Son of Man by watching and serving Christ.[17] On the Two Gospel Hypothesis Luke had knowledge of the text of Matthew because in Luke 12:42-46, Luke edited very carefully the Matthean version (24:45-51) of the parable of the Chief Servant and Slaves into his composition.[18] All that remains is to explain how Luke also incorporated the parable of the Thief at Night (Matt 24:42-44) into his account.

As the basis for the unit of Luke 12:35-40 in Luke 12:35-38 Luke uses two parables on the general theme of "girding the loins." This should be understood as a metaphor on preparation for service.[19] Being guided by the linguistic term γρηγορεῖν, which Luke (12:37) had apparently found in the source material, Luke then utilized in his composition a block of source material in Matthew (24:42-44) that also emphasized watchfulness and preparation. In Matthew 24:42, 43, γρηγορεῖν appears twice. To avoid redundancy, Luke (12:39) started at Matthew 24:43 and incorporated the Matthean account of the Thief in the Night and the Matthean ending on preparing for the coming of the Son of Man directly into the account (Lk 12:39-40 ‖ Matt 24:43-44). Then Luke finished out the unit by using the parable of the Chief Servant and Slaves (Matt 24:45-51 ‖ Lk 12:42-46).

Luke is making a moralistic point. Since the Lord is the one who will return to serve (Lk 12:37b) so his followers are to be characterized by watchful service (12:35, 40, 42-48). Luke 12:39 should probably be read in the same way. For Luke the emphasis is not, as in Paul, the unexpected suddenness of the coming

---

[17]I. Howard Marshall, *The Gospel of Luke: A Commentary on the Greek Text*, NIGTC (Grand Rapids: Eerdmans, 1978) 532.

[18]Perhaps Luke has in mind the entire text of Matt 24:36–25:13 because of its repeated allusions (24:36, 37, 39, 42, 44, 50; 25:13) to the coming of the Son of Man.

[19]The compositional history of these verses is explained by A. J. McNicol, W. R. Farmer, D. L. Dungan, J. B. Orchard, D. B. Peabody, "The Two Gospel Hypothesis Textual Discussion: The Composition of the Synoptic Eschatological Discourse," in *The Interrelations of the Gospels*, BETL 95, ed. David L. Dungan (Leuven: Leuven University Press/Peeters; Macon GA: Mercer University Press, 1990) 163-67. (Henceforth this article will be referred to as McNicol, "Composition of the Eschatological Discourse.") Luke has fused together two parables: the parables on "Slaves Waiting for the Coming of the Master" (Lk 12:36-37a) and on "Being Prepared to Serve" (Lk 12:35,37b-38).

of the thief in the night, but the need to be prepared to prevent the burglar from doing damage, by faithful watching at all times.[20]

As a result of this initial overview of the literary parallels between 1 Thessalonians 5:2 and Matthew 24:42-43 ‖ Luke 12:39 we have come to some preliminary conclusions. There is not enough verbatim evidence to indicate that there was direct copying between Paul and Matthew. It is far more likely that Paul and Matthew utilized a common tradition on the Thief at Night, and that Luke used the Matthean version of this parable as the basis for his composition of Luke 12:39-40. The fact that Luke in his prologue acknowledges use of earlier narratives and that there is extensive verbatim agreement between Luke and Matthew serves to support this conclusion of literary dependence of Luke upon Matthew in this instance.

First Thessalonians 5:3 and the Use of Jesus Tradition

After Paul has stated that the Day of the Lord comes suddenly and unexpectedly (1 Thess 5:2), Paul adds some additional teaching in 5:3 about its coming.

He states that whenever people say "Peace and safety," then sudden destruction will come upon them. This assertion is an extension of the description of the coming of the Lord given in the previous verse. Then the text asserts that the Day of the Lord will bring imminent destruction, and it is compared to the birthpang of a woman about to give birth to a child. In both instances the point of suddenness is highlighted. The unit ends with a claim that there is no escape from this reality.

What is especially striking about this passage is the number, for Paul, of unusual words which occur here. The following list is notable.[21]

	Paul	Pastorals	New Testament
ἐφιστάναι	1	2	21
γαστήρ	1	1	9
ὠδίν	1	-	4
ἀσφάλεια	1	-	3
αἰφνίδιος	1	-	2
ἐκφεύγειν	3	-	8

---

[20]Thus, the change from φυλακῇ (Matt 24:43) to ὥρᾳ (Lk 12:39). Other editorial changes by Luke are insignificant. Marshall, *Luke*, 538, claims that Luke's opening τοῦτο is secondary to Matthew's ἐκεῖνο (Matt 24:43 ‖ Lk 12:39; cf. Lk 10:11). For a discussion on whether the Matthean γρηγορεῖν should be read in the text of Lk 12:39, see McNicol, "Composition of the Eschatological Discourse," 164.

[21]Cf. Lars Aejmelaeus, *Wachen vor dem Ende: Die Traditionsgeschichtlichen Wurzeln von 1. Thess 5:1-11 und Luk 21:34-36*, SFEG 44 (Helsinki: Finnische Exegetische Gesellschaft, 1985) 8-9, has noted the basic evidence.

While this vocabulary is unusual for Paul, a number of these words occur in important eschatological texts in the LXX.[22] These abundant echoes and reminiscences of the language of the LXX, along with several instances of unusual language for Paul, has caused Tuckett to claim that Paul used a tradition as a basis for his composition in 1 Thessalonians 5:3.[23] We will also argue in favor of the assessment that Paul drew on a tradition attributed to Jesus which he alluded to in his composition.[24]

First Thessalonians 5:3 opens abruptly with a subordinate clause introduced by ὅταν followed by a plural verb with an indefinite subject. This use of the plural verb λέγωσιν ("some say") with an indefinite subject is not characteristic of Paul's linguistic usage.[25] The idea that the phrase "Peace and safety" is an ironic reference to the propaganda of the early Principate is unlikely.[26] This kind of derisive comment on the work of the Roman government is not typical of Paul (cf. Rom 13:1-7). Rather, Paul seems to be quoting a more substantive tradition that opens with a statement about those who have a false sense of security. With its reference to peace the text echoes Jeremiah 6:14 (LXX).[27] In addition, the reference to ἀσφάλεια ("safety") occurs in Isaiah 8:15 preceded in 8:14 by παγίς ("snare"), a word which will be of some importance in our discussion below. In Isaiah 8 we are told that the opponents addressed there lacked ἀσφάλεια ("safety") and were in danger of falling into a snare. The terminology of Isaiah 8:14-15 resurfaces in tradition that Paul recovered and was

---

[22]Most notable is the frequently used ἀσφάλεια (3 times, in Is 8:15; 18:4; 34:15) and ἐν γαστρὶ ἔχουσα and similar motifs in numerous places including Is 13:8.

[23]Tuckett, "Synoptic Tradition in 1 Thessalonians?" 174. This view differs from the position of Aejmelaeus, *Wachen*, 38-47, who views this as Pauline composition based on LXX reminiscences.

[24]The formulation τότε . . . ὥσπερ is probably Pauline. Cf. J. Plevnik, "1 Thess 5,1-11: Its Authenticity, Intention, and Message," *Biblica* 60 (1979): 83.

[25]This is one of the unusual linguistic uses that has been noted by commentators as a sign that Paul is using tradition. Cf. E. Best, *A Commentary on the First and Second Epistles to the Thessalonians*, HNTC (New York: Harper & Row, 1972) 207. A list of linguistic usages in 1 Thess 5:1-10 not characteristic of Paul, and thus possibly indicating the presence of tradition, is supplied by Collins, *Studies on the First Letter*, 110.

[26]H. Koester, "From Paul's Eschatology to the Apocalyptic Schemata of 2 Thessalonians," in *The Thessalonian Correspondence*, BETL 87, ed. R. F. Collins (Leuven: Leuven University Press/Peeters, 1990) 449-50.

[27]Καὶ λέγοντες Εἰρήνη εἰρήνη. Again, the use of peace here is unusual for Paul. Paul normally uses εἰρήνη to describe the situation of blessedness for the believer in Christ (cf. Rom 5:1). Here peace is used in the general sense of safety in a time of eschatological crisis. This is another indicator that Paul is using tradition. For similar echoes in the LXX see Ezek 13:10 and Mic 3:5.

taken over in 1 Thessalonians 5:3 to describe the false security of some before the parousia.[28]

As we have observed, the warning against false security is followed by two comments to the effect that sudden destruction will come upon the unprepared. Paul appeared to have edited the warning against false security into a complete sentence through the use of the τότε . . . ὥσπερ formula.

With regard to the first announcement of sudden destruction commencing with τότε, the unusual wording, for Paul, of αἰφνίδιος ("sudden") and ἐφιστάναι ("to appear") is an additional strong sign that he was continuing to invoke tradition. And when we turn to the second announcement, we see that in the comment introduced by the ὥσπερ formula as a point of a comparison this wording also seems to have come from tradition. Thus the sudden coming of the Day of the Lord (1 Thessalonians 5:2,4) was likened by Paul to the sudden stab of pain of a pregnant woman at the onslaught of child birth. This latter image is a strong echo of Isaiah 13:6-8 where the Day of the Lord and destruction (συντριβή) from God was supposed to hit the Babylonians with the same severity as a woman in the throes of giving birth. It is interesting to note that the cognate συντρίβειν occurs in Isaiah 8:15. Thus, an interpreter could easily have connected Isaiah 8:15 and 13:6-4 through this linguistic link. Finally, we learn from 1 Thessalonians 5:3 that, at the Day of the Lord, οὐ μὴ ἐκφύγωσιν ("there will be no escape") from this turmoil. This image of no escape was also an echo of Isaiah 24:17-18 (LXX) where we are told that those who try to escape (φεύγειν) the eschatological judgment will ultimately end up in a trap (παγίς).

Thus, what we have in this verse is Paul's echoing a tradition of eschatological judgment of what will happen at the last day based on terminology drawn from a catena of passages in Scripture. It is in continuity with his reminder in 1 Thessalonians 5:2 that he shares a knowledge of this common tradition with his readers. The tradition utilizes terminology drawn from Jeremiah 6:14, Isaiah 8:14-15; 13:6-10, and 24:1-20. Since much of the wording of 1 Thessalonians 5:2b and Matthew 24:42-43 can be clearly identified as Jesus tradition, the presumption is that an earlier version of the closely connected 1 Thessalonians 5:3, another passage reflecting massive use of tradition, was also received and handed on by Paul as Jesus tradition as well. That leads us to a discussion of the

---

[28]The exact referent of the subject of λέγωσιν (1 Thess 5:3) is a point of some importance. In pre-Thessalonian tradition this may refer to unbelievers in Christ or those who did not heed prophetic preaching. But Paul has changed the usage to warn believers (note the parenesis of 1 Thess 5:4-10) that their failure to be ready for the parousia will result in severe consequences for them.

relationship between Paul's use of this tradition in 1 Thessalonians 5:3 and the apparent emergence of the same tradition in Luke 21:34-36.

Similar Jesus Tradition in 1 Thessalonians 5:3 and Luke 21:34-36

1 Thessalonians 5:3	Luke 21:34-36

	³⁴προσέχετε δὲ ἑαυτοῖς μήποτε
	βαρηθῶσιν ὑμῶν αἱ καρδίαι ἐν
	κραιπάλῃ καὶ μέθῃ καὶ μερίμναις
	βιωτικαῖς καὶ ἐπιστῇ ἐφ' ὑμᾶς
τότε <u>αἰφνίδιος</u> αὐτοῖς ἐφίστα-	<u>αἰφνίδιος</u> ἡ ἡμέρα ἐκείνη
ται ὄλεθρος ὥσπερ ἡ ὠδίν . . .	³⁵ὡς παγὶς ἐπεισελεύσεται γὰρ
	ἐπὶ πάντας τοὺς καθημένους
	ἐπὶ πρόσωπον πάσης τῆς γῆς.
	³⁶ἀγρυπνεῖτε δὲ ἐν παντὶ καιρῷ
	δεόμενοι ἵνα κατισχύσητε <u>ἐκφυ-</u>
καὶ οὐ μὴ <u>ἐκφύγωσιν</u>	<u>γεῖν</u> ταῦτα πάντα τὰ μέλλοντα
	γίνεσθαι καὶ σταθῆναι ἔμπροσθεν
	τοῦ υἱοῦ τοῦ ἀνθρώπου.

Embedded in Luke 21:34-36 appears to be a more extensive version of the same tradition that was echoed by Paul in 1 Thessalonians 5:3.[29] We will now attempt to substantiate that claim and draw some conclusions about the history of this tradition.

David Wenham has furnished a useful display illustrating the close parallel linguistic structure between certain phraseology in 1 Thessalonians 5:3 and Luke 21:34-36.[30]

Luke: ἐπιστῇ ἐφ' ὑμᾶς αἰφνίδιος . . . ὡς παγίς . . . ἐκφυγεῖν
Paul: αἰφνίδιος αὐτοῖς ἐφίσταται . . . ὥσπερ (ὠδίν) . . . ἐκφύγωσιν[31]

In both cases the subject is the Day of the Lord (1 Thess 5:2; Lk 21:34). This Day is said to come suddenly (the only occurrences of αἰφνίδιος in the New Testament). Both Luke and Paul use the same verb (ἐφιστάναι) to refer to the coming of the Lord. Outside of the Pastorals that verb is used only here in the writings of Paul. Furthermore, the point of comparison in both Paul (ὥσπερ ἡ ὠδίν) and Luke (ὡς παγίς) has some important common affinities. Hartmann has observed that behind παγίς stands a Hebrew word for

---

[29]There are several punctuation, word order, and textual problems in this verse which will be discussed in the analysis of Lk 21:34-36 in the chapter on Luke, below.

[30]Wenham, *Rediscovery of Jesus' Eschatological Discourse*, 110.

[31]The word ὠδίν does not appear in Wenham's display as noted above.

"rope", or "snare;" but if that word is vocalized differently it means "travail."[32] A similar linguistic phenomenon appears in Aramaic. Therefore, παγίς and ὠδίν may be Greek translation variants. Wenham has noticed that παγίς and ὠδίν stand in parallelism with each other in Ps 17:6 of the LXX.[33] More significantly, the two words are connected in the same catena of texts on eschatological distress drawn from Isaiah, which we have identified as being echoed in 1 Thessalonians 5:3.[34] Thus, the plural form of ὠδίν is found in Isaiah 13:8. And παγίς appears in Isaiah 24:17-18. Whether this is a case of translation variants from a Semitic *Vorlage* or Paul was echoing Isaiah 13:8 (LXX) and Luke was echoing Isaiah 24:17-18 (LXX), there seems to be indication of the use of a common scriptural tradition at this point by both Paul and Luke. Finally, both Luke and Paul use the relatively rare word ἐκφεύγειν. These close verbal and syntactical parallels constitute evidence to indicate that there is either a literary connection between 1 Thessalonians 5:3 and Luke 21:34-36 or that both authors were using a similar tradition. We will argue in favor of the latter hypothesis.

Given conventional dating, one could be inclined to conclude that Luke used Paul freely by editing 1 Thessalonians 5:3 to compose Luke 21:34-36. But other evidence makes this conclusion highly unlikely. There are two places, *independent of 1 Thessalonians 5:3*, where Luke 21:34-36 echoes strongly the text of Isaiah 24:1-20 (especially 24:17-20). First, in Luke 21:34 Luke uses the collocation ἐν κραιπάλῃ καὶ μέθῃ ("in intoxication and drunkenness") as part of his warning against a life of dissipation before the coming of the Son of Man. Similar terminology is found in an eschatological context in Isaiah 24:20. Although Luke frequently echoes language of the LXX, since we have evidence that Luke was using tradition at this point, most likely Luke found this phrase not in the LXX but in a body of tradition that was also known independently by Paul. This is a more understandable explanation than arguing that Luke used Paul as his source, and then, somehow, knowing that Paul echoes Isaiah 24, turned to compose his account atomistically utilizing various additional material from Isaiah.[35]

---

[32]Lars Hartman, *Prophecy Interpreted: The Formation of some Jewish Apocalyptic Texts and of the Eschatological Discourse. Mark 13 Par.*, ConBNT 1 (Lund: C. W. K. Gleerup, 1979) 192.

[33]Wenham, *Rediscovery of Jesus' Eschatological Discourse*, 112.

[34]According to some commentators, there is no evidence in the LXX that παγίς was a translation of the Semitic *Vorlage* for travail. Aejmelaeus, *Wachen*, 121; cf. Tuckett, "Synoptic Tradition in 1 Thessalonians?" 174-75.

[35]The fact that Paul uses various forms of the verb μεθύειν in 1 Thess 5:7 (cf Lk 21:34) is totally congruent with our thesis. Paul, having this terminology in his tradition, echoes it as part of his parenesis. The point is that Paul does not have the rare κραιπάλη which only occurs in the New Testament at Lk 21:34. Thus, Luke could not have drawn κραιπάλη from Paul. Also it is worthwhile to note that the unusual μεθυόντων occurs

Second, Luke 21:35, with its statement that the Day of the Lord will come suddenly ἐπὶ πάντας τοὺς καθημένους ἐπὶ πρόσωπον τῆς γῆς ("upon all those who reside upon the face of the earth"), seems to echo Isaiah 24:1, 18 (LXX). In Isaiah 24:1 it was promised that the eschatological judgment of God was coming upon the whole face (πρόσωπον) of the habitation. All these things (ταῦτα πάντα, Is 24:13/Lk 21:36) will come upon the earth (Is 24:13, 18/Lk 21:35).

Therefore, we conclude that the most likely explanation for the similar linguistic terminology between 1 Thessalonians 5:3 and Luke 21:34-36 is that Luke has used a source on eschatological matters for the composition of 21:34-36;[36] and this same source was echoed (earlier) by Paul in 1 Thessalonians 5:3. This source was filled with reminiscences and echoes of a catena of LXX texts based on Isaiah 24:1-20, but which also included elements of Jeremiah 6:14; Isaiah 8:14-15, and 13:6-10.

It is not our purpose to attempt to reconstruct either its precise form or tradition history. However, from what we have identified as use of tradition in 1 Thessalonians 5:3 and Luke 21:34-36 we can say: (a) it included a strong warning against false security (b) a statement that the Day of the Lord would come suddenly upon all; (c) there would be no escape.

Although this does not affect the material results of this research, it could be noted that on the grounds of coherence with what was generally considered to be the eschatological message of Jesus, and multiple attestation of witnesses, a case could be made that the essence of this tradition came from Jesus.

Preliminary Summary

Thus we come to a preliminary conclusion that Paul in 1 Thessalonians 5:2 utilized a Jesus tradition on the Day of the Lord coming as a Thief in the Night. This appears to be fused with another tradition that is echoed in 1 Thessalonians 5:3 which involved a statement that in an unexpected time the suddenness of the Day of the Lord would come as the sharp birthpang of the woman before childbirth, and there would be no escape.

Matthew (24:42-43a) utilized the first tradition in the composition of the Thief in the Night. On the Two Gospel Hypothesis, Luke, probably, following Matthew 24:42-43a, also utilized the tradition of the Thief in the Night in Luke 12:39. But Luke was also familiar with the second tradition utilized by Paul in

---

in Matt 24:49 (cf. μεθύσκεσθαι in the parallel at Lk 12:45). Could Luke (Lk 12:45) on the Griesbach Hypothesis, having used Matt 24:45-51 at Lk 12:41-48, come to use the tradition behind Lk 21:34-36 on the basis of this repeated terminology?

[36]A discussion on how Luke likely has composed on the basis of this source will be given in the chapter on Luke.

1 Thessalonians 5:3. Luke used this second tradition as the basis for the composition of Luke 21:34-36.

Analysis of this textual evidence appears to lead to the conclusion that Paul (presumably before the composition of the Synoptic Eschatological Discourses) knew and assumed familiarity among his converts with the existence of a body of several teachings on eschatological matters that were attributed to Jesus. More than likely these teachings were used in the regular catechesis given to the mission churches.

First Thessalonians 4:15-17 ‖ Matthew 24:30b-31a: A Common Origin within the Jesus Tradition?

An additional section in 1 Thessalonians 4:13-5:11 that has been associated with Jesus tradition is Paul's reference to the word of the Lord in 4:15. Here Paul alludes to a word of the Lord as his warrant for arguing that the dead ones (in Christ) will participate jointly with those who are alive in a meeting with the Lord at the time of the parousia.

It is generally accepted that there are six references in Paul to traditions that are specifically connected with a word or command from what Paul calls "the Lord" (1 Cor 7:10-11, 25; 9:14; 11:23-26; 14:37; and 1 Thess 4:15). The specific terminology in these passages is worthy of notice.

In 1 Corinthians 7:10-11 Paul appeals to a Jesus tradition on divorce οὐκ ἐγὼ ἀλλὰ ὁ κύριος ("not I but the Lord").[37] This tradition is similar to the teaching of Jesus on the same subject in the Synoptics (Matt 19:9 ‖ Mk 10:11; Matt 5:32 ‖ Lk 16:16). Paul uses it as the basis for his ethical instruction to the married believers in Corinth. In 1 Corinthians 9:14 Paul asserts that the ὁ κύριος διέταξεν ("the Lord commanded") that those who proclaim the gospel should live by means of the gospel—a saying that appears in Matthew 10:10/Luke 10:7. And in 1 Corinthians 11:23-26 Paul uses the formula παρέλαβον . . . παρέδωκα ("I received . . . I handed over") to refer to his reception and transmission of liturgical tradition about the Lord's Supper. Here the wording of the liturgical tradition is close to that of Luke 22:18-20. In 1 Corinthians 7:25 Paul asserts that he has no command (ἐπίταγην) from the Lord on a particular matter. That is, he has no word that can be attributed to the Lord on the subject. And finally, Paul in addressing the charismatics in Corinth (1 Cor 14:37), claims that he writes with the Lord's authority (ἃ γράφω ὑμῖν ὅτι κυρίου ἐστὶν ἐντολή).

---

[37]Paul uses παραγγέλειν (cf. 1 Thess 4:11) as a way of introducing this ethical instruction which alludes to Jesus' word.

These passages indicate that Paul knew enough about the verbal traditions attributed to Jesus that he could quote from them. The first three passages have specific analogues in the Synoptics. In the fourth instance Paul says he has no word. So, this leaves us with a basis for a presumption that when Paul refers to or speaks about the commandment (1 Cor 14:37) or word (1 Thess 4:15) of the Lord, he has in mind, in these two latter references, that his teaching has an authority based on some text or tradition that could be verified as coming ultimately from the Lord Jesus.[38]

This is precisely what I believe can be shown in 1 Corinthians 14:37 and 1 Thessalonians 4:15. Since the former text is not the focus of this monograph we will deal with it only briefly.

Commencing in 1 Corinthians 14:26 Paul was concerned to give a series of regulations about correct decorum in the assembly. In keeping with a community of the new creation he argues that the church should be governed by the principles of decency and order (14:40) and mutual submission to each other (cf. 14:32-34). Instructions along these lines were given to those who spoke in tongues (14:27-28) and also to the prophets (14:29-32). Paul then turned to the matter of giving instructions to the wives (14:33-36).[39] His instructions were similar to the other groups stressing their need to be silent and to show submission especially when the spiritual gifts were being exercised in the assembly.

This demand to show restraint is backed up in 14:34 by Paul's appeal to the law (ὁ νόμος).[40] In short, he warrants his claim by an appeal to scripture. In 14:36 he chastizes the Corinthians for their vaunted and overrated claims to knowledge of the word of God (ὁ λόγος τοῦ θεοῦ). And then he comes to 14:37 where he argues that which he writes in the letter is the commandment of the Lord.[41] He seems to be making the claim that his understanding of this

---

[38]In 1 Thess 1:8 and 2 Thess 3:1 Paul uses "the word of the Lord" as synonym for the gospel. However, this does not seem to shed much light on the meaning of the term "by a word of the Lord" (ἐν λόγῳ κυρίου) in 1 Thess 4:15. Cf. E. Best, *First and Second Epistles to the Thessalonians*, 191.

[39]We assume 1 Cor 14:34-35 is part of the original text of 1 Corinthians. For an extended discussion that deals judiciously with the textual issue see E. E. Ellis, "The Silenced Wives of Corinth (1 Cor. 14:34-35)," in *New Testament Textual Criticism, Its Significance for Exegesis: Essays in Honour of Bruce M. Metzger*, ed. E. J. Epp and G. D. Fee (Oxford: Clarendon Press, 1981) 213-20.

[40]Most likely Paul does not refer to Gen 3:16 as argued by C. K. Barrett, *A Commentary on the First Epistle to the Corinthians*, HNTC (New York: Harper & Row, 1968) 330, but to both Gen 1:26ff. and 2:21ff. which Paul understands as the intended model of the creator for the order of his creation now restored proleptically in the church. Cf. F. F. Bruce, *1 and 2 Corinthians*, NCB (Greenwood SC: Attic Press, 1976) 136.

[41]That is, this teaching is in keeping with the real intent of Scripture. Whether we accept the Western reading of the text that omits ἐντολή at 1 Cor. 14:37 is not crucial

Scripture will be corroborated by any (genuine) prophet or spiritual person as the true word of the Lord.[42] In short, what Paul is saying comes ultimately from the Lord, being anchored in the word of the Lord *in a text*—in this case—the call in Genesis for the woman to accept her appropriate role in the created order.

Formally, this is precisely what we see happening in 1 Thessalonians 4:15-17. There, we will argue, Paul claims that what he is saying has dominical authority (ἐν λόγῳ κυρίου). In this case, we maintain, his teaching is anchored in the words of Jesus rather than the word of the Lord in the text of Genesis.

In order to substantiate this claim we intend do two things. First, we will show that although 1 Thessalonians 4:15-17 is primarily Pauline composition, it incorporates a small body of non-Pauline apocalyptic Jesus tradition. Second, this non-Pauline apocalyptic tradition is similar to that which was incorporated by the author of Matthew into his Eschatological Discourse (Matt 24:30b-31). Thus, in 1 Thessalonians 4:15-17, Paul claims to be speaking with or by dominical authority. As the source of dominical authority, this body of Jesus tradition served as Paul's basic authority for his statements in 4:15-17.

Tradition and Composition in 1 Thessalonians 4:15-17

First Thessalonians 4:15, 16b-18 as Not Derived from Tradition

Observation of the grammatical structure in 1 Thessalonians indicates that Paul has written in the first person plural from 4:13-15. At 4:15a Paul states that *we* say this (τοῦτο) by a word of the Lord. The total Greek sentence is 4:15-18. It is used to explicate the "this" (τοῦτο) which is affirmed on dominical authority. Since we have already noted that 4:18 (cf. 4:1, 5:11) is characteristic of Pauline parenesis, reinforcing the point already made, we will discuss first, the overall structural unity of 4:15-17, and then separate Paul's own wording from his use of tradition.

---

for our purposes. Actually, the omission of ἐντολή would bring the meaning of 1 Cor 14:37 slightly closer to "by the word of the Lord" in 1 Thess 4:15. In either case, Paul claims that he was giving these instructions "from the Lord." C. H. Dodd, "Ἔννομος Χριστοῦ," in *More New Testament Studies* (Grand Rapids: Eerdmans, 1968) 143, suggests that 1 Cor 14:37 (without ἐντολή) means that Paul is claiming that any genuine prophet will recognize that Paul's ruling on this matter of the silence of the wives bears the stamp of approval of the risen Christ and carries dominical authority. We concur. Our point, however, stresses that what Paul claims as coming from the Lord is based on a text of Scripture; and that, in the context of the new messianic age, his interpretation of God's word already had the status of an authoritative tradition (cf. 14:33-34).

[42]R. H. Gundry, "The Hellenization of Dominical Tradition and Christianization of Jewish Tradition in the Eschatology of 1—2 Thessalonians," *New Testament Studies* 33 (1987): 173.

The major verb of the sentence at 4:15 λέγομεν ("we say") is linked closely with a repeated construction ἡμεῖς οἱ ζῶντες ("we the living") to form a tight structural unity to 4:15-17. In 4:15 we are told that the living do not have precedence over those who have died. And in 4:17, the living are joined by others (the ones who have been resurrected from the dead) to meet the Lord in the air. The repeated construction is supplemented by a πρῶτον ("first") and ἔπειτα ("then") formula to describe the order of events at the parousia. Thus, the reference to this (τοῦτο) in 4:15 turns out to be a claim that at the parousia the dead in Christ will be raised first. Then, they along with the living will be caught up to meet Christ in the air.

The vocabulary of 1 Thessalonians 4:15b is characteristic of Paul's linguistic usages. The phraseology ἡμεῖς οἱ ζῶντες is widely recognized as Pauline (cf. 2 Cor 4:11; 6:16; Rom 14:8-9). The use of οἱ περιλειπόμενοι ("the ones who are left") is found only in Paul in this repeated construction in 1 Thessalonians 4:15-17. Statistically it is un-Pauline. Here, however, this rare word functions as part of Paul's writing vocabulary and was especially appropriate to describe this particular situation. As such it can hardly be called "un-Pauline." We conclude that the phrase probably is Pauline composition and does not reflect his use of tradition.

In addition, the use of parousia (of the Lord/Christ) is found elsewhere in Thessalonians (1 Thess 2:19; 3:13; 5:23; cf. 2 Thess 2:1). Although Paul usually uses φθάνειν in the sense of "to attain," or "to arrive" (1 Thess 2:16; 2 Cor 10:14), it can denote, as here, precedence.[43] Paul can use οὐ μὴ ("under no circumstances") besides using it in LXX quotations;[44] and the use of κοίμασθαι is thoroughly Pauline. All in all, there is little or no evidence that Paul is using tradition in 4:15.

In 1 Thessalonians 4:16b-17 characteristic Pauline linguistic terminology continues to appear. We will return shortly to 4:16a to argue that it is a piece of separate tradition. Only the use of ὁ κύριος to refer to the coming Jesus represents characteristic Pauline terminology in 4:16a. It is found elsewhere five times in 1 Thessalonians alone (2:19; 3:13; 4:17 [anarthrous]; 5:23) and must be Pauline.[45] With respect to 1 Thessalonians 4:16b, the phraseology οἱ νεκροί ἐν Χριστῷ is uncontestably Pauline. And although Paul's use of ἀναστή-

---

[43]Ibid.; cf. Gal 5:16; 1 Cor 8:13; and as we have noted 1 Thess 5:3.

[44]Gerd Lüdemann, *Paul Apostle to the Gentiles: Studies in Chronology*, trans. F. S. Jones (Philadelphia: Fortress, 1984) 222 (cf. 1 Thess 4:13-14).

[45]Lüdemann, *Apostle to the Gentiles*, 223. Besides the frequent use of this word in Paul, as Lüdemann notes, the πρῶτον and ἔπειτα formula that occurs in 1 Thess 4:16-17 also occurs in a similar apocalyptic context marked by Pauline composition in 1 Cor. 15:46 (cf. 15:23).

σονται ("they will be raised") is unusual, it may have come into the text through association with ἀνέστη in 4:14. In 1 Thessalonians 4:17a the use of ἔπειτα is thoroughly Pauline.[46] Likewise the ἅμα σύν construction has been convincingly shown to be Pauline. The only other wording in 1 Thessalonians 4:17a is the repeated terminology of 4:15: ἡμεῖς οἱ ζῶντες οἱ περιλειπό-μενοι. Although this is a rare usage, we concluded above that this terminology did, most likely, not come from tradition.

Finally, in 4:17b we need to look carefully at the collocation ἁρπαγησό-μεθα ἐν νεφέλαις εἰς ἀπάντησιν τοῦ κυρίου εἰς ἀέρα ("we will be snatched up on the clouds for a meeting with the Lord in the air"). On the grounds of rare usage in Paul the collocation has been identified as Paul's appropriation of tradition.[47] Thus ἁρπάζειν is found in 2 Cor 12:2, 4 where Paul describes a man (perhaps a circumlocution for the apostle himself) who is transported in ecstasy to the third heaven. Likewise, νεφέλη and ἀήρ are rare in Paul's writing; and ἀπάντησις does not occur elsewhere in Paul. While it is uncontested that the phraseology of the rest of 1 Thessalonians 4:17b-18 commencing with καὶ οὕτως ("and thus") is Pauline, it does appear that a case can be made for claiming that the reference to being "snatched up in the air to meet the Lord on the clouds" is "un-Pauline."

However, an alternative view that this is Pauline composition has been put forward. Robert Gundry has made a strong case on behalf of the position that this phraseology must be viewed against the background of the portrayal of an imperial visit in the Hellenistic world; that is, upon the visit of a ruler to a city, important dignitaries and other interested parties would go outside the city, meet the ruler, and accompany him into the city on the last leg of his journey.[48] The argument is that Paul has appropriated this terminology to describe the coming of the heavenly κύριος (Jesus) in 1 Thessalonians 4:17. On this festive occasion his people are snatched up in the air for a meeting (ἀπάντησις) with him. Presumably the idea is that the Thessalonians are being told that they will accompany the returning Lord on the last leg of journey to reclaim his creation.

At the very least Gundry has shown that this image was used in the higher circles of Greco-Roman culture. We presume it would be intelligible to the Thessalonians. It is less likely that this image constituted tradition that emerged out of a Palestinian mileau. This conclusion is fortified by the fact that a description of the snatching up of believers to meet a heavenly figure in the air is without precedent in the early Jesus tradition. Therefore it is doubtful that this terminology funtioned as tradition. Gundry's conclusion that 1 Thessalonians 4:17b

---

[46]Ibid., 223-24.
[47]Ibid.
[48]Gundry, "Hellenization," 166-69.

represents Paul's special contribution to his Hellenistic readers with respect to the doctrine of the parousia may be accepted.

First Thessalonians 4:16a: Paul's Reflection of Tradition

However, there does remain one block of apocalyptic material in this unit found in 1 Thessalonians 4:16a that is unusual for Paul. Coincidentally, it seems to echo material found in Matthew 24:30b-31. This can be set forth in the following display.

Matthew 24:30b-31a	1 Thessalonians 4:16a
1. τὸν υἱὸν τοῦ ἀνθρώπου ἐρχόμενον ἐπὶ τῶν νεφελῶν τοῦ <u>οὐρανοῦ</u>	1. ὅτι αὐτὸς ὁ κύριος (καταβήσεται ἀπ' <u>οὐρανοῦ</u>)
2. μετὰ δυνάμεως καὶ δόξης πολλῆς	2. ἐν κελεύσματι
3. καὶ ἀποστελεῖ τοὺς ἀγγέλους	3. ἐν φωνῇ ἀρχαγγέλου καὶ
4. μετὰ <u>σάλπιγγος</u> μεγάλης	4. ἐν <u>σάλπιγγι</u> θεοῦ

First, it should be noted that the key terminology found in 1 Thessalonians 4:16a is practically nonexistent elsewhere in Paul.[49] Moreover, the terminology is very congruent with descriptions of the end in Jewish apocalypses, and it is well within the realm of possibility that these statements could either attach themselves to Jesus tradition, or may even have come from Jesus himself on the subject of the apocalyptic coming of the Son of Man.

What is significant is that the major features of 4:16a, aside from the shift of order of καταβήσεται ἀπ' οὐρανοῦ ("he will descend from heaven") for purposes of display, stand in sequential parallelism with material found in Matthew 24:30b-31a. This sequential parallelism does not occur in Mark or Luke.

We will note briefly the major features of this striking case of sequential parallelism. First, with reference to the initial parallel, granted that the use of Son of Man by Matthew and κύριοι by Paul are linguistic features of these respective writers to refer to Jesus, for both, the theophany is narrated as coming

---

[49]This has been argued definitively by Lüdemann, *Apostle to the Gentiles*, 222. Καταβήσεται ἀπ' οὐρανοῦ is not found elsewhere in an apocalyptic sense in Paul; κέλευσμα is a hapax legomenon in the New Testament; ἐν φωνῇ ἀρχαγγέλου occurs only in Jude, a writing that may contain early Palestinian material; and ἐν σάλπιγγι θεοῦ appears only in Paul elsewhere at 1 Cor 15:52—a similar apocalyptic unit.

from heaven. In addition, in Matthew, the Son of Man comes upon the clouds. In an inversion on this theme, in the explanatory teaching (4:17) Paul has the cloud; but for him the cloud is the vehicle for the believers to meet the Lord.

Second, in Matthew the Son of Man comes in power and great glory. Paul has the Lord coming ἐν κελεύσματι, ("under the authority of the commander's cry"). What is significant is that Paul pulls together into one event, by use of ἐν with attendant circumstances, the commander's cry, the voice of the archangel, and the sound of the trumpet. The linkage is traditional in Jewish apocalyptic;[50] and since κελεύσμα is an hapax legomenon in Paul this is a strong indication that Paul was using tradition. Indeed, this may be an instance where both Paul and Matthew preserve different parts of the same tradition. (κελεύσμα = Paul; μετὰ δυνάμεως καὶ δόξης πολλῆς ["with power and great glory"] Matthew).[51]

The third and fourth sequential parallels refer to the role of the angels and the blowing of the trumpet at the parousia. The fact that Matthew has angels and Paul an archangel should be viewed in light of the understanding that the archangel, as the leader of the angelic host, under metonymy, can stand for the whole group.[52]

This extensive case of sequential parallelism between 1 Thessalonians 4:16a and Matthew 24:30b-31 may suggest to some that there exists a direct literary connection between the two texts. But this is not likely. On conventional dating, one may entertain the notion that Matthew used Paul. But, since Matthew continues his narrative in 24:31b, with a considerable block of apocalyptic material on the gathering of the elect not alluded to by Paul, one would presume that all of Matthew 24:30-31 is part of a more extensive source utilized by Matthew. And, on the other hand, since there is no substantial body of literary evidence to support the view that Paul copied Matthew, this instance of striking but isolated sequential parallism is not strong enough to warrant positing a direct literary relationship. It would appear that, at this point, it is most reasonable to conclude that Paul and Matthew are using a common tradition. However, the precise nature of that tradition has not been definitively resolved.

Our conclusion is that for the basis of the composition of 1 Thessalonians 4:15-17 Paul has referred to a tradition (1 Thessalonians 4:16a) on the appear-

---

[50]G. Friedrich, "σάλπιγξ," *Theological Dictionary of the New Testament*, vol. 7, ed. G. Kittel and G. Friedrich, trans. G. F. Bromiley (Grand Rapids: Eerdmans, 1971) 84, notes several connections between the commander's cry and the end of the age in Jewish sources. Adam and Eve Apocalypse (i.e., Greek Text Apoc. Mos.) 37-38; 4 Ezra 6:23; Sib Or 4:174. cf. Dan 12:1-2.

[51]Cf. Wenham, *Rediscovery of Jesus' Eschatological Discourse*, 305.

[52]Μέγας (Matt 24:31) occurs 20 times in the text of Matthew. It is also found in O. T. apocalyptic traditions (cf. τῇ σάλπιγγι τῇ μεγάλῃ in Is. 27:13 LXX).

ance of the Lord/Son of Man at the end of history found also at Matthew 24:30b-31. Formally, this is in accord with the way Paul utilizes tradition; especially in 1 Corinthians 14:37. In 1 Corinthians 14:37 Paul claims that the interpretation of the word of the Lord (Scripture) which he brought to Corinth has dominical authority and will be vindicated by the prophets. Likewise, on the basis of a word of the Lord in 1 Thessalonians 4:16a

> Under the authority of the commander's cry, with the call of the archangel, and the sound of the trumpet of God, the Lord himself will descend from heaven

Paul warrants his remarks for claiming that the dead will be raised first, and that they will join believers to meet the returning Lord in the air. Thus Paul has underwritten with dominical authority a body of teaching that goes well beyond the actual claims of the tradition to which he alludes. As in 1 Corinthians 14:37, there is no question that, in his view, this interpretation of the "word of the Lord" was correct and was normative for the church.

So, Paul's interpretation of the tradition for his Hellenistic audience in Thessalonica goes far beyond its actual claim which merely presumes the coming of the Lord to some kind of a final gathering of the elect at the end.[53] This allows Paul to give comfort by claiming that the dead in Christ will not be disadvantaged, but will be raised first, and with the believers who are alive, will meet the returning Lord in the air. With this understanding the Thessalonians are exhorted to encourage one another (4:18). As Paul used the formula κυρίου ἐστὶν [ἐντολή] ("that this is [a commandment] from the Lord") in 1 Cor 14:37 to refer to scripture which warrants his instruction to the Corinthians, in 1 Thessalonians 4:15, Paul uses the formula ἐν λόγῳ κυρίου ("by the word of the Lord") to appeal to Jesus tradition to undergird the authority of his instructions to Thessalonica.[54]

---

[53]That Matt 24:30-31 was taken to refer to resurrection can be seen by Did 16:6. There the third sign (cf. Matt 24:30) of the appearance of the Lord after the ἐκπετάσεως in heaven, and the sound of the trumpet, was the resurrection of the dead. C. M. Tuckett, "Synoptic Tradition in the Didache," in *The New Testament in Early Christianity*, BETL 86, ed. J.-M. Sevrin (Leuven: Leuven University Press/Peeters, 1989) 208, concluded that the pattern of parallels between the Didache and Matthew is thus most easily explained if the Didache here presupposes Matthew's finished Gospel. This conclusion is well substantiated despite the claim of considerable recent secondary literature that Matthew and the Didache are using common tradition. Cf. esp. J. S. Kloppenborg, "Didache 16, 6-8 and special Matthaean Tradition," *Zeitschrift für die neutestamentliche Wissenschaft* 70 (1979): 54-67.

[54]Otfried Hofius, "Unknown Sayings of Jesus" in *The Gospel and the Gospels*, ed. P. Stuhlmacher (Grand Rapids: Eerdmans, 1991) 338-42, has shown that ἐν λόγῳ κύριου is a phrase utilized in the LXX as a term either for the legitimacy of a direct

First Thessalonians 4:15-17 is definitely not an agraphon of Jesus.[55] But neither is it a word totally disconnected from the Jesus tradition. Rather, presuming the existence of the Jesus tradition (1 Thess 4:16a) it represents a bold attempt to use this tradition as the authority to deal with new realities.

The Understanding of 1 Thessalonians 4:13–5:11
as a Word on Eschatological Matters
Based on the Dominical Authority of Jesus Tradition

Our analysis has indicated that Paul, under the general rubric of treating eschatological matters, has dealt with two *topoi* in 1 Thessalonians 4:13-5:11. First, he has dealt with the reality of those Christians who have died with a view to their situation at the parousia (1 Thess 4:13-18); and second, he has dealt with the appropriate attitude for believers in approaching the timing of the parousia (1 Thess 5:1-11). In both cases Paul creatively draws upon Jesus traditions similar to some which are found in the Synoptic eschatological discourses as a way of buttressing his argument (1 Thess 4:16a ‖ Matt 24:30b-31; 1 Thess 5:2 ‖ Matt 24:42-43 ‖ Lk 12:39; 1 Thess 5:3 ‖ Lk 21:34-36).

In this final unit in our discussion of 1 Thessalonians, we will attempt to state succinctly what Paul is saying in 4:13-5:11 based on these appeals to Jesus tradition.

Purpose of the Topos (4:13)

The purpose of the *topos* is to discuss the fate of "the dead ones" in such a way that there should be no concern on their behalf by the believers at Thessalonica who were still alive and who expected to join Christ in the new world. The context clearly indicates that "the dead ones" were believers in Jesus. It does not specify that the concern of the Thessalonians was over a specific local situation. Indeed, the field of vision of Paul and the Thessalonians in this instance may well have covered at least Macedonia. Perhaps a recent death in the

---

prophetic word to him or the prophet's assertion of divine authority for what he says. Something similar to the latter seems to be happening with Paul. Although the apostle does not claim to receive the word direct from the risen Lord, he does claim that his interpretation of the (verbal) tradition has divine authority.

[55]The view that Paul is alluding to an otherwise unknown saying of Jesus seems very unlikely. The case has been argued by J. Jeremias, *Unknown Sayings of Jesus* (London: S.P.C.K., 1958) 5, 64-67. But, on its face, it can never be proven or disproven. If a plausible case could be made that this word is echoed elsewhere in the gospel tradition (as we believe we have done), on methodological grounds, the agraphon thesis ought to be discarded. Likewise, the view that Paul is alluding not to the tradition behind Matt 24:30b-31, but to John 11:25-26 (cf. Gundry, "Hellenization," 164), is not very plausible.

church at Thessalonica provoked special eschatological concerns that were building for some time among the believers in Macedonia over the fate of their dead. In this case, it is quite noticeable that Paul uses the present tense with the participle τῶν κοιμωμένων ("those who have fallen asleep"). At any rate the concern of the Thessalonians was real and deep-seated. It was not merely a philosophical or theoretical point.

Paul's statement on the topic of how to handle the grief process consequent to the loss of loved ones takes on a particular nuance in relation to the way this topic was treated by ancient rhetoricians. His stance was to contrast the hope of the Christian over against the lack of hope of the Gentile without Christ. He seemed to mean in 4:13b, starting with the clause ἵνα μὴ λυπῆσθε ("that you may not grieve") that the believers in the gospel have a hope in God's new creation that is qualitatively superior to anything that can be offered in the pagan world. It is hard not to hear this as yet another example of Paul's grim assessment of pagan life without the gospel which can be seen very clearly in 1 Thessalonians 4:4-5 (cf. Rom 1:18-32). For Paul, there was no assurance of a life beyond death that was on a par with the Christian hope built on the resurrection of Christ. This leads Paul into his argument in 4:14 which will serve as a statement that the hope of the believer for life beyond death rested on the resurrection of Christ.

Confession of the Resurrection of Jesus (4:14)

The confessional formula of 4:14 is stated in the form of a conditional sentence. The protasis, "since we believe that Jesus died and was raised" constitutes the essence of the confession. God is the subject of ἀνέστη ("was raised") and thus the transition is made to 14b where the subject is restated.[56] The apodosis of the sentence traditionally is susceptible to two very different interpretations which must be discussed exegetically. The essence of the exegetical dispute is over the grammatical construction of the phrase διὰ τοῦ Ἰησοῦ ("through Jesus").

---

[56]R. C. Tannehill, *Dying and Rising with Christ: A Study in Pauline Theology*, BZNW 32 (Berlin: Alfred Töpelmann, 1967) 130-34, makes the interesting observation that 1 Thess 4:14 and 5:10 are unusual in Paul because they connect the death and the resurrection of Jesus with the parousia. Paul regularly uses the motif of death and resurrection to describe the believer dying and rising with Christ to a new ethical life. The stress is on participation in the death of Christ because to die with Christ is the necessary precondition for rising with Christ to a new life. Nevertheless, since dying and rising with Christ is a dynamic process for Paul, by extension, Paul's application of this motif to the culminating point of the parousia appears to be consistent with his theological thinking.

One view is that this phrase modifies the participle τοὺς κοιμηθέντας ("the dead ones"). The phrase διὰ τοῦ 'Ιησοῦ would then be either a genitive of attendant circumstances[57] ("the dead ones who have died [as martyrs?] for Christ") or a genitive of specification ("the ones who have died in Christ").[58] The thrust of the clause would be to assert that those who have died with their faith in Christ will at a future point of time be raised (just as Jesus was raised) and will share fulness of life σὺν αὐτῷ ("with him [i.e., the Lord]").

The second view construes the phrase διὰ τοῦ 'Ιησοῦ as directly modifying the verb ἄξει ("he will bring").[59] In this instance, the meaning would be that God will bring through the instrumentality of Jesus' parousia to him (σὺν αὐτῳ) the ones who have fallen asleep.

Both these ways of construing the text present difficulties. With regard to the first position, since there is no real evidence that Paul is talking about believers dying under some unique circumstance we will dismiss the view that διὰ τοῦ 'Ιησοῦ ("through Jesus") is a genitive of attendant circumstances. Second, we can also dismiss the view that Paul is using διὰ τοῦ 'Ιησοῦ as the functional equivalent of ἐν Χρίστω ("in Christ"). Paul knew the difference between the two phrases, and since ἐν Χρίστω is one of his most characteristic linguistic usages (note 4:16), he certainly could have used it in 4:14 if that were his intention.

This leaves us with the latter position. We believe it is the correct view. It is true, as often noted by the commentators, that the apodosis of 4:14b is somewhat imbalanced and that σὺν αὐτῷ constitutes a slight redundancy. But this problem can easily be overcome if we understand that both the protasis and apodosis of the sentence should be joined together by repetition of the verb πιστεύομεν ("we believe"). Paul is saying that since we believe that God raised the dead Jesus from the grave, οὕτως ("thus") or "it necessarily follows" that we believe that God, through the instrumentality of Jesus' parousia will likewise bring the dead ones in Christ to himself also. Therefore, 4:14 functions as a thesis sentence of the *topos*. It is an anticipation of the final conclusion of 4:16-17, where Paul incorporates a dominical word, that the new world, when it

---

[57]C. F. D. Moule, *An Idiom Book of the New Testament Greek*, 2nd ed. (London: Cambridge University Press, 1959) 57.

[58]As noted by several of the commentators (below n. 59); their point is that the phrase διὰ τοῦ 'Ιησοῦ is the functional equivalent to 1 Thess 4:16, οἱ νεκροί ἐν Χριστῷ (cf. 1 Cor 15:18).

[59]E. Best, *First and Second Epistles to the Thessalonians*, 188-89; T. Holtz, *Der Erste Brief an die Thessalonicher*, EKKNT 13 (Zürich: Neukirchen-Vluyn, 1986) 193; Bruce C. Johanson, *To All the Brethren: A Text Linguistic and Rhetorical Approach to 1 Thessalonians*, ConBNT 16 (Stockholm: Almquist and Wiksell International, 1987) 122.

comes, will not only be for those believers who are alive, but also for those who have died.

Here we come to the crux of Paul's argument on the *topos* of the dead ones. Given the fact that Christians believe that Jesus was raised from the dead and that the faithful living would share in Jesus' reign in the new world at his parousia (1 Cor 6:1-3), if there were no place for the dead Christians, their earlier miserable circumstances as Gentiles would have been compounded by their conversion. This is so, because through the sheer caprice of the delay of the end, they would miss out on the benefits of the new world while the rest of the believers would attain them. On this reading, Paul had on his hands a pastoral problem with the families of the deceased ones. His answer, of course, was to argue that the dead believers would be raised and granted equal participation in the new world with the living at the time of the parousia. In 4:15-17 he bolsters this argument with "a word of the Lord."

Jesus Tradition on the Resurrection of the Believers (4:15-17)

In 4:15-17 Paul presents in one sentence his pastoral response to the crisis over the fate of the dead ones. He states that the living at the time of the parousia will not have precedence over the dead (4:15). Utilizing Jesus tradition to describe the coming of the Lord (4:16a), Paul claims that at the parousia the dead in Christ will be raised first (4:16b). Then, joined by the entire complement of believers who are alive at the time, together they will meet the Lord in the air to welcome him in his return in triumph (4:17).

Closing Word (4:18)

In 4:18 Paul continues showing his pastoral concern for the believers in Thessalonica. In place of their natural concern over the deaths of their fellow believers and their deepened sense of anxiety as to whether these fellow believers would participate in the new world, Paul urges his readers to reflect upon the word of 4:15-17 and comfort one another with it. Instead of having anxiety over the fate of the dead ones, Paul the pastor exhorts the Thessalonians to look to the future coming of the Lord with hope based on the confession of 4:14 and the word of the Lord in 4:16-17.[60]

---

[60]K. Donfried, "The Cults of Thessalonians," 347-348, notes that the triadic formula to faith, hope, and love is used by Paul in 1:3 and 5:8, but Timothy in his report on the spiritual condition of the Thessalonians only mentions their faith and love (3:6). The suspicion is that although the Thessalonians have an intellectual belief in the resurrection and future parousia of Christ, they have not pushed it to its logical conclusion that those who have died in him share the hope for postresurrection life and an appearance at the parousia.

A Further Appeal to Tradition (5:1-3)

In 5:1-3 Paul alludes "to the times and the seasons." Clearly this is a reference to eschatological matters. Discussion of certain eschatological points had been the subject of the previous *topos* (4:13-18). Just as the delay of the parousia and the subsequent death of some of the believers had caused the problem which was addressed in the previous *topos*, apparently there was still a further problem to be discussed: namely something to do with "the times and the seasons" (5:1).

Precisely when was the parousia supposed to take place? If the Lord is coming why does he delay? Was this interpretation of history that Paul had taught them credible? This was not just a doctrinal matter. As with the previous *topos* it was clearly a matter of pastoral concern. There was a very thin line between believing that they would participate in a renewed life with Jesus in a new world and rejecting Paul's whole perspective as foolishness.

Paul's response was to give parenesis which carried subtle allusions and reminders of the Jesus tradition that they had already been taught on these matters. By reminding them of the fundamental reality that the parousia (Day of the Lord) was coming suddenly and without notice they needed to be ready.

Thus in 5:1b, if they would take the time to recollect the tradition, there was no need to write further on the matter. The Thessalonians indeed knew the tradition well (5:2a). The use of οἴδατε constitutes a technical term for Paul (1 Thess 1:5; 2:1, 2, 5, 11; 3:3, 4; 4:2). It refers back to the time when Paul was with the Thessalonians. Part of what took place, then, was Paul's teaching of the tradition (4:1-2). Probably the unusual ἀκριβῶς ("accurately") in 5:2a is Paul's point that on the matter of the timing of the eschatological events at the end of history they were taught well. Now they should heed this teaching.

In 5:2b-3 Paul alludes to what the Thessalonians were actually taught. As we have already seen, this involves allusions to a body of Jesus tradition on eschatological matters. This coheres with our view that 5:1-2a refers to the giving to the Thessalonians of the Jesus tradition at an earlier time on eschatological matters— along with other information.

The emphasis of Paul is on the startlingly different phenomenon of the parousia to any event that preceded it. Thus it is compared with the sharp and sudden stab of pain of the pregnant woman who has come to full term rather than the period of eschatological horrors of tribulation that was often perceived in apocalyptic circles as preceding the end of history.

The sudden destruction will be concurrent with the full term of the pregnant woman (i.e., the time of the actual parousia of Jesus himself). Perhaps the emphasis was made for pastoral purposes of encouraging the Christians to keep on keeping on; or, as is often said, to defuse undue eschatological enthusiasm. In any case, by the referring of the labor pains to the actual parousia Paul put an emphasis on an actual reversal of the normal state of affairs at the parousia and not on the terrible tribulations of the tough times that precede it. This then sets the tone for 5:4-10. There the mood is one of encouragement for the present in light of the swift, sudden, and sure vindication of the faithful at the parousia.

Parenesis Based on the Jesus Tradition (5:4-10)

Having made his point that the current events did not necessarily portend the immediate occurrence of the parousia, Paul then moved to give a brief description of what the attitude of the Thessalonians should be in light of this reality. He commences in 5:4 with the strong adversative (ὑμεῖς δέ). He transfers the metaphor of day (of the Lord) from the eschatological arena to the terminology of moral exhortation. This transposition takes place in 5:4-5a. The Thessalonians are reminded that they are people of "the day" and not of "the night." And, again faintly echoing the shared Jesus tradition (cf. Matt 24:43/Lk 12:39), Paul argues that if they live as people of light the end will not come upon them unexpected, like a thief. Paul reinforces this exhortation in 4b-8 by shifting back to his use of the first person plural. And in 5:6 Paul uses γρηγορεῖν ("to watch") and καθεύδειν ("to sleep") in a strong moral sense to accentuate the difference between believer and unbeliever.

Paul, at 5:6, 10, with his use of γρηγορεῖν seems to be echoing again the tradition of the parable of the thief, which we identified as being behind 1 Thessalonians 5:2, and was part of the tradition which Paul taught to the Thessalonians.[61] On the other hand while μεθύσκεσθαι ("to become intoxicated") in 1 Thessalonians 5:7 and καθεύδειν (5:6,7,10) are also somewhat unusual words for Paul, it is probably the case that they function as part of a general vocabulary on moral exhortation at the time.[62]

Paul brings this moral exhortation to a resounding crescendo in 1 Thessalonians 5:8-10. Because God has destined his people to salvation through the death of Christ, his people are to manifest the virtues of faith, hope, and love. Whether

---

[61]In the Matthean version, Matt 24:42-43, γρηγορεῖν appears twice. It is generally regarded as a linguistic characteristic of Matthew. See D. G. Tevis, *An Analysis of Words and Phrases Characteristic of the Gospel of Matthew* (Ann Arbor MI: University Microfilms, 1983) #229, 173. But, if our understanding of the history of the source tradition is correct, this word was in the source before it was utilized by Paul and Matthew. The only other occurrence of γρηγορεῖν in the Pauline corpus is at 1 Cor 16:3 and Col 4:2. The twofold use of it here is compatible with the view that Paul is echoing common tradition.

[62]The fact that μεθύειν (μεθύσκεσθαι) is found in Matt 24:49 ‖ Lk 12:45 is not strong evidence that there was a link in the Jesus tradition known by Paul between the Parable of the Thief in the Night (Matt 24:42-43 ‖ Lk 12:39-40) and the Chief Servant and the Slaves (Matt 24:45-51 ‖ Lk 12:42-46). The same point can be made with respect to the appearance of καθεύδειν in Matt 25:5 and Mk 13:36.

the believer is alive ("watching") or is deceased ("sleeping"), he will be united with the Lord at the parousia (5:10, cf. 4:17).[63]

Concluding Word (5:11)

As in 4:18, Paul brings this second *topos* on eschatological matters to an end with parenesis. The Thessalonians should not ultimately be concerned about either the oppressiveness of the current times or special problems that they have concerning the parousia. An opportunity is available as they wait for the parousia for them to exercise spiritual development. Paradoxically, it is in the cultivation of spiritual growth that they will be most prepared for the sudden, unexpected return of Jesus. This should be the basis for their encouragement and building up of one another in the faith.

Summary and Conclusion

Our study of similar Jesus tradition in the Synoptic Eschatological Discourse and in 1 Thessalonians is now complete. We have discovered three instances where both Paul and the Synoptic writers used a similar tradition.

Paul (1 Thessalonians 5:2) and Matthew/Luke (24:42-43 ‖ 12:39) both utilized the parable of the Thief in the Night. Paul (1 Thessalonians 5:3) and Luke (21:34-36) utilized a similar tradition on the *Sudden Calamity of the End* from which there is no escape. Finally, Paul (1 Thessalonians 4:16a) and Matthew (24:30b-31) used a common apocalyptic tradition on the coming of the Lord/Son of Man at the end.

In none of these instances does the evidence require direct literary dependency between Paul and Matthew/Luke. Rather, in each instance, it is more likely that Paul and the Synoptic writers were utilizing common Jesus tradition.

Assuming the Synoptics were composed after Paul wrote 1 Thessalonians, the literary evidence allows us to conclude that Paul, as a traditioner, knew Jesus tradition on eschatological matters and passed this tradition on to his converts. However, the literary evidence does not warrant that, at the time that he wrote 1 Thessalonians, he knew an extensive eschatological text which could qualify as a *proto* or *Ur* version of the Synoptic Apocalypse. We would be comfortable with the conclusion that the evidence warrants the claim that Paul had a knowledge about a certain collection of sayings of Jesus on the end time; but we have been unable to find any convincing indication that the material form of the

---

[63]This latter reference to "sleeping" should probably be understood more in light of 1 Thess 4:17 rather than being a specific reference to a moral situation as was the case in 1 Thess 5:6, 7. Cf. Tannehill, *Dying and Rising*, 133-34.

collection of these sayings closely paralleled our Synoptic versions of Jesus' Last Eschatological Discourse.

However, there is another body of material in 2 Thessalonians 2:1-12 which also must be factored into the discussion. We will now examine carefully that body of material in order to determine what relevance it has for an understanding of the history of the formation of the Synoptic Eschatological Discourse.

3.
Second Thessalonians 2:1-12

The Sequence and Situation of 2 Thessalonians

When the second letter to the Thessalonians was written the situation in the church at Thessalonica had changed since the time of the composition of the earlier letter.[1] The focus of the change centers on a greater awareness by the writer of the letter about the grave suffering that had taken place among the Christians in Thessalonica. Early in the letter this is stated explicitly in 1:14b; and a similar refrain can be seen throughout the composition (1:5-6,11; 2:15; 3:1-3). By adopting a general deliberative rhetorical style of writing Paul gives advice to the Thessalonians. He states that he identifies fully with their situation because he likewise suffers (2 Thess 3:1-2).

The perception of the depth and pervasiveness of the hostility toward the gospel, resulting in the suffering of believers, is the underlying new reality that faces the writer of 2 Thessalonians. It leads the author to place this opposition

---

[1]This presumes the letter was written after 1 Thessalonians. Indeed, this does seem to be the most reasonable position to take. Jewett, *Thessalonian Correspondence*, 21-30, discusses at length the history of the debate over the sequence of the letters and concludes that the letters were written in the canonical sequence. His argument is that the rhetoric of 1 Thessalonians presumes only one founding visit to Thessalonica, a hasty departure, and a relatively brief period of separation before the composition of 1 Thessalonians. 2 Thess 2:15 is most easily understood as a reference to an earlier letter despite rigorous arguments to the contrary. Cf. C. A. Wanamaker, *The Epistles to the Thessalonians: A Commentary on the Greek Text*, NIGTC (Grand Rapids: Eerdmans, 1990) 37-45. However, the presumption that a relatively brief period of time transpired between the writing of the first and second letters is not warranted. A more promising argument, in our view, is that 2 Thessalonians represents a later response, after some years, to certain developments, which included intense persecution at Thessalonica. Certainly, since the time of W. Wrede, it has been noticed that the author responds by writing a letter strongly echoing both the vocabulary, style, and themes of the first letter. (cf. 1 Thess 1:1–2 ∥ 2 Thess 1:1–2; 1 Thess 5:14 ∥ 2 Thess 3:6-12; 1 Thess 2:13; 4:1 ∥ 2 Thess 2:15; 3:6). The writer of 2 Thessalonians is especially concerned to state that this letter is an authentic word from Paul (2 Thess 3:17; cf. 2:15) as opposed to certain inauthentic communications that the Thessalonians have received over time (2 Thess 2:2). This seems to presume that some years had elapsed between the first and second letter so that a debate had arisen over what Paul taught on eschatological matters. The writer now seeks to present an authoritative response on the matter.

in the context of a statement on the universal punishment of those who oppose the gospel (1:5-12). In other words, opposition to the word is directly linked with a promised final judgment that will expose the enemies of the Gospel at the end of the age. A similar connection between an outburst of terrible wickedness and the coming of the Day of the Lord is made a major focus in 2:1-12.

As in 1 Thessalonians, where Paul is concerned to address the pastoral situation, the writer asserts that in this time of great persecution it is necessary to hear his teaching clearly and obey the tradition he has already imparted to them (2 Thess. 1:10-12; 2:13-15; 3:6, 11-15). Upon understanding that God would definitively punish evil in the future the readers could accept, for the present, that the grace of God would suffice to sustain them in their suffering (1:3-4; 11-12; 2:16-17; 3:2-3, 5, 16). And, in fact, the tough times, although not specifically an indication that the Day of the Lord had come, do have a purpose in that they will eventually produce deeper faith, hope, and love in the community (1:11;2:13, 16; 3:5). Thus, both with respect to the present and for the future, the letter argues that the Christian faith offers hope for the readers.

It is not necessary for our purposes to give the definitive word on whether or not this letter was a pseudonymous work.[2] If we can anticipate the conclusion of this chapter, we tend to think that 2 Thessalonians came from within the Pauline circle from a coworker (perhaps Timothy) on behalf of Paul from a period late in his life.

What is more significant for our study is the question of the time and circumstances of its composition. The reference to the expectation of the man of lawlessness making an appearance in the temple of God (τὸν ναὸν τοῦ Θεοῦ), in 2:4, seems to preclude a date after 70 CE. The arguments, often made,

---

[2]The work of W. Trilling has had the effect of causing a major swing in recent scholarly opinion against Pauline authorship in favor of a view that 2 Thessalonians is an imitation of 1 Thessalonians and is a pseudonymous work. Cf. W. Trilling, *Untersuchungen zum zweiten Thessalonicherbrief*, ETS 27 (Leipzig: Benno, 1972); *Der Zweite Brief an die Thessalonischer*, EKKNT 14, (Zürich: Neukirchen, Benziger, 1980); "Literarische Paulusimitation im 2. Thessalonicherbrief," in *Paulus in den neutestamentlichen Spätschriften: Zur Paulusrezeption im Neuen Testament*, ed. K. Kertlelge (Freiburg: Herder, 1981) 146-56. The most comprehensive response to Trilling from one who claims 2 Thessalonians was a genuine letter from Paul is still the work of I. H. Marshall, *1 and 2 Thessalonians*, NCB (Grand Rapids: Eerdmans, 1983) 28-45. A point that is often overlooked is that 1 and 2 Thessalonians claim to come from Paul, Silas, and Timothy (1 Thess 1:1; 2 Thess 1:1). Some differences in terminology, style, and theological outlook in 2 Thessalonians from the earlier letter may be the result of authorship by one of the circle of Paul's coworkers. Cf. K. Donfried, "2 Thessalonians and the Church of Thessalonica," in *Origins and Method: Towards a New Understanding of Judaism and Christianity Essays in Honour of J.C. Hurd*, JSNTSS 86, ed. B. H. Mclean (Sheffield: JSOT Press, 1993) 143-44.

that the language of 2:4 is so traditional and pictorial that the end of the Jerusalem temple did not form any obstacle for its use in a literary work post 70 are implausible.[3] More compelling is the argument of Martin Hengel, that the language of 2 Thessalonians 2:4 sounds very similar to widespread concerns at the time of the political crisis in the Roman Empire in the latter part of the decade prior to 70 CE.[4] This period of great upheavals, starting with the great fire at Rome, the instability of Nero and his successors, and the subsequent problems of harassment of the church, provide a plausible *Sitz im Leben* that may well have nourished an anticipation of the kind of scenario described in 2 Thessalonians 2:1-12. The writer (ostensibly Paul) has suffered from the opposition of unbelievers (3:2-3); and a greater manifestation of lawlessness may well be at hand before the eschatological crisis is finally resolved (2:6-10). In this intervening time the believers are exhorted to hold to the Pauline traditions (3:6-13). If they do this they will not be shaken by the extravagant claims of contemporary prophets (2:2, 9-10), but will be a participant in the ultimate eschatological triumph of Christ (1:5-10). Thus, although we cannot be absolutely certain of the time of the composition of this letter, a date in the late sixties of the first century seems to be congruent with the textual evidence.

Second Thessalonians 2:1-12 in the Structure of 2 Thessalonians

Structurally, the letter is built around the call of Paul to the Thessalonians to heed the traditions they were taught. In turn, these traditions were to provide them with the necessary fortitude to survive at the last day. Thus, in the opening segment (2 Thess 1:3-12) the crisis of persecution is acknowledged, but the evidence of faith confirms the Thessalonians true calling in Christ which ultimately will be vindicated at the end. This leads to both the statement of the issue facing the Thessalonians and its resolution in 2:1-12. The writer addresses a major misunderstanding on eschatological matters. Appearances to the contrary, he reminds his readers that the Day of the Lord has not come. Rather it is a specific event which will not take place until certain eschatological occurrences have run their course. Finally, the concluding parenesis of 2:13-3:15 is a call to continual sober living built on the proposition that one needs to adhere to Paul's words to cultivate the kind of spiritual development that will stand the test at the last judgment.

---

[3]Cf. L. Hartman, "The Eschatology of 2 Thessalonians as included in a Communication," in *The Thessalonian Correspondence*, BETL 87 (Leuven: Leuven University Press/ Peeters, 1990) 482-83, who argues that 2 Thess 2:4 is so "traditional" and "pictorial" that the destruction of the Temple does not affect its use here.

[4]M. Hengel, *Studies in the Gospel of Mark* (Philadelphia: Fortress, 1985) 19-20.

Second Thessalonians 2:1-12 falls into four distinct sections. In an opening unit, 2:1-3a, Paul set forth his essential argument: namely, that it is an error to believe that the Day of the Lord has come. Then, in 2:3b-5, he gives the first of three reasons to substantiate his claim. The Day of the Lord has not come because certain eschatological events have not taken place. Prominent among them is the arrival of the apostasy and the appearance of the man of lawlessness in the temple. Second, in 2:6-7, through the work of τὸ κατέχον/ων ("the thing/one restraining"), the actual coming of the man of lawlessness is being held back. Since it is the time of restraint, and the man of lawlessness has not appeared, one should conclude that the Day of the Lord has not yet come. Finally, in 2:8-12, the readers are told that the full manifestation of the man of lawlessness will precipitate the parousia of Christ. Since the manifestation (parousia) of the man of sin has not come, neither has the parousia of Christ. This constitutes the third reason given to prove that the Day of the Lord has not arrived. The conclusion is that any belief that the Day of the Lord has come is not warranted.

These arguments fit well into the general theme that the present is a time of testing and development of spiritual growth for the people of God. But in good time those who continue to show fortitude will be vindicated at the last day.

The Use of Jesus Tradition in the Composition of 2 Thessalonians

Second Thessalonians 2:1-12, with its reference to a final eschatological crisis before the parousia, including the appearance of false prophets, and the epiphany of the evil man of lawlessness in the holy place, has a number of formal parallels with the major features of both the Matthean and Markan versions of Jesus' Last Eschatological Discourse. The question thus inevitably arises, "Is there a direct literary connection between these works?" Or, could these separate works reflect dependence on a common tradition?[5]

In order to make a judgment on this matter, we will examine, piecemeal, the major literary parallels between 2 Thessalonians 2, and its closest Synoptic parallel, the Matthean version of the Eschatological Discourse. Links to Mark's version of the Discourse, where it appears to come closer to Paul, will be discussed in the text. Having done this, we will summarize the evidence and end the discussion by drawing our conclusions.

---

[5]Hartman, *Prophecy Interpreted*, 201-202, after a lengthy analysis, is convinced the author of 2 Thessalonians 2 was aware of a version of the Eschatological Discourse that was also utilized by the writers of the Synoptic Eschatological Discourse. He has made some strong arguments that are often too quickly dismissed in the secondary literature.

Second Thessalonians 2:1 || Matthew 24:3b, 31: The Topic of the Parousia

2 Thessalonians 2:1	Matthew 24:3b, 31
	³ᵇκαὶ τί τὸ σημεῖον (cf. 30)
ὑπὲρ τῆς <u>παρουσίας</u>	τῆς σῆς <u>παρουσίας</u> . . . (cf. 27)
τοῦ κυρίου ἡμῶν	
<u>καὶ ἐπισυναγωγῆς</u> ἐπ' αὐτόν	³¹<u>καὶ ἐπισυνάξουσιν</u>
	τοὺς ἐκλεκτοὺς αὐτοῦ . . .

Both units open with a specific reference to the parousia. 2 Thessalonians 2:1-12 begins by indicating that it is Paul's desire to set forth a specific topic of doctrine ὑπὲρ τῆς παρουσίας τοῦ κυρίου ἡμῶν Ἰησοῦ Χριστοῦ καὶ ἡμῶν ἐπισυναγωγῆς ἐπ' αὐτόν ("concerning the coming of our Lord Jesus Christ and our gathering to him"). Already this linkage between the coming parousia of Christ and a gathering of believers to him had surfaced in 2 Thessalonians 1:7-10. Certainly, this same motif is a chief feature of 1 Thessalonians 4:13-5:11, which the author probably has in mind.[6]

The use of παρουσία and ἐπισυνάγειν ("to gather") frames a major segment of Matthew's version of the Eschatological Discourse (Matt 24:3b, 31). The disciples ask Jesus for a sign of (your) parousia (24:3b). It turns out as the narrative unfolds with its rich discussion of eschatological events that a final definitive sign is given: the sign (τὸ σημεῖον) of the Son of Man in heaven (24:30). Then, immediately upon the coming of the sign, the Son of Man will send the angels to gather (ἐπισυνάξουσιν) the elect. Thus, as in 2 Thessalonians 2:1, Matthew links the parousia with a gathering of believers to meet the Lord of the church.[7] The parallel is quite striking.

Second Thessalonians 2:2a, 3, (11) || Matthew 24:4b, 6b:
The Warning Not to be Deceived or Disturbed

2 Thessalonians 2:2-3,11	Matthew 24:4, 6
²ᵃμηδὲ <u>θροεῖσθε</u> . . .	⁴ᵇβλέπετε
³<u>μὴ τις ὑμᾶς</u> ἐξαπατήσῃ . . .	<u>μὴ τις ὑμᾶς πλανήσῃ</u> . . .
	⁶ᵇ<u>μὴ θροεῖσθε</u> . . .

---

[6]G. S. Holland, *The Tradition that You Received from Us: 2 Thessalonians in the Pauline Tradition*, HUT 24 (Tübingen: J. C. B. Mohr [Siebeck], 1988) 44.

[7]The word ἐπισυναγωγή occurs only twice in the N.T. (2 Thess 2:1; Heb 10:25). The rare usage of the noun (2 Thess 2:1) combined with the fact that the verbal form does occur in a context with parallel subject matter (Matt 24:30) is modest evidence that either Matthew is echoing Paul or Paul is echoing tradition similar to that found in Matthew. In our view, the preponderance of evidence will lead us towards the latter conclusion.

²:¹¹καὶ διὰ τοῦτο
πέμπει αὐτοῖς ὁ Θεὸς
ἐνέργειαν πλάνης

After the announcement of the topic of the parousia in 2 Thessalonians 2:1 there follows sequentially a warning not to be disturbed (Θροεῖσθε) by a deceptive report that the Day of the Lord has come (2 Thess 2:2). This warning is immediately followed by another warning not to be deceived (ἐξαπατᾶν) on this matter (2 Thess 2:3).

Similarly, in both Matthew and Mark, Jesus' first response to the disciples request for a sign (Matthew has parousia) is accompanied by a warning not to be deceived (πλανήσῃ: Mt 24:4, Mk 13:5). This warning is repeated (Mt 24:5; Mk 13:6) in the call not to be deceived by those who claim to come bearing the title ἐγώ εἰμι ("I am"). (Matt 28:5 has even specified the "I am" to be "the Christ.") Then, in the next verse (Mt 24:6/Mk 13:7), there follows the warning not to be disturbed (Θροεῖσθε). Here the specific sources of disturbance are wars and rumors of wars.

Thus, in both Matthew/Mark and 2 Thessalonians there is a call not to be deceived and disturbed. In the case of the latter, in both Matthew/Mark and 2 Thessalonians the same word (Θροεῖσθε) is used. Elsewhere in the New Testament this word is found only at Luke 24:37. This rare use of Θροεῖσθε is an additional modest indicator that a literary relationship exists between the two bodies of material.

However, we cannot say definitively that the call not to be deceived (different Greek words in Matthew 24:4 and 2 Thessalonians 2:2) is Jesus tradition.[8] It could be stock apocalyptic phraseology on not being led astray. Nevertheless, the similar linkage of not being disturbed and led astray (deceived) which is found in these two texts that have other close thematic connections, does invite further inquiry.

This inquiry may be pursued if we note that in 2 Thessalonians 2:2 the warning against being disturbed and led astray is given with reference to a belief that the Day of the Lord has come (ἐνέστηκεν). The author is concerned to state that whether this belief had its origin among the Thessalonians, by the utterance of a prophet through the Spirit (διὰ πνεύματος), or through a written teaching (δι' ἐπιστολῆς), it must be rejected in favor of receiving the tradi-

---

[8]But note the phraseology ἐνέργειαν πλάνης ("powerful delusion") 2 Thess 2:11 uses to describe those who come under the power of the man of lawlessness. Here the word πλάνη does correspond to Matt. 24:4. The verbal form of πλάνη occurs four times in the Matthean version of the Eschatological Discourse as a warning to the readers not to be deceived or led astray (Matt 24:4 ‖ Mk 13:15; Matt 24:5 ‖ Mk 13:6; Matt 24:11 [in reference to false prophets]; 24:24).

tions transmitted by the author of this letter.[9] In other words, 2 Thessalonians claims to give the definitive word of Paul that the Day of the Lord has not come; it will not come until a certain set of events takes place. It is interesting to note that the Last Discourse of Jesus in the Synoptics (Matt 24:5/Mk 13:6; cf. Matt 24:26) is, among other things, concerned to refute a belief that the Christ is somehow secretly present in the world. Likewise, the parallel in Luke 21:8, with its additional statement of the deceivers who say the time has come (ὁ καιρὸς ἤγγικεν),[10] makes a similar point.

Thus we are confronted here with analogous language and concerns in both 2 Thessalonians 2:2-3,11 and Matthew 24:4,6 and parallel places in the synoptic versions of the Last Eschatological Discourse of Jesus. In both bodies of material a scenario is given to refute the belief that the critical events of the end time have taken place. In place of such a belief a detailed scenario of the time leading up until the parousia of Christ is sketched. Indeed, in our next unit we will note that there are close similarities in content between Paul and the Jesus in the Last Eschatological Discourse with regard to the details of these events.

Second Thessalonians 2:3b-4 || Matthew 24:11-12, 15: The Time of Apostasy

2 Thessalonians 2:3b-4	Matthew 24:11-12, 15
³ᵇὅτι ἐὰν μὴ ἔλθῃ ἡ ἀποστασία πρῶτον καὶ ἀποκαλυφθῇ ὁ ἄνθρωπος τῆς ἀνομίας	¹¹⁻¹²καὶ πολλοὶ ψευδοπροφῆται ἐγερθήσονται καὶ πλανήσουσιν πολλούς καὶ διὰ τὸ πληθυνθῆναι τὴν ἀνομίαν ψυγήσεται ἡ ἀγάπη τῶν πολλῶν. . . .
ὁ υἱὸς τῆς ἀπωλείας, ⁴ὁ ἀντικείμενος καὶ ὑπεραιρόμενος ἐπὶ πάντα λεγόμενον θεὸν ἢ σέβασμα, ὥστε αὐτὸν εἰς τὸν ναὸν τοῦ θεοῦ καθίσαι ἀποδεικνύντα ἑαυτὸν ὅτι ἐστὶν θεός.	¹⁵ὅταν οὖν ἴδητε τὸ βδέλυγμα τῆς ἐρημώσεως . . . ἑστὸς ἐν τόπῳ ἁγίῳ. . . .

---

[9]The author, of course, claims to be Paul. The wording ἃς ἐδιδάχθητε εἴτε διὰ λόγου εἴτε δι᾽ ἐπιστολῆς ἡμῶν of 2 Thess 2:15 forms a beautiful inclusio with 2:2. Apparently there has been some dispute over actual or perceived misrepresentation about the Pauline teaching concerning the Day of the Lord. 2 Thess 1:5-10 has made it clear that the final eschatological Day has not yet arrived. A similar point constitutes the burden of the discussion between 2:2 and 2:15.

[10]This phraseology probably employs ἐγγίζειν to mean the "very near coming of the end." Cf. J. Bradley Chance, *Jerusalem, the Temple, and the New Age in Luke-Acts* (Macon GA: Mercer University Press, 1988) 93.

Second Thessalonians 3b-4 is not a complete sentence. The sentence is conditional with the statement of the protasis ἐὰν μὴ ἔλθῃ ἡ ἀποστασία; but no apodosis is given to conclude the sentence. It is generally understood that the apodosis is "the Day of the Lord has not come." This would be implied from the phraseology at the end of 2 Thessalonians 2:2.[11] Thus Paul is saying, "Except certain events take place, which I will enumerate, The Day of the Lord will not have come."

It is quite noticeable that Paul set out two important events which, although they may overlap to some extent, are supposed to occur before the Day of the Lord. First, there comes in 2:3 the "falling away (ἀποστασία). Second, also in 2:3, the "falling away" has as its central feature the manifestation of an evil figure known as the man of lawlessness (ὁ ἄνθρωπος τῆς ἀνομίας).[12] This figure is destined to be seated in power in the temple of God and receive acclaim that is only appropriate for a divine figure (2 Thess 2:4). Coincidentally, upon his manifestation, the man of lawlessness will be destroyed by the parousia of Christ (2:8).

This sequence of the appearing of a "falling away" or apostasy culminating in a final definitive manifestation of rebellion against God in the temple is found in Matthew 24:11-12, 15. The description of "the falling away" is stated eloquently in Matthew 24:11, and in 24:12, it is called lawlessness (τὴν ἀνομίαν).[13] Of course, lawlessness has always been present, to some degree, in the world. However, Matthew seems to be referring to an intensified expression of it that is qualitatively different to anything that has happened before. Thus, it is reasonable to equate πληθύνειν ἀνομίαν (Matt 24:12) with ἀποστασία in 2 Thessalonians 2:3.

As in 2 Thessalonians, this burst of lawlessness as described by Matthew has, as its culminating point, the appearance of the ultimate manifestation of evil. This occurs at Matthew 24:15. In the holy place of the temple there will be

---

[11]Cf. Holland, *2 Thessalonians in the Pauline Tradition*, 107.

[12]This figure is also given the title, ὁ ἄνομος (2:5). The use of πρῶτον underscores that these two events occur before the coming of the Day of the Lord.

[13]This word occurs four times in Matthew and is not found elsewhere in the gospel tradition. Normally, this would count as strong evidence that this is a Matthean linguistic usage and is consequently Matthean composition. However, D. Wenham, "A Note on Matthew 24:10-12," *Tyndale Bulletin* 31 (1980) 160-61, has observed that the phraseology πληθύνειν ἀνομίαν, which occurs only in Matthew, at 24:12, is found in a polemic against idolatry in Ezek 16:51 (LXX). There is much in Matt 24:10-12 that reflects the O.T. terminology of polemics against apostasy (esp. in Daniel 12). Thus, it is quite possible that the appearance of ἀνομία may, in Matt 24:12, reflect a use of biblical tradition, and account for the parallel with 2 Thess. 2:3.

found the Horrible Desecration (τὸ βδέλυγμα τῆς ἐρημώσεως).[14] More than likely this does not mean anything more than "the ultimate expression of idolatry."[15] The terminology, of course, is most directly dependent on the description, found in the text of Daniel, when Antiochus Epiphanes profaned the temple (Dan 9:26; 11:31ff.; 12:11; cf. 2 Macc 6:1ff.). But, more than a recapitulation of that horrendous event, for Matthew, it represents the very climax of a process of human profanation and idolatry that had already fully occupied the attention of the Old Testament prophets.

Although, as indicated by the display, the linguistic parallels between 2 Thessalonians 2:3-4 and Matthew 24:10-12, 15 are sparse, and definitely not strong enough to indicate direct copying, there is a striking similarity in themes.[16] In both cases we have an eschatological description where the parousia is preceded by a two-stage event. First, there is a great apostasy. Second, this apostasy develops into another stage, wherein at a *chairos*, there occurs a terrible manifestation of evil in the temple of God—presumably in Jerusalem. These striking sequential parallels are of sufficient impact to lead us to the conclusion that both 2 Thessalonians 2:3b-4 and Matthew 24:11-12, 15 are dependent upon a common tradition. As we have already indicated, this tradition on the time of apostasy, which is used by the writer of 2 Thessalonians, appears to be part of a wider collocation of material that has echoes throughout the Synoptic Eschatological Discourse. We have already shown that 2 Thessalonians 2:1 echoes material sim-

---

[14]D. Wenham, "Paul and the Synoptic Apocalypse," in *Gospel Perspectives: Studies of History and Tradition in the Four Gospels* 2, ed. R. T. France and D. Wenham (Sheffield: JSOT Press 1981) 352, suggestively interprets the οὖν of Matt 24:15 to function as a connective to mean that the appearance of the Horrible Desecration represents the conclusion of the argument from Matt 24:11f. As such Matt 24:15f. explicates the highest manifestation of the "multiplication of lawlessness," as described in Matt 24:10-12.

[15]Wenham, "Note on Matthew 24," 160. He has found in Ezek 11:21 LXX a close linkage between βδέλυγμα and ἀνομία (cf. Ezek 11:18). In Ezekiel there are frequent references to ἀνομία in Jerusalem. And twice (Ezek 8:16-17; 44:6, 7) similar terminology is connected with idolatrous abominations in the temple.

[16]On our hypothesis, Mark is dependent upon the text of Matthew. It is not infeasible that Mark also had access to the text of 2 Thessalonians. If this were the case it may explain the Markan use (Mark 13:14) of the grammatically difficult ἑστηκότα ὅπου οὐ δεῖ. This apparent use of the perfect masculine participle to modify a noun in the neuter gender may have been a daring attempt by Mark to reconcile a difficulty he found in the two traditions. Anticipating our conclusion in chap. 6, it may well have represented Mark's attempt to come to grips with the actual historical circumstances at the time. That is, in Matthew the ultimate expression of evil is an event, whereas in Paul evil comes in a person. At any rate, Wenham, *Rediscovery of Jesus' Eschatological Discourse*, 193-94, commendably warns against embracing quickly the view that Mark clumsily preserves an older tradition and that Matthew and Luke have corrected it grammatically in their own particular ways.

ilar to that found in the Matthean version of his discourse both at its beginning and towards its climax (Matt 24:3, 30-31). And 2 Thessalonians 2:2 echoes Matthew 24:4, 6 with its twofold warning not to be led astray and disturbed by the time of crisis. This literary evidence leads us to the tentative conclusion that the basic contours of the version of the Eschatological Discourse which appears in Matthew/Mark are echoed in 2 Thessalonians 2:1-12.[17]

Glenn Holland has noted that Matthew/Mark has placed Jesus' Last Discourse in "a three-part eschatological scenario."[18] The first stage is the beginning of the birthpangs of the end (Matt 24:5-9 ‖ Mk 13:6-10). This stage is highlighted both by the calamities which characterize an eschatological crisis and the appearance of false prophets and messianic pretenders.[19] The second stage is the actual terrible tribulation (θλῖψις).[20] This is found in Matthew 24:10-29a/Mark 13:14-23. The appearance of the Horrible Desecration, more false prophets, and great tribulation, is the central focus of this era. Third, there is the parousia of the Son of Man (Matt 24:29b-31/Mk 13:24-27).[21]

A similar three-stage scenario on the end also informs the composition of 2 Thessalonians 2:1-12. This threefold scenario, which the writer perceives will unfold chronologically, may be called the present crisis, the eschatological crisis, and the parousia of Jesus and last judgment at the end of the age.[22] Before we draw conclusions about the use of these similar eschatological traditions in both 2 Thessalonians and the Synoptic Eschatological Discourse, we will set forth an analysis of 2 Thessalonians 2, and show how this tradition with its threefold scenario on the end was of critical importance in its composition.

---

[17]A fuller explication of *all* of the echoes of Jesus tradition in 2 Thessalonians, found in the Synoptic Eschatological Discourse, will be given when we study the source tradition of Matthew in the next chapter.

[18]Holland, *2 Thessalonians in the Pauline Tradition*, 134-35.

[19]Ibid.

[20]Ibid.

[21]Ibid.

[22]Here we take issue with one aspect of the otherwise excellent discussion by Holland, ibid., 134. Holland claims that the author of 2 Thess 2:1-12 organizes his eschatology into a scenario of present crisis, the Day of the Lord, and the parousia. I would substitute "the final crisis" for the "Day of the Lord." Despite Holland's extended argumentation in his monograph in favor of the view that the Day of the Lord is an earlier separate crisis preceding the parousia of Jesus at the end of the age, his analysis of the text proves just the opposite (cf. ibid., 101-103). The Day of the Lord is the parousia in 1 Thessalonians. We see nothing in the second letter to indicate that this view has changed.

Second Thessalonians 2:1-12:
The Problem of the Delay of the Day of the Lord
Addressed by the Use of Tradition

The Problem (2:1-3a)

The writer opens in 2:1-2 by invoking the common hope for the parousia and the assembly of the righteous ones to meet Jesus. He asserts that the Thessalonians should not allow themselves to be shaken or disturbed by an alternative position that held that the Day of the Lord had come. The readers are reminded that they had received teaching on this matter earlier (2:5). And in 2:15 the position, contrary to the view that the Day of the Lord has already come, is reinforced.

The Synoptic passages Matthew 24:5-6 (cf. 24:24-26) || Mark 13:5-6 || Luke 21:8, seem to presuppose that there were some who held that the Messiah was secluded in secret and would soon be revealed at his day—a propitious time. Another posibility is that, more than likely, the Thessalonians in question considered that the "Day of the Lord" was not a specific day but a short period of horrors surrounding the parousia itself.[23] At any rate, the two situations are not mutually incompatible. What is certain is that the advocates of such positions referred to, both in the Synoptics and 2 Thessalonians, had already been refuted by the plain teaching of 1 Thessalonians. It was the essence of the message of 1 Thessalonians that the parousia will be an event of universal import; it cannot be veiled in obscurity. That is the point which the writer of 2 Thessalonians picks up and wishes to emphasize from the teaching of the former letter. Furthermore, this is backed up by the earnest, emphatic assertions of 2 Thessalonians 2:3, 5, 15; 3:6, 17, that such teaching was genuinely the word of Paul.

The Crisis before the End (2:3b-5)

In this sentence which functions as an anacolouthon, through the medium of a lengthy protasis, Paul explains that the Day of the Lord will not come until two major connected events will have taken place. There must occur before the Day both the apostasy and the appearance of the man of lawlessness (2:3). The adverb first (πρῶτον) refers to the coincidental events of the apostasy and appearance

---

[23]The view of Gundry, "Hellenization," 170-71, is that the current period of suffering had caused the Thessalonians to deduce that this very situation was the time of the birth pangs of the new age (Matt 24:8 || Mk 13:8). According to this view, just as the birth pangs of the woman indicate that the child is about to be born, so the current sufferings indicated that the parousia was as good as here. This scenario is plausible but, as Best, *First and Second Epistles to the Thessalonians*, 276-78, notes, it is ultimately unprovable.

of the man of lawlessness *preceding* the Day of the Lord.[24] Here Paul focuses on
the second of a three-stage tradition on the end: (1) the time of present eschatological crisis noted throughout the letter; (2) *the brief final climax of evil;* (3) the
resolution of the crisis on the Day of the parousia of Jesus Christ.

The brief final climax of evil features the appearance of the apostasy; it is
important to see that this term has its background in a set of incidents that
surrounded the activity of Antiochus Epiphanes IV in Judea in the second century
before Christ.[25] In an attempt to enforce the Jews to adopt Hellenistic customs
and habits, Antiochus' crusade ended with a cultic shrine dedicated to Zeus
Olympias being placed in the temple. This vigorous attempt to make the Jews
abandon their exclusive loyalty to the one God of Israel was labelled by the
author of 1 Maccabees as apostasy (1 Mac 2:15). This is clearly the understanding of Daniel as well (Dan 8:23). In keeping with esoteric exegesis, after the
time of Daniel, the words of the book are considered prophetic and pregnant with
meaning for any future eschatological era. The concept of a brief final rebellion
marked by great blasphemy toward God in the holy city was part and parcel of
eschatological thinking in Judaism by the first century of our era (1 Enoch 91:7;
Jubilees 23:14-23 cf. Asc. of Isaiah 2:4). The author (supposedly Paul the Jew),
having received a word on this matter through tradition, regarded such an
occurrence as an inevitable part of the culmination of eschatological events.
Since 2 Thessalonians 2:5a claims the Thessalonians were taught about these
things, and these specific events had not taken place, the author believes that he
is well within bounds to claim that the Day of the Lord had not come.

A second element of this final eschatological climax of evil that the writer
discusses is the appearance of the man of lawlessness.[26] This evil figure's title

---

[24]F. F. Bruce, *1 & 2 Thessalonians*, WBC 45 (Waco TX: Word Books, 1982) 167.

[25]Various discussions as to whether this is a Jewish or Christian apostasy completely
miss the point. Paul himself would not perceive that there were a distinction. As N. T.
Wright notes saliently in *The Climax of the Covenant: Christ and the Law in Pauline
Theology* (Minneapolis: Fortress, 1991) 125-36, Paul was essentially a Jewish theologian
who incorporates his belief in Jesus as Messiah into his foundational views on
monotheism and election which were nourished in his ethnic heritage in the people of
God. For Paul all theology emerges out of the situation of this heritage in Israel.

[26]The language used to describe the man of lawlessness was drawn heavily from Old
Testament terminology of the opponents of God. As much Old Testament terminology for
a deliverer is referred to Christ, so key language about opposition to God is consolidated
in the description of the lawless one. Especially in 2 Thess 2:4 the language parallels
most closely terminology used to describe Gentile kings who were part of another mythic
system in absolute opposition to God. Examples may be seen with Antiochus IV (Dan
11:36) and the kings of Babylon (Isaiah 14:12-13) and Tyre (Ezekiel 28:2-3). This is all
standard polemic against a human figure who embodies and supports some other form of
ultimacy rather than that of Yahweh. A particularly striking instance is given in the

may have been derived from a combination of the description of Antiochus IV (in Dan 11:35-36) and his allies (Dan 12:10, ἄνομοι in Theodotian). By similar language one can go to Isaiah 57:3-4 where the LXX links the plural υἱοὶ ἄνομοι ("lawless sons") with τέκνα ἀπωλείας ("children destined for destruction"). Probably the title ὁ υἱὸς τῆς ἀπωλείας (2:3) can also be explained by this derivation; and finally, if we move by means of repeated vocabulary ἄνομοι to Isaiah 66:3-6, there we find that the ἄνομοι were described as ἀντικείμενα ("adversaries"). These ones were called to account by the Lord from his inner sanctuary (ναός) in the holy city. In 2 Thessalonians 2:4 the man of lawlessness was described as ὁ ἀντικείμενος who set himself up and exalted himself above God in the inner sanctuary (ναός).

The use of such strong biblical terminology to describe the arch opponent of the way of God should be understood in its eschatological setting. The man of lawlessness would have his seat of power in the inner sanctuary which was housed in Jerusalem: Jerusalem was the traditional site for the critical events of the turn of the ages. Certain attempts to place the Roman standards of Caligula (40 CE) in Judea, in this setting, no doubt would have been viewed by many as a harbinger of what would be the ultimate Gentile expression of opposition to the divine claims. But it was equally clear to the author that such a blasphemous event as the man of lawlessness taking residence within the inner sanctuary had not yet taken place. Therefore, it should be self-evident to his readers that the Day of the Lord had not come.

Upon giving this concrete explanation for the delay of the Day of the Lord, the author (ostensibly Paul) reinforces his argument with the plaintive query, "Do you not remember that while I was with you, I was accustomed (ἔλεγον being a customary imperfect) to instruct you in these things" (2:5). This sentence serves as a closure to the anacolouthon. Now, Paul (note the first person) having raised the issue of the final crisis, and having reminded the readers of his earlier teaching on these matters, is ready to return to the existing situation at the time of writing the letter (cf. 2 Thess 2:1-3a).

The Work of the Delaying Power/Restrainer (2:6-7)

Having utilized the anacolouthon (2:3b-5) to remind his readers of the two key components of the brief final climax of evil before the end. The writer now returns to discuss the present situation (stage one of the final crises) in 2:6-7. The passage is replete with a plethora of exegetical difficulties. But the overall thrust

---

description of the king of Tyre in Ezek 28:2-3. There, in 28:2 (LXX), the king says of himself θεός εἰμι ἐγώ. This is the same terminology used to describe the man of lawlessness as he takes his seat in the inner sanctuary (2 Thess 2:4).

of the argument is relatively clear; a mysterious eschatological power delaying the occurrence of the apostasy and the man of lawlessness was actively at work in the world. If one were aware of this reality there would be no question about the implausibility of a claim that the Day of the Lord had come.

Structurally, the unit opens with an emphatic καὶ νῦν (2:6a). This emphatic expression "and now" contrasts the present time with the future appearance of the man of lawlessness who will be revealed in his own time (2:6b; cf. 2:8a). In turn, the coming revelation of the man of lawlessness will both precede and precipitate the parousia of Christ which will end the cycle of eschatological events (2:8b). Here we have set forth the author's three-stage scenario of eschatological events; first, the present time of the work of the Delaying or Restraining Power (τὸ κατέχον); second, the full manifestation of the apostasy and the coming of the man of lawlessness; third the parousia of Christ.

A thorough discussion of all the interpretative possibilities within this passage would take us well beyond the purposes of this monograph. We will rest content in making the case for a specific understanding of the meaning of the Delaying Power (τὸ κατέχον) and demonstrating that a close reading of the details of the text presumes a three stage scenario of present crisis, final crisis, and parousia.

With reference to the present time, καὶ νῦν (2:6), the writer refers to it as the time of the work of the τὸ κατέχον. There are at least two exegetical problems here. First, the actual identification of τὸ κατέχον. Second, why can τὸ κατέχον (a neuter participle) be substituted by use of the masculine participle ὁ κατέχων ("The Restrainer") in 2:7b?

We will note the second problem first. It is evident that the emphatic καὶ νῦν (2:6a), which speaks about the present work of τὸ κατέχον, stands in apposition with τὸ γὰρ μυστήριον ἤδη ἐνεργεῖται τῆς ἀνομίας of 2:7a ("For already the secret working of lawlessness is at work"). In short, the writer perceives that just as the persecution and evil of the present crisis (secret working of lawlessness) can be characterized impersonally, but will become personalized in the final crisis with the appearance of the lawless one (ὁ ἄνομος) as is noted in 2:8a; so, τὸ κατέχον starts out impersonally, but at the time of its removal (2:7b) is delineated in personal terms. Thus the shift from neuter to masculine (τὸ κατέχον to ὁ κατέχων) is not determined so much by different referents, but by the pattern of argumentation with respect to the intensification of events of the end.[27]

With this in mind, we are in a position to discuss briefly the meaning of τὸ κατέχον. Despite the efforts of C. H. Giblin, who has argued another position,

---

[27]Holland, *2 Thessalonians in the Pauline Tradition*, 112.

it seems best to understand τὸ κατέχον to mean "the Power to restrain or delay."[28] Following the claim that the readers had already been taught on this subject (2:5), the writer resumes in 2:6a to say, "And now you know what we mean by the Delaying Power."[29] What does he mean by his reference to τὸ κατέχον ("the Delaying Power")?

Two major views have been set forth on this matter. First, there is the view that the Roman state is the power "to restrain or delay."[30] Such a view may have some plausibility if we thought that 2 Thessalonians were written before 65 CE But if we date it after 65 CE, the view is beset by an inner contradiction. A system that had already produced a Caligula, and now a Nero, although often treated benignly by the early Paul, could hardly be perceived to be a stabilizing factor delaying the appearance of "the man of lawlessness."

It is far more plausible to understand κατέχον/ων to refer to a work of the Spirit especially in the preaching of the Gospel and growth of the early Christian movement.[31] Indeed the generalized view that κατέχον/ων is the work of the Spirit enpowering mission is fruitful for two reasons. First, it is true that in the Pauline tradition Paul's whole missionary strategy was viewed in the context of God's eschatological plan to bring the Gentiles to the praise of God on the grounds of the coming of the Messiah.[32] Such an interpretation of Paul was

---

[28]C. H. Giblin, *The Threat to Faith: An Exegetical and Theological Re-Examination of 2 Thessalonians 2*, An Bib 31 (Rome: Pontifical Biblical Institute, 1967) 167-248, understands the term to refer not to any restraining power but to the activity of seizure/seizer as in spiritual possession. In his later restatement he responds to criticism from various authors such as Best, *First and Second Epistles to the Thessalonians*, 298-302; cf. Giblin, "2 Thessalonians 2 Re-Read as Pseudepigraphal: A Revised Reaffirmation of the Threat to Faith," in *The Thessalonian Correspondence*, BETL 87, ed. R. F. Collins (Leuven: Leuven University Press/Peeters, 1990) 461-68. Giblin still argues that the verb κατέχειν means "possess" and cannot mean "restrain" in the sense of "hold off/prevent." However, Giblin now concedes that it may possibly mean "restrain" in the sense of "detain." As far as I can see, that is not that much different from our position.

[29]What is being delayed is "the apostasy" and primarily "the appearance of the man of lawlessness," i.e., αὐτόν (2:6). The antecedent of αὐτόν must be the "man of lawlessness" because he is linked by the author with ἀποκαλύπτειν both in 2:3 and 2:8.

[30]Bruce, *1 & 2 Thessalonians*, 171-72, is the most well-known modern advocate of this position. Reading it in association with Rev 17:12-14, and following Tertullian, Bruce argues that the breakup of the empire accompanied by great turmoil will precipitate the advent of the man of lawlessness. Thus, the coherence of Rome prevents the rise of the man of lawlessness. The breakup of Rome facilitates his rise.

[31]Giblin, "2 Thessalonians Re-Read," 466, admits this position has much to commend it, although he thinks it comes too close to the view that this benign power or forces "holds off" or "restrains" the man of lawlessness, which is unacceptable for him.

[32]Rom 15:16-22; cf. E. P. Sanders, *Paul, the Law, and the Jewish People* (Philadel-

commonplace in the ancient church.[33] And, given the eschatological framework operative in early Christianity (cf. texts such as Lk 21:24), it is easy to conceive that many may have thought that the time of mission was limited. This brings us to a second reason. Between Matthew 24:10-12, 15, a passage which we have identified as being based on a source tradition common to Matthew and 2 Thessalonians, stands Matthew 24:14.[34] This verse states that the gospel of the kingdom will be proclaimed to all the nations and then the end will come. More discussion on Matthew 24:14 will come in the next chapter.[35] It is enough for us to say now that if the writer of 2 Thessalonians had access to the text of Matthew 24:10-15, or, more likely, a similar tradition behind 24:10-15, this interpretation of τὸ κατέχον as the proclamation of the gospel that delays the end would comport well with the total context.

Finally, such an interpretation sheds light on another *crux interpretum,* the meaning of The Restrainer of the lawless one being "taken out of the way" (ἕως ἐκ μέσου γένηται) in 2 Thess 2:7b. This oblique parenthesis should be understood to say that the power of the Restrainer, perhaps as especially evident in the mission of certain spirit endowed figures in the Church, delays the appearance of the man of lawlessness until the eschatological proclamation to the nations is complete. In brief, the text is saying until the word is proclaimed to all the nations, it is only Christian mission which restrains the appearance of the lawless one. Grammatically, the appearance of the lawless one is the implied object of κατέχων; the referent to ἕως ἐκ μέσου is the proclamation to the nations.

Thus, in 2 Thessalonians 2:6-7 the writer has given further explication about his understanding of God's eschatological plan. This was done to reinforce his argument that the Day of the Lord has not yet come. Indeed, the apostasy and appearance of the man of lawlessness, which *precedes* that day, had yet to take place. The secret power of lawlessness was at work in the present crisis (2:7). But the mysterious eschatological power of delaying these end time events in the

---

phia: Fortress, 1985) 171-99. Cf. R. D. Aus, "God's Plan and God's Power: Isaiah 66 and The Restraining Factors of 2 Thess 2:6-7," *Journal of Biblical Literature* 96 (1977): 540.

[33]A list of interpreters on behalf of such views can be found in J. Munck, *Paul and the Salvation of Mankind* (Richmond: John Knox, 1959) 37.

[34]The significance of the placement of this verse is noted by Wenham, *Rediscovery of Jesus' Eschatological Discourse,* 285.

[35]It may be noted that J. Jeremias has argued that the substance of Matt 24:14 represents genuine Jesus tradition. Jeremias, *Jesus' Promise to the Nations,* SBT 24, trans. S. H. Hooke (repr. Philadelphia: Fortress, 1982 = 1958) 23; cf. L. Gaston, *No Stone on Another: Studies in the Significance of the Fall of Jerusalem in the Synoptic Gospels* NovTSup 23 (Leiden: Brill, 1970) 20. If it can be merely sustained that it is tradition and not Matthean composition, this would tend to confirm that we are on the right track.

work of τὸ κατέχον/ων was also operative. In the view of 2 Thessalonians, not until the work of mission had been fully complete would the end come. Thus, hypothetically, either Matthew 24:14, or a tradition behind Matthew 24:14 is echoed in 2 Thessalonians 2:6-7. It is possible that 2 Thessalonians 2 does echo the text of Matthew. But this would almost certainly mean a post 70 CE date of composition of 2 Thessalonians. As noted earlier, in our judgment, the presupposition of 2 Thessalonians 2:4 that the temple is still standing makes this highly unlikely. Thus we take the position that possibly 2 Thessalonians 2:6-7 is echoing a similar tradition that was also used by the author of Matthew 24:14.

The Culmination of History (2:8-12)

After he has reminded his readers of his earlier teaching about the delay of the appearance of the man of lawlessness (2:6-7), the writer returns to his description of the sequence of eschatological events he initially alluded to in 2:3b-4. In 2:3b-4 the emphasis was on the initial appearance of the lawless one. In 2:8-12 the emphasis is on his fate. With 2:8-12 the third stage of the final eschatological scenario has arrived; the Day of the Lord has come.

The pericope opens in 2:8a with καὶ τοτέ ("and then") which is a temporal reference to the future when Paul expects two connected events to occur. First, there will be a brief manifestation of the man of lawlessness and his allies 2:8a, 9-12. Second, the appearance of the lawless one will have its dramatic counterpoint in the parousia of Christ who will destroy the ultimate rebel against God (2:8b).

In keeping with the emphasis on tribulations and sufferings in 2 Thessalonians, the description of the final appearance of the lawless one is given considerable emphasis. In 2:9 the appearance of the lawless one is actually said to be a parousia. This is a bizarre parody of the parousia of Christ. Also, in 2:9 the man of lawlessness is thought to produce lying signs and wonders (cf. Matt 24:24 ‖ Mk 13:22).[36] He has absolute control over his coterie of followers who ultimately will share his fate (cf. 1:7-10).

On the other hand, the word is sure that the appearance of Jesus Christ will bring an end to the deceitful activity of the lawless one. In 2:8b the appearance of Christ is described in terminology which echoes Isaiah 11:4, a passage which is a direct counterpoint to the description of the king of Babylon in 14:12-14, and

---

[36]The reference to the σημεῖα and τέρατα in both 2 Thessalonians and Matthew/Mark (cf. Did. 16:4) can be explained as a use of common eschatological terminology. Nevertheless, if Matthew/Mark and 2 Thessalonians used a common tradition, or the author of 2 Thessalonians knew the text of Matthew, such an echo would be perfectly understandable.

which, in turn, probably furnished some of the background for the description of the man of lawlessness.

With the description of the triumph of Christ over his enemies at the end of the era the author of 2 Thessalonians brought his discussion about the future eschatological events to an end. This discussion was precipitated by the current crisis which he and the Thessalonians faced. The Thessalonians were wrong in thinking that the Day of the Lord had come. A review of the eschatological teaching the author imparted to them in the past should bring them to see that the end was being held back and that the man of lawlessness must be revealed before the parousia. They should make no mistake about it. When the man of lawlessness is revealed and the Lord makes his appearance there will then be no doubt that the Day of the Lord has come.

Summary and Conclusion

Our analysis of the parallels between 2 Thessalonians 2 and the Synoptic Eschatological Discourse is now complete. This analysis has furnished some concrete results.

In summary, we have identified three strong sets of literary parallels between two bodies of material. First, in 2 Thessalonians 2:1 || Matthew 24:3b, 31, on the topic of the parousia, both units use almost identical terminology to link the coming of the parousia with a gathering of believers to meet the Lord of the church. Second, in 2 Thessalonians 2:2a (11) || Matthew 24:4b, 6b, there is an identical double warning for the church not to be deceived and disturbed by the current crisis. Third, in 2 Thessalonians 3b-4 || Matthew 24:11-12, 15, there is a striking parallel on the emergence of a time of apostasy when both writers expect it to culminate with the appearance of a desolating sacrilege in the temple in Jerusalem. The appearance of this sacrilege will precipitate the parousia of Christ. In addition, in 2 Thessalonians 2:6-7 we have detected an echo of a parallel with Matthew 24:14. In both authors (2 Thessalonians 2 and Matthew 24) a three stage tradition about the future is presupposed. First, there is the present time of grave eschatological crisis. Second, the apostasy and desolating sacrilege/man of lawlessness must appear. Third, the parousia of Christ will be instrumental in defeating the man of lawlessness and bringing deliverance to the elect.

Our conclusion is this. The text of 2 Thessalonians 2:1-12 echoes a number of words and phrases also found in Matthew 24:3-31 and, to a lesser degree, Mark 13:3-27. The echoes are both linguistic and thematic. However, the linguistic evidence is not strong enough to warrant the conclusion that the writer of 2 Thessalonians had the text of Matthew and used his version of the Eschatological Discourse as a basis for argumentation. This is so for two reasons: first, although several linguistic parallels between Matthew 24 and 2 Thessalonians 2 are quite striking, given the fact that there is little linguistic evidence elsewhere to indicate a direct correlation between the two works, the parallels are not of sufficient quantity for us to conclude that there is a direct literary connection. Second, although both writers do refer to the parousia, it is interesting to note that there are no echoes of the parousia in 2 Thessalonians from Matthew 24:27, 37-38, 39, three units that are structurally very similar and may have been brought by Matthew into his version of the Eschatological Discourse from a separate source tradition.

Neither is it likely that Matthew used 2 Thessalonians as a direct source. There is not enough linguistic evidence to posit a direct literary conection between the two works. Moreover, it will be observed in the next chapter that nearly all the echoes in Matthew with 2 Thessalonians 2 occur in what we will identify on other grounds as Matthew's major source for his account of the Eschatological Discourse.

Thus, we arrive at a preliminary conclusion, which will be substantiated by source analysis of Matthew in the next chapter. We tentatively conclude that the author of 2 Thessalonians based his argument on an eschatological tradition similar to that which was used in Matthew 24:5-6, 10-15, and 30-31 when he wrote 2:1-12.

If 2 Thessalonians were written by the late 60s, it could mean that already by the time of the last days of Nero there circulated among the churches a coherent body of eschatological tradition highlighted by a three-stage scenario on the future. The material is attributed to Jesus in Matthew 24 and also functions as authoritative tradition for the author of 2 Thessalonians 2:1-12. In due time others within the canon (Luke, Mark, Revelation) and outside (Didache 16), will also have cause to discuss similar themes. Commencing with a study of the compositional history of the Matthean usage of these traditions, which were incorporated in Matthew's Eschatological Discourse, we will now examine more carefully the origin of this tradition and its process of development within the Synoptic Gospels.

II

The Formation
of the Eschatological Discourses
in the Synoptic Gospels

4.
The Matthean Version
of the Last Eschatological Discourse

Our analysis in the previous chapters has led to the conclusion that the Thessalonian correspondence reflects knowledge of a body of Jesus tradition on eschatological matters which has a number of verbal parallels and echoes with certain pericopes in Matthew 24.

As we have established in an earlier chapter, preserved in Matthew 24 is a body of Jesus Tradition that is also echoed in 1 Thessalonians. Thus, 1 Thessalonians 5:2 echoes the parable of the Thief in the Night which is found in Matthew 24:42-43. Also, 1 Thessalonians 4:16a assumes knowledge of a Jesus Tradition on the coming of the Lord/Son of Man that also is preserved in Matthew 24:30b-31. A study of these parallels produced insufficient evidence to allow us to conclude that there was any direct literary relationship between Matthew and 1 Thessalonians. And, as there is little other evidence of literary parallels between the two writings, we do not believe that Matthew used 1 Thessalonians as a direct source or that 1 Thessalonians was dependent upon Matthew. It is more likely that both Matthew and 1 Thessalonians were dependent on a common tradition in eschatological matters and utilized this tradition for their own particular purposes.

When we come to 2 Thessalonians, although the literary evidence is more extensive, we reached a similar conclusion. In Matthew 24:4b-6, 10-12, 14-15, 29-31, the textual evidence indicates that there are both verbal parallels and thematic echoes with 2 Thessalonians 2:1-12 and a consistent threefold eschatological pattern of: (1) concern over a present eschatological crisis; (2) anticipation of an apostasy culminating in the appearance of a horrible desecration in the temple in Jerusalem; (3) and a belief that the apostasy would be resolved by the parousia of Christ.

This evidence, while insufficient to support a theory of direct literary relationship, suggests that Matthew knew of a similar tradition on eschatological matters to the one which was known to the author of 2 Thessalonians 2:1-12. In this chapter we will argue that it was this very tradition, supplemented by another verbal source, several parables, and Sondergut, that was utilized by Matthew to compose the Olivet Discourse of Jesus. Later the authors of Luke, Mark, and probably the Didache would draw upon this Matthean composition as a major source for their own versions of the same Discourse. Thus, Matthew stands at the pivotal stage between the circulation of various early collections of verbal Jesus tradition on eschatological matters for catechetical purposes in the church and the formulation of these collections into an organized composition, which we now know as the Olivet Discourse or Jesus' Last Eschatological Discourse. We will focus on this Discourse in this chapter through an analysis of its composition.

The Genre and Structure of Matthew

As far as the popular mind is concerned it has always been taken for granted that the four gospels of the New Testament were biographies of Jesus. However, since the emergence of form criticism early in the century, until recently, most biblical scholars would have questioned this assessment.[1] The position is now changing. Several important works have been written which have substantially increased our knowledge of the biographical literature of the Greco-Roman world.[2] It is now frequently argued that Hellenistic biographical literature was not produced within the confines of a tightly structured genre with its own inflexible set of conventions, but was very flexible, continuously developing, and was freely adapted for the particular settings in which it was produced. The author of a widely used handbook now claims that the New Testament gospels should be designated as "a subtype of Greco-Roman biography."[3]

The issue is important because if it could be determined that the gospels were biographies, then, as with any other genre of literature, one may look for certain common traits and conventions within them and this could provide important clues enabling us to determine the basic rhetorical structure of a whole work.

However, there still remains considerable discussion over what form of Greco-Roman biography served as the basic model for the writers of the canonical gospels. Do the gospels reflect primarily the influence of biographical conventions found in the literature of the pagan Greco-Roman world or that found

---

[1]David E. Aune, *The New Testament in its Literary Environment*, LEC 8, ed. Wayne Meeks (Philadelphia: Westminster, 1987) 22; Charles Talbert, "Seminar on Gospel Genre: Introduction," *Colloquy on New Testament Studies: A Time for Reappraisal and Fresh Approaches*, ed. Bruce Corley, (Macon: Mercer University Press, 1983) 197-202; idem, "Ancient Biography," *Anchor Bible Dictionary* 1 (New York: Doubleday, 1992) 745-49.

[2]Foundational for the new interest in the diversity of the biographical literature in the Greco-Roman world is the work of Arnaldo Momigliano, *The Development of Greek Biography* (Cambridge: Harvard University Press, 1971); Albrecht Dihle, *Studies zur griechischen Biographie* (Göttingen: Vandenhoeck und Ruprecht, 1956); Richard A. Burridge, *What Are the Gospels? A Comparison with Graeco-Roman Biography* (Cambridge: Cambridge University Press, 1992) 3-190.

[3]Aune, *New Testament Literary Environment*, 46.

in contemporary Jewish biography which, although influenced by Hellenism, had its own literary history and theological concerns?

When we come to discuss the possible impact that conventions of Greco-Roman biography had upon the author of Matthew we may begin by taking note of the important work of Philip Shuler.[4] Shuler has argued convincingly that Matthew was composed in keeping with the conventions of Greco-Roman epideictic oratory. Specifically, Shuler claims that Matthew was conceived as a work of praise or an encomium.[5]

Yet, it is an obvious fact that the gospels tell the story of the Jew, Jesus of Nazareth, not that of Heracles or Achilles. For the communities that nourished the early Christian story, a more immediate precedent for the biography of a holy man would be the accounts of such figures as Moses, Elisha, the Servant of Isaiah 52:13–53:12 in the Scriptures, Philo's Life of Moses, and his other works on Abraham, and Joseph.[6] At the very least, it can be argued that both the biographical accounts of important figures in Scripture and their analogues in Hellenistic Judaism supplemented by the use of Hellenistic biographical conventions, formed an ethos of writing that makes the appearance of such a work as the first gospel in the first century of our era very plausible. Given the widespread use of the Hellenistic biographical conventions in the literate culture of the First Century, it would be remarkable if Matthew had not been at least indirectly influenced by them.

Nevertheless, it is evident at this juncture that genre analysis of the gospels as biographies has not yet reached the stage whereby it can inform us reliably as to the principles operative in the compositional arrangements of the various peric-

---

[4]Philip Shuler, *A Genre for the Gospels: The Biographical Character of Matthew* (Philadelphia: Fortress, 1982); idem, "The Genre(s) of the Gospels," in *The Interrelations of the Gospels*, BETL 95, ed. David Dungan (Leuven: Leuven University Press/Peeters; Macon GA: Mercer University Press, 1990) 459-83.

[5]Shuler, *Genre*, 37, 55-56, 88-106. He established that such literary conventions as noble birth, personal advantages of childhood, and spiritual excellence were part and parcel of encomiastic literature. These conventions were also used in the composition of Matthew as were certain rhetorical techniques such as amplification and comparison. The net effect is that Shuler gives a credible rationale for Matthew's use of the birth narratives, the comparison between Jesus and John the Baptist, and certain features of Jesus' ministry. As one can immediately determine something of the educational skills and background of the writer by the style of his or her letters, Shuler has shown that the first gospel definitely, in terms of its general structure, bears the imprint of one who was knowledgeable about the conventions of Hellenistic rhetoric.

[6]An interesting attempt to discuss genre in the context of Greco-Roman Jewish biography is Meredith Kline, "The Old Testament Origins of the Gospel Genre," *Westminster Theological Journal* 38 (1975): 1-27. However, this work places too much emphasis on covenant, a theme that is hardly explicit in the narrative of the gospels.

opes in such a work as Matthew. Thus, for the present, we are still mainly dependent for our knowledge of the structure of Matthew on those works that have approached the book mainly from the standpoint of traditional historical criticism.

In this connection there is widespread disagreement among the commentators as to the principle informing the compostional structure of the various pericopes in Matthew.

Traditionallly, throughout the twentieth century, the view of the Yale scholar B. W. Bacon has carried great weight.[7] Bacon argued that Matthew had a prologue (chapters 1–2) and epilogue (26:3–28:20). In between Matthew was divided into five units analogous to the five "books" of the Pentateuch. Each book was made from (1) narrative material and (2) a major discourse, in that order. Each discourse ended with a formulaic saying, "And when Jesus finished. . . . " The formulaic sayings (7:28-29; 11:1; 13:53; 19:1; 26:1) were the chief markers around which Matthew was supposed to have developed the structure of the Gospel. In recent years this plan has been modified in various ways with some scholars arguing that the discourses precede the narrative units[8] or follow a chiastic structure.[9]

A major difficulty with this division of Matthew into five separate units of narrative and discourse is that the sections identified as either narrative or discourse are neither entirely narrative or discourse. For example, according to Bacon's thesis, 8:1-34 is narrative material; but interspersed within are considerable portions of discourses (8:10-12; and 8:20-22). And when one turns to what is claimed to be discourse material (9:36–10:42), much of this is arranged in the form of a narrative. It is not very clear how Bacon's thesis can account for the arrangement of the very diverse literary materials in Matthew from 11:2 to 17:21, a very difficult nut to crack on any structural arrangement of Matthew.

Nevertheless, the Baconian view of Matthew's structure has one abiding feature that continues to commend it. It is clear that Matthew does contain five great bodies of Jesus' teachings: the Sermon on the Mount (5:1–7:27); the Mission Discourse (10:5-42); the Parable Discourse (13:1-52); the Rules for the Community (18:1-35); and the Discourse on the Last Things (24:3–25:46). This observation has to be foundational for any analysis of the structure of Matthew.

---

[7]B. W. Bacon, "The 'Five Books' of Matthew against the Jews," *The Expositor* 15 (1918): 56-66.

[8]Philippe Rolland, "From the Genesis to the End of the World: The Plan of Matthew's Gospel," *Biblical Theology Bulletin* 2 (1972): 155-76. Thus, the prologue ends at 4:16; book 1 at 9:34; 2 at 12:50; 3 at 17:27; 3 at 23:39; and 5 at 28:20. Note also B. Rod Doyle, "Matthew's Intention as Discerned by His Structure," *Revue Biblique* 95 (1988): 34-54.

[9]C. H. Lohr, "Oral Techniques in the Gospel of Matthew," *Catholic Biblical Quarterly* 23 (1961): 403-35.

The major alternative view on the structure of Matthew in recent years has been that set forth by Jack Kingsbury.[10] Kingsbury has argued that Matthew may be divided into a threefold structure. Matthew 1:1–4:16 introduces Jesus to the reader. In this unit Kingsbury places considerable stress on a perceived Matthean emphasis on Christology. At the center of the opening unit is the revelation of Jesus as God's Son (3:17). The redactional clause "from then Jesus began" (ἀπὸ τότε ἤρξατο ὁ Ἰησοῦς), occurs at 4:17 to open the second section of the book, and is repeated again in 16:21 to open the third and final unit. The second part of the division, according to Kingsbury, highlights both Jesus' public ministry to Israel in teaching, preaching, and healing, and Israel's repudiation of Jesus. The third section deals with Jesus' journey to Jerusalem and his suffering, death, and resurrection.

There is much here to commend this view of Matthew's structural arrangement. However, a question remains as to whether so much weight can be placed on the single formula ἀπὸ τότε ἤρξατο ὁ Ἰησοῦς to function as the crucial foundation for the entire structural arrangement of the Gospel. What is there in this formula, as opposed to the fivefold "And when Jesus finished these sayings" or other formulaic statements that makes this one so crucial? The debate on this issue has reached something of an impasse. Clearly, no structural outline has been produced by the commentators that compels widespread assent.[11]

This forces a difficult question. Did the author of Matthew have a clear overarching structural arrangement in mind when he produced his gospel? At present, we are in no position to give a resounding "yes" in response. Indeed, the issue may prove to be insoluble. Therefore, in this work, we will not venture to offer any great new proposal as to the structure of Matthew. Rather, at this stage we will be content to return to something that is fairly minimal and obvious about Matthew, namely to draw attention again to the reality of the five great teaching discourses, and to note that each represents a progression from the emergence of

---

[10]Jack Dean Kingsbury, *Matthew: Structure, Christology, Kingdom* (Philadelphia: Fortress, 1975) 1-39; idem, "The Figure of Jesus in Matthew's Story: A Literary Critical Probe," *Journal for the Study of the New Testament* 21 (1984): 3-36; idem, "The Figure of Jesus in Matthew's Story: A Rejoinder to David Hill," *Journal for the Study of the New Testament* 25 (1985): 61-81.

[11]See David R. Bauer, *The Structure of Matthew's Gospel: A Study in Literary Design*, JSNTSS 31 (Sheffield: Almond Press, 1988); Also, William R. Farmer, *Jesus and the Gospel: Tradition, Scripture, and Canon* (Philadelphia: Fortress, 1982) 138-40, has argued for another version of a literary structure of Matthew based on the geographical movements in Jesus' ministry redactionally stated in 4:18, 23; 13:1; 15:29; and 19:1. However, it is clear that for Farmer this outline serves as more of a "house" in which other major themes such as the Servant passages, and exhortations to martyrdom find a resting place, rather than a foundational structure for everything that occurs in Matthew.

Jesus as the Teacher to the formation and development of a new community within Israel.

At the very center of Matthew, Jesus states expressly his desire to found a new community in Israel (16:18-19). All of the major speeches of Jesus dovetail into this theme.

In opposition to other Jewish interpretations of God's demand current in the first century (5:17-48), the Sermon on the Mount states Jesus' norms for the community. The Mission Discourse stresses that the community began with the mission to the lost sheep of the house of Israel (9:35–10:43). The Parable Discourse indicates what life would be like in this new community and stresses that the course of the community and the outcome of its mission would have a major impact upon the eschatological events at the last day (13:1-52). After the new community was inaugurated (16:13-23), lengthy advice was given for situations that would arise in it day-by-day, hence the composition of the Community Discourse (18:1-35). Finally, the Last Discourse (24:3–25:46), set within the wider perimeters of a universal eschatological vision of reality, is an anticipation about the future course and ultimate destiny of the community.

Therefore, it is clear that for Matthew part of telling the story of the coming and martyrdom of Jesus the Messiah as the flesh and blood Son of God is to insert into his biography five strategic discourses that connect his life with the origin, *raison d' être*, fortunes in history, and ultimate destiny of the new community founded by him. Matthew 24–25 is important because, as the last in this series of discourses, it anticipates the ultimate impact of the Jesus story, that climaxes in the death, burial, and resurrection, will be at the end of the age. It reminds us that Jesus' story must be viewed from a wider perspective. As Matthew tells it, after the birth of the Messiah, a new community was inaugurated during his ministry; this community will continue to uphold his story until the end of the age. Matt 24–25 gives a preview of the author's view of its ultimate destiny.

The Scope of the Matthean Version
of Jesus' Last Eschatological Discourse

At the outset there is a problem defining the scope of Jesus' Last Discourse in Matthew vis-à-vis the other versions of the Discourse in Mark and Luke.

The usual procedure in contemporary scholarship, dominated by the Two Source Theory, is to say that the speech delivered from the Mount of Olives in Mark (13:3-37) is the oldest form of the Discourse in the Synoptics. On this view, Matthew has made some significant additions and editorial alterations to reproduce the Discourse in 24:3-36; and Luke, although exercising considerably greater compositional freedom in the use of Mark in his composition, has done something similar with the composition of 21:5-36. But when one looks at the text of Matthew as a thing in itself, without the assumption of Markan priority, a very different picture develops. The section of Matthew that parallels Mark 13 and Luke 21 is part of a much more comprehensive set of discourses of Jesus (23:1–25:46). Central to these discourses are questians relating to the legitimacy of the leadership and the ultimate destiny of the people of God.

From 23:1 to 24:2 Matthew has a collection of strong statements by Jesus against the Jewish leadership in Jerusalem highlighted by a list of seven woes against the Scribes and Pharisees (Matt 23:13-33). In many ways this stinging critique summarizes Jesus' relationship with Israel from the beginning of his ministry until the end of his life. This is logically followed by the Olivet Discourse which centers on a discussion of the situation and conditions betweeen the time of Jesus and the parousia (24:3-36). It concludes with what appears to be seven parables of warning about the need for preparedness and faithfulness given the delay of the parousia of the Son of Man and a sweeping panoramic description of the final Judgment (24:37–25:46).[12] Thus, the entire text of Matt 23:1–25:46 seems to be internally coherent. This structural coherence also reflects a unity of theme centering around the preunderstanding that God has forsaken the contemporary leadership of Israel in Jerusalem and his presence has shifted to being among the disciples of Jesus, who in their mission unto the ends of the earth, now function as transparencies for the leadership of the Matthean community which constitutes the true leadership of the people of God.

This can be seen, in particular, in the shifts of Jesus' audience in 23:1–25:46. Matthew opens 23:1-12 with a discourse of Jesus both to the crowds and the disciples. He reminds this audience that because of their practices the Scribes and Pharisees do not live up to their confession (Matt 23:3-7). Conversely, the true people of God reflect absolute dependence upon the benevolence of a gracious heavenly Father (23:8-9, 11-12).

Then in 23:13-33 there is a change in subject. In this section of the seven woes Jesus addresses directly the Scribes and Pharisees. As a result of their practices they have forfeited the right to lead the people of God. A parenthetical addendum to the seven woes (23:34-39) brings this prophetic critique to a climax. The present generation of leaders in Jerusalem will inherit not only judgment for their own failures but will receive the just dues of the disobedient leaders in earlier times as well. The temple is pronounced as already forsaken (23:38).

It is noteworthy that within this parenthetical addendum there is the opening of an inclusio (23:36) that ends in 24:34. In 23:36, the full force of Jesus'

---

[12]The parables or similes are: Noah's Flood (24:37-39); The Two in the Field (24:40); The Two at the Mill (24:41); The Thief at Night (24:43-44); The Faithful and Unfaithful Servants (24:43-51); The Ten Virgins (25:1-13); The Talents (25:14-30); and the account of the Judgment of the Nations (25:31-46).

prophetic judgments regarding ταῦτα πάντα ("all these things") is threatened to come upon the current generation (cf. the end of the broad inclusio 24:34 [cf. 24:2, 3, 33], which functions for chapter 24 as 23:36 functions for chapter 23). Then, in 23:37-39, we learn that this word of judgment will remain in effect until the reappearance of the Messianic One. The pronouncement of this coming appearance of the Messiah, in the Matthean narrative world, is an anticipation of the appearance of Jesus at the end (cf. Matt 21:9).

Matthew 24:1-2 follows in a clear thematic sequence upon chapter 23 and stands as the connecting link to the Olivet Discourse. In 24:1a Jesus leaves the temple as if to indicate that he has left the former established order of Israel's leadership. Jesus' disciples then draw near to him on two successive occasions (24:1b, 3). They constitute the nucleus of the new order of leadership. First, in 24:1b-2, Jesus speaks a prophetic word of doom against the temple itself. The phrase ταῦτα πάντα, used in 23:36 to refer to the judgment coming upon the Scribes and Pharisees, resurfaces (24:2). Clearly, in 24:2, the specific reference now is to the destruction of the actual temple complex in Jerusalem. But the reader knows it refers to much more. It refers to the leadership of Israel which has control of these facilities. This is so, because of the strategic placement of this pericope which comes, immediately after the denunciation of the Pharisees in chapter 23, as well as Jesus' deliberate evacuation of the temple precincts in 24:1. Thus we arrive at the real turning point of the whole unit which will come in 24:3 with the question of the disciples about the future. Just as the Scribes and Pharisees represented the leadership of the old order of the people of God in 23:13-24:2, so in 24:3-25:46, the disciples, who now are the recipients of Jesus' message, represent the vanguard of leadership of the new order of the people of God.

When the disciples come a second time to Jesus, now at the Mount of Olives, they ask the question, "When will these things (ταῦτα) be?" (24:3). That is, "When will your prophetic judgments be consummated?" The future coming of the Messianic One (23:39) and the end of the temple (24:1b-2) were a powerful set of constructs for the disciples to comtemplate, for throughout the first Gospel the author presumes the continued existence of the temple and its cultic operation (cf. 5:23-24; 17:24-27). By taking up the disciples' question, Matthew moves the reader into a future trajectory not only from the earthly Jesus' time but from the time of the composition of Matthew itself. The presupposition is that this trajectory will culminate when the end of the age, with both the appearance of the Messiah and the judgment upon Jerusalem, will be accomplished.

As we will see in our analysis below, Matthew 24:3 is of critical importance for understanding the interpretation of the entire unit of 23:1-25:46. In this verse, Matthew has united the disciples' question, in respect to Jesus' saying in 24:2

(the end of the temple), with the time of the parousia of Jesus and the end of the age. The two events of both the end of the age and the end of the temple are totally interlocked by the author of Matthew. This author appears unable to conceive that the one event can be different from the other. Thus, Matthew 23:1–24:2, which climaxes in the announcement of the end of the temple system, and 24:3–25:46, which deals with the eschatological events that lead up to the end of the age when the temple will be destroyed, form a comprehensive unit. The attempt to drive a wedge between Matthew 24:2 (understood as eschatological time until the Fall of Jerusalem in 70 CE) and 24:3 viewed as a reference to the future sign of the parousia and the end of the age will be shown in our analysis as not warranted by the text.[13]

For the author of Matthew, the time of the end of the old order was coterminous with the appearance of the coming of the Son of Man. It was expected to take place within a generation of Jesus' ministry (24:34; cf. 23:36). In the era before the end, the focus is on the disciples, presumably now the functional leaders of the restored people of God, and the fortunes of their mission especially to the nations (24:14; cf. 25:31-46). The various similes and parables on patient and productive waiting for the culmination of the eschatological events (24:37–25:30) is a fitting climax to the argument of this whole section that plots the transition in the leadership of the people of God. With this in mind, it would seem somewhat arbitrary to say that the Olivet Discourse must be strictly identified as Matthew 24:3-36.[14]

Specifically, the Discourse is an integral part of an entire unit that goes from 23:1 to 25:46. That will be our presupposition in this study. However, since in

---

[13]As argued in the analysis of Fred W. Burnett, *The Testament of Jesus-Sophia: A Redaction-Critical Study of the Eschatological Discourse in Matthew* (Lanham MD: University Press of America, 1981) 198-225.

[14]Kurt Aland, *Synopsis Quattuor Evangeliorum*, 13th ed. (Stuttgart: Deutsche Bibelgesellschaft, 1984) 409, has a major heading immediately preceding Matt 24:36 entitled "Parables about Coming which Supplement the Eschatological Discourse (According to Matthew)." This is even too much for Frank Beare, "The Synoptic Apocalypse: Matthean Version," in *Understanding the Sacred Text: Essays in Honor of Morton S. Enslin On the Hebrew and Christian Beginnings*, ed. John Reumann (Valley Forge: Judson, 1972) 131, who, commenting on an earlier edition of Aland's heading, says, "It is only because we attribute too much importance to the priority of Mark that we can even think of the long non-Markan conclusion to the discourse in Matthew as a mere 'supplement' to the apocalyptic section which he has taken over from Mark." Nevertheless, many scholars continue to put forth the view that the discourse functionally ends at 24:36. Thus J. Lambrecht, "The Parousia Discourse: Composition and Content in Matthew, XXIV-XXV," in *L'Évangile selon Matthieu: Rédaction et Theologie*, ed. M. Didier, BETL 29 (Gembloux: Duculot, 1972) 324-25. John P. Meier, *The Vision of Matthew: Christ, Church, and Morality in the First Gospel* (New York: Paulist, 1978) 173.

fact a new phase of the Discourse does commence on the Mount of Olives in response to a question in 24:3 and our focus in later chapters of this monograph will be on the composition of the Lukan and Markan versions of this section of the Discourse, it will only be necessary to enter into a detailed analysis of Matthew 24:3-36 since Matthew 24:37–25:46 (especially Matt 25) only functions peripherally as far as Luke 21 and Mark 13 are concerned.

Source Tradition behind the Composition of Matthew 24:3-51

In this section we will argue that when the author of the first gospel began to compose an account of the Last Discourse of Jesus he used two major collections of Jesus traditions on eschatological matters which were part of the larger body of Jesus tradition that circulated in the earliest Christian communities in greater Syria. An important part of our task is to set forth the general scope of these two major collections. In the case of the first gospel, we are not prepared to assume that Matthew utilized as the major sources for his composition, Mark and Q.[15] Our own presuppositions on the source question, and our analysis of the use of Jesus traditions on eschatological matters in the Pauline materials leads us in a new direction. We wish to frame the hypothesis that Matthew has utilized two major collections of Jesus tradition on eschatological matters in the composition of chapter 24. Henceforth, we will refer to these collections as "sources."

First, Matthew utilized a source on eschatological matters which we may term, *On the Final Crisis of the Era*. This source was also known by the writer of 2 Thessalonians. We will argue that this source may be found embeddded in Matt 24:4b-6, 10-12, 14-15, 21-24, 29-31.

Second, we will argue that Matthew has also utilized a second major source for the composition of this chapter. We name this source *On the Coming of the Son of Man*. There is no evidence that this collection was known or used by Paul and it does not appear in Mark. This source stands behind Matthew 24:27, 37, 38-39, (44). Besides these major sources, Matthew, of course, used Sondergut and several similes or parables as the basic source materials for the composition of his narrative. One notable parable that Matthew did use is the Thief in the Night (Matt 24:42-43). As our analysis in chapter 2 has already indicated, Matthew there utilized common source material also echoed by Paul in 1 Thessalonians 5:2.

---

[15]Beare, "The Synoptic Apocalypse," 118-19, gives a precise chart diagramming what he perceives to be the sources Matthew drew primarily from Mark and Q in the composition of his Discourse. Needless to say, our view of the sources utilized by Matthew is very different.

Source One: On the Final Crisis of the Era
(Matthew 24:4b-6, 10-12, 14-15, 21-24, 29-31)

In the previous chapter we have stated the case for the view that material echoed in Matthew 24:(3b), 4b-6, 10-12, 15, and 30-31 also formed a coherent perspective on eschatological matters which was known and utilized by the author of 2 Thessalonians. Since these verses constitute key segments of the Matthean Olivet Discourse, the question needs to be raised as to whether these verses can be identified as a coherent source utilized by the author of Matthew; and, if so, what was the scope of this source?

We set forth three basic bodies of evidence that lead us to the determination that the author of Matthew has utilized a source for the composition of 24:4b-31 that involves many of these verses. First, in this passage, there are a number of key vocabulary items (often repeated) that do not appear, or appear very irregularly, in other places in Matthew. This linguistic evidence is so strong that one may reasonably be inclined to conclude that, at this point, the author has not composed but has used a source. Second, there is evidence that these verses identified by the linguistic evidence have a unity of theme, and it is the same theme that has been identified as being embedded in a source behind 2 Thessalonians 2:1-12, a separate work. Third, the evidence of redaction by the author of Matthew indicates (especially at 24:3) that a compositional framework was constructed to embed the source into our Matthew 24. This procedure seems to be broadly consonant with how the author of Matthew utilized source material elsewhere in the first gospel.

In light of the analysis of Matthew 24:4b-31, it may well be that the scope of the source extended slightly beyond the sections in Matthew which we had identified in our study of 2 Thessalonians in the previous chapter. At the end of this discussion, we will summarize the evidence and will revise our earlier preliminary assessment of the scope of the source.

Of course, we cannot reconstruct the precise wording of a hypothetical source. But by being rigorous in our use of the above methodology, we believe the chief contours of the source should appear and be clearly recognizable.

Repetition of Key Vocabulary Items

A number of key vocabulary items occur very frequently in certain verses of Matthew 24:4b-31 that are different from the characteristic vocabulary of Matthew found throughout the rest of the gospel.[16] We claim that the number and

---

[16]Primarily, we will use as the basis of study for the linguistic characteristics of Matthew: Hawkins, *Horae Synopticae: Contributions to the Study of the Synoptic Problem,*

repetition of vocabulary items in this one unit which are different from the linguistic characteristics of Matthew provide evidence for the existence of a source used by the author of Matthew. With respect to the evidence, first, there are a number of words that only appear at this juncture in Matthew. Among these, in Matthew 24:6, there is the twofold use of πόλεμος ("war"). This word occurs nowhere else in Matthew. On the Two Gospel Hypothesis it cannot be drawn from the parallel in Mark 13:7 or Luke 21:9. Furthermore, the occurrence of πληθυνεῖν ("to multiply") in 24:12 is the only appearance of this word in the whole of the gospels. Also, ψύχειν ("to grow cold") in 24:12 is a hapax for the whole of the New Testament. Finally, κολοβοῦν ("to cut short") twice in 24:22, ψευδόχριστος (24:24), and ἄκρον ("boundary") in 24:31 occur only at this point in the text of Matthew.[17] This alerts us to the fact that there is a considerable amount of unusual vocabulary, for Matthew, in certain verses of this source.

Second, we have two out of three occurrences of ψευδοπροφήτης (Matt 7:15; 24:11, 24) in this unit.

Third, we find that there are three instances of the five uses of ἐκλεκτός ("chosen") in Matthew found in this unit (24:22, 24, 31). The other two occurrences appear to be a doublet of a gnomic statement of Jesus (20:16; 22:14).

Fourth, a very important vocabularly item in the unit is θλίψις ("distress"). The unit furnishes two out of the four appearances of this word in Matthew (24:21, 29). This word appears a third time in Matthew 24:9.[18] The composer of Matthew at 24:9 may have been inclined to use this word because of its appearance in the source.

Fifth, we have the fourfold repetition of πλανεῖν ("to deceive") in this text (24:4, 5, 11, 24). This constitutes four of the eight appearances of the word in Matthew. The multiple use of this word in the unit is so striking that it has caused Luz to say that it is a *Leitwort* of Matthew 24:4-24.[19]

2nd ed. rev. and supplemented (London: Oxford University Press, 1909); and D. G. Tevis, *Words and Phrases*. Also several times we have noted Ulrich Luz, *Matthew 1-7: A Commentary*, trans. Wilhelm C. Linss (Minneapolis: Augsburg/Fortress, 1989), who has a handy list of Matthean vocabularly (51-77), and Goulder, *Midrash and Lection*, who has made scattered comments on Matthean linguistic characteristics throughout his book.

[17]The latter three words are paralleled in Mk 13:20, 22, and 24 respectively.

[18]There is no parallel to Matt 24:9 in Mark. Several of these linguistic items have already been noted by S. Brown, "The Matthean Apocalypse," *Journal for the Study of the New Testament* 4 (1979): 2-27.

[19]Luz, *Matthew 1-7*, 66; it is worthy of note that this word occurs three other times in Matt 18:12-13. With such limited distribution throughout the gospel it can hardly be called a linguistic characteristic of the author of Matthew, yet it seems to be the work of

Sixth, the frequent use of (οἱ) πολλοί ("the many") in various case forms is most striking. It appears in 24:5 (twice), 10, 11 (twice), and 30. These are the only occurrences of πολύς ("much, many") between Matthew 22:14 and 25:19.[20] Πολύς is generally not thought to be a Matthean linguistic characteristic.

What we discover here is that these unusual Matthean vocabulary items tend to cluster in a set of verses. These verses are Matthew 24:4b-6, 10-12, 14-15, 21-24, 29-31.

In addition, there is a paucity of characteristic Matthean vocabularly items in these particular verses. We note that, apart from Matthew 24:14-15, Tevis cites only ὁρᾶτε μή (Matt 24:6) and some apocalyptic phraseology in 24:30 as coming from a single writer—who may or may not be the author of Matthew.[21]

The only two other vocabularly items found in this unit which are characteristic of Matthean vocabulary are ἀνομία ("lawlessness") in 24:12, and ἀστήρ ("star") 24:29. The use of the former is often thought to be Matthean redaction. We will not contest this conclusion. However, as we will note in our analysis, in this instance, because it echoes an Old Testament text, even this usage may not necessarily be redaction. We can learn little for source analysis from use of the latter word (ἀστήρ) since it is part of stereotypical apocalyptic description of the end.

---

a single author—the writer of a source used by Matthew?

[20]Also Matt 22:14 features the use of ἐκλεκτός which we have noted was a characteristic vocabularly item of our source.

[21]With reference to the use of ὁρᾶτε μή, Tevis, *Words and Phrases*, #214 on p. 158, notes that the construction ὁράω + μή is used in several different contexts in Matthew (8:4; 9:30; 18:10; 24:6). Aside from synoptic parallels at Matt 8:4 and 24:6 this construction appears elsewhere in the N.T. only at 1 Thess 5:13. We conclude that it is most likely Matthean composition because of its distribution in various parts of different contextual material in Matthew. In 24:30, 31 Tevis notes two apocalyptic constructions that are noteworthy. First, there is the phraseology ὁ υἱὸς τοῦ ἀνθρώπου + ἀποστελεῖ + τοὺς ἀγγέλους αὐτοῦ (#227 on p. 171). This phraseology occurs in Matt 24:30, 31; it also is found in Matt 13:41 which does not have a parallel in the Synoptics. These elements do not occur elsewhere in the N.T. They most likely come from a single writer; this is as much as we can conclude on sheer linguistic evidence. Similarly, the collocation of a form of ὁράω + Son of Man + ἐρχόμενον which occurs in 24:30, 16:28, and 26:64 (Tevis #312 on p. 211) probably is the work of a single writer; it may well be from a source because of its special apocalyptic usage. If this were the case, it would be additional confirmatory evidence of the hypothesis that Matt 24:30-31 is Matthean source material. With respect to Matt 24:14-15 we will discuss this further below. It suffices now to say that it has been well argued that Matt 24:14, in some form, has had a long compositional history before it was used by the author of Matthew; and the phraseology τὸ ῥηθὲν διὰ Δανιὴλ τοῦ προφήτου (24:15) is clearly characteristic phraseology of the author of Matthew and can be easily separated from the rest of the verse.

Generally, we would agree with those who argue that source traditions are very difficult to locate based on patterns of usage of vocabulary items. Nevertheless, in the texts under discussion, the combination of both these large numbers of recurrent vocabulary items scarcely found elsewhere in Matthew and, the sparse appearance of linguistic characteristics of Matthew in the same text, is compatible with a view that a preexistent source was incorporated by the author of Matthew into the construction of 24:4b-31. This observation is solidified when we see that this hypothetical source overlaps very closely the subject matter of 2 Thessalonians 2:1-12. Tentatively, the pattern of linguistic evidence leads us to conclude that the scope of the preexistent source appears to be Matthew 24:4b-6, 10-12, 14-15, 21-24, 29-31.

Unity of Theme

In this body of material we find a coherent argument both about the situation preceding the parousia and about its occurrence. Also, this source tradition has, in its details, a very similar eschatological view of the end time, coming in three stages, which is implicit in the tradition embedded within 2 Thessalonians 2:1-12.

As the source opens we find that it describes as present a time of eschatological crisis where we learn that the faith of the disciples will be greatly tested (24:4b-6, 10-12). This will be followed by a horrible act of blasphemy at the temple in Jerusalem accompanied by terrible distress for a short while (24:15, 21-24). In turn, there will follow the coming of a heavenly figure (24:29-31). This is a simple three-stage eschatological explanation of the end which is specifically paralleled in 2 Thessalonians 2.

Specifically, as far as the first stage of the crisis is concerned, Matthew 24:4b-6 is a warning not to be deceived by false messiahs and false claims about the end. All of this is indicative of the present eschatological crisis (24:10-12). But while this period does constitute an era of great testing for the disciples, it is also a time of mission where the message is taken to the whole of creation (24:14). This is the first stage of the end.

Second, in 24:15, 21-24, the second stage, the final crisis, has arrived. The horrible desecration takes place in the holy place (24:15 cf. 2 Thess. 2:3b-5, 9). This time of terrible crisis (24:21) is referred to as the θλῖψις μεγάλη ("Great Tribulation"). The false messiahs and prophets even intensify their efforts for doing σημεῖα μεγάλα καὶ τέρατα ("great signs and wonders") cf. 2 Thessalonians 2:9. This is the second stage of the end.

Then, the final stage is described in 24:29-31. By virtue of the revelation of θλίψις ("a time of testing") 24:21, 29, there is a very easy transition from Matthew 24:21-24 to 29-31. In the latter pericope, attention is turned away from the terrible time of crisis, and ever present danger of apostasy, to the definitive appearance of the Son of Man who will cause the tribes of the earth to mourn.

This final section of the source, heavily dependent on the apocalyptic terminolo-gy of Old Testament texts, asserts that the coming of the Son of Man will be on the clouds of heaven in contrast to the locale of Judea which, as the place of the false prophets and messiahs, was the center for the final crisis.[22]

Before we close this discussion on the thematic unity of the source, the reference to the sign in 24:3b, 30, a very difficult question, should be taken up.[23] Is it Matthean redaction or did it come from Matthew's source tradition?

First, a similar exegetical tradition on the final appearance of the Lord which brings travail upon the tribes of the earth, based on Zechariah 12:10-12 is found in Revelation 1:7. However, the author of Revelation does not refer to a sign of the Lord in the heavens. Since, there is a possibility that Revelation 1:7 repre-sents a variation on the same exegetical tradition as Matthew 24:30, there being no substantive evidence that the author of the Apocalypse shows direct literary dependence upon Matthew, we infer that there is insufficient evidence to con-clude that the reference to the "sign of the Son of Man in heaven" was an inherent part of the tradition.[24] It may have been a separate item of tradition used by Matthew or have come later from the hand of the author of Matthew.

Second, although Didache 16:6-8 asserts that at the last day there will appear a set of three σημεῖα ("signs"), namely, a cleavage in heaven, the sound of a trumpet, and the resurrection of the dead, since we have already taken the posi-tion that the Didache does show literary dependence upon Matthew, we conclude that what is present in Didache 16:6-8 is an exegetical expansion of Matthew 24:30. Thus, this passage cannot be counted against the view that the reference to the "sign of the Son of Man in heaven" is from the hand of the composer of Matthew.

Third, we will show immediately below that Matthew 24:3b appears in a verse that shows considerable redactional activity by the author of Matthew. This strengthens the possibility that σημεῖον, in the connected Matthew 24:30, may be part of this redaction.

On the other hand, the fact that σημεῖον occurs in a verse that we have identified as a source (24:30) provides some evidence that it is consonant with

---

[22]The background to this connection between signs and the eschatological events is found as early as Isa 11:2 (LXX). There the future son of Jesse will gather the dispersed of Israel from the four corners of the earth (cf. Matt 24:31) as a sign of the final triumph of Yahweh. Already in Isaiah (18:3) this tradition is linked with the sound of the trumpet. Later it is linked with the resurrection of the dead (Dan 12:1-2; cf. 1 Thess 4:15-17).

[23]Burnett, *Testament of Jesus*, 338-41, gives the list of the basic possibilities held by interpreters for understanding the nature of the sign.

[24]Barnabas Lindars, *New Testament Apologetic: The Doctrinal Significance of the Old Testament Quotations* (London: SCM Press, 1961) 126, argues cogently that the sign was a separate item from this exegetical tradition.

the possibility that this phraseology may have been source material for Matthew. The fact that a reference to σημεῖον is also found in 2 Thessalonians 2:9 may mean that its appearance there was an echo of a tradition lying behind a source also used by Matthew. We conclude that it is unclear whether σημεῖον was in source material used by Matthew. It is a very difficult matter to decide. We tend to lean towards the view it was Matthean redaction, but we cannot rule out the possibility it was embedded in the Matthean source.

Evidence of a Seam:
Matthew 24:3 as the Composition of the Author of Matthew

Matthew 24:3 is a verse that both linguistically and compositionally serves to set the stage for Matthew's transition into a source.

Tevis has determined that the phraseology καθημένου δὲ αὐτοῦ ἐπὶ τοῦ + noun + verb + pronoun + noun + a participial form of λέγω ("while he was sitting on the Mount of Olives the disciples came to him alone, saying") occurring in Matthew 24:3, also has the same grammatical elements in Matthew 27:19; this collocation does not occur elsewhere in the New Testament.[25] He draws from this the conclusion that it is likely the work of a single writer; and it is likely this phrase came from a redactor.[26]

In addition, this potential evidence of redactional activity is supplemented by a construction that uses προσέρχομαι followed by a noun or pronoun in the dative case ("the disciples came to him").[27] The appearance of this construction in Matthew 24:3a is one of twenty five instances of this usage in Matthew. This grammatical construction does not occur elsewhere in the New Testament except for some Synoptic parallels, and thus is deemed by Tevis as the work of a redactor.[28] This means that all of Matthew 24:3a can be identified as containing linguistic characteristics of a single author—most likely a redactor. Since Matthew 24:3a is at a seam (immediately preceding a long discourse), it is reasonable to conclude that the redactor was the primary author of our present text.

Moreover, we have already determined above by our own analysis that in Matt 24:3, 30, the word τὸ σημεῖον could be Matthean redaction. In addition, since the phraseology συντελείας τοῦ αἰῶνος ("end of the age") is linguistic terminology characteristic of the text of Matthew, and occurs in the immediate vicinity of other redactional passages in Matthew, (13:39, 40 (twice) 28:20), and with the exception of Hebrews 9:26, nowhere else in the New Testa-

---

[25]Tevis, *Words and Phrases of Matthew*, #46 on p. 72.
[26]Ibid.
[27]Ibid., 20, 43-44.
[28]Ibid.

ment, there is a good possibility that this can be considered as also coming from a redactor.[29]

There seems to be no valid reason not to conclude that the final redactor of Matthew 24:3 was the author of Matthew. Thus, in Matt 24:3a the author has Jesus sit on the Mount of Olives with his disciples. The disciples ask Jesus a question about the end of the temple and the time of his parousia and the end of the age. This compositional framework serves as an appropriate introduction to the whole Olivet Discourse.

In contrast to the elaborate compositional framework constructed in Matthew in 24:3, enabling the author to connect this narrative to a major source, which serves as the basis for the whole Discourse, there is no evidence of a seam when Jesus' answer to the question of 24:3b ends in 24:31. Instead, Matthew is able to make an easy transition to the parable of the fig tree (24:32-33). This parable, with its emphasis on the rapid movement from the time the bud comes forth to the final harvest, provides a fitting conclusion to the description of the working out of eschatological events which Matthew anticipates will soon culminate in the end of the age. Thus the suture between different source traditions in 24:31 and 32 is accomplished very easily and unobtrusively.

Scope of Source

Our study of the linguistic characteristics of the source, its theme, and analysis as to how the author of Matthew placed the source into the narrative framework of the Olivet Discourse is now complete. Initially, because of the observation of close linguistic parallels and a common theme between Matthew 24:4b-31 and 2 Thessalonians 2:1-12, we were led to investigate whether both writers were utilizing earlier traditions. In the case of 2 Thessalonians 2:1-12 we argued that indeed this was the case. Now, on the basis of the study of special vocabularly items and internal thematic coherence, it appears that a similar tradition was utilized by the author of Matthew in the composition of the Olivet Discourse. Our analysis of the initial linguistic evidence supports the thesis that the author may have drawn on this source in Matt 24:4b-6, 10-12, 14-15, 21-24, 29-31. Further details about how this source was incorporated into the composition of Matt 24:3-25:46 will be given in the final section of this chapter.

---

[29]Ibid., #135 on p. 135. The discussion of the appearance of παρουσία in Matt 24:3 will be discussed below.

A Second Source: On the Coming of the Son of Man
(Matthew 24:27, 37, 38-39, [44])

In Matthew 24:27, 37, 38-39, there appear three formulaic statements *On the Coming of the Son of Man*. These formulaic statements appear in literary units that have a pattern of similar structural and verbal agreements. The common structure and vocabulary of these verses give the impression that they are either the creation of a single author or come from a special source. We will argue that the latter is most likely the case.

The three units (Matt 24:27, 37, 38-39) are not paralleled in Mark. They are found in Luke 17:24, 26-27. The pattern of these agreements can be seen in the display.

Matthew 24:27	Luke 17:24
²⁷ὥσπερ γὰρ ἡ ἀστραπὴ	²⁴ὥσπερ γὰρ ἡ ἀστραπὴ
ἐξέρχεται ἀπὸ ἀνατολῶν	ἀστράπτουσα ἐκ τῆς ὑπὸ τὸν οὐρα-
καὶ φαίνεται ἕως δυσμῶν,	νὸν εἰς τὴν ὑπ' οὐρανὸν λάμπει,
οὕτως ἔσται ἡ παρουσια τοῦ υἱοῦ	οὕτως ἔσται ὁ υἱὸς τοῦ ἀνθρώπου
τοῦ ἀνθρώπου.	[ἐν τῇ ἡμέρᾳ αὐτου].

Matthew 24:37	Luke 17:26
³⁷Ὥσπερ γὰρ αἱ ἡμέραι τοῦ Νῶε,	²⁶καὶ καθὼς ἐγένετο
	ἐν ταῖς ἡμέραις Νῶε,
οὕτως ἔσται	οὕτως ἔσται καὶ
ἡ παρουσία τοῦ υἱου	ἐν ταῖς ἡμέραις τοῦ υἱου
τοῦ ἀνθρώπου.	τοῦ ἀνθρώπου.

Matthew 24:38-39	Luke 17:27, 30
³⁸ὡς γὰρ ἦσαν ἐν ταῖς ἡμέραις	
ἐκείναι ταῖς πρὸ τοῦ κατακλυσμοῦ	
τρώγοντες καὶ πίνοντες	²⁷ἤσθιον, ἔπινον,
γαμοῦντες καὶ γαμίζοντες,	ἐγάμουν, ἐγαμίζοντο,
ἄχρι ἧς ἡμέρας	ἄχρι ἧς ἡμέρας
εἰσῆλθεν Νῶε εἰς τὴν κιβωτόν,	εἰσῆλθεν Νῶε εἰς τὴν κιβωτόν,
³⁹καὶ οὐκ ἔγνωσαν	
ἕως ἦλθεν ὁ κατακλυσμὸς	καὶ ἦλθεν ὁ κατακλυσμὸς
καὶ ἦρεν ἅπαντας,	καὶ ἀπώλεσεν πάντας.
οὕτως ἔσται καὶ	³⁰κατὰ τὰ αὐτὰ ἔσται
ἡ παρουσία τοῦ υἱου τοῦ ἀνθρώπου.	ἦ ἡμέρᾳ ὁ υἱός
	τοῦ ἀνθρώπου ἀποκαλύπτεται.

Before we enter into a source analysis of these texts, it should be noted that, with respect to Matthew, we have already shown earlier through a study of 1 Thessalonians 5:2 that a source tradition on the Thief at Night rests behind

Matthew 24:42-43. Matthew 24:44 concludes with a reference to the coming of the Son of Man! Although it is questionable, it is possible that Matthew found his source for 24:44 in the same source that supplied 24:27, 37-39—a series of sayings on the coming of the Son of Man. We will return to this point later in the chapter.

In order to state the evidence for the hypothesis that Matthew 24:27, 37-39, (44) comes from a single source, we will now examine several of the linguistic features of this text. Our goal is simply to confirm the hypothesis that the entire block of Matthew 24:27, 37-39, as well as perhaps verse 44, comes from a single source which Matthew incorporated into his account of Jesus' Olivet Discourse.

We believe such a project can be undertaken without first resorting to the hypothesis that both Matthew and Luke used the same or a similar source tradition independently.[30] On the contrary, we believe it can be argued plausibly that not only did Matthew utilize source tradition, but also that there is good literary evidence to indicate that Luke did know and was dependent upon the text of Matthew for his composition.[31] We will now turn to examine in detail each of these three units of the textual evidence.

Matthew 24:27 || Luke 17:24

Structurally, Matthew 24:27 has been identified as an "As it was . . . So will . . . " formulation.[32] This formula is a common literary feature of Matthew 24:27, 37, 38-39; but, as the display below indicates, it is also found elsewhere in Matthew.

---

[30]This, of course, is the usual position of those who adhere to the Q hypothesis. Adherents of this hypothesis generally have tended to see the wording of Luke as being closer to the original form of the source and have viewed the Matthean differences from Luke as Matthean redaction. Some even see all of Lk 17:23, 24, 26-30, 34-35, 37 as an internally coherent apocalypse drawn from Q. cf. John S. Kloppenborg, *The Foundation of Q: Trajectories in Ancient Wisdom Collections* (Philadelphia: Fortress, 1987) 154-66.

[31]Much of this evidence is given in McNicol, "Composition of the Eschatological Discourse," 168-73. A major argument that supplements this body of evidence should be noted with respect to the appearance of ὥσπερ in Lk. 17:24. This word occurs at least ten times in Matthew and is labelled by Hawkins, *Horae Synopticae*, 8, as a linguistic characteristic of the first gospel. On the other hand, ὥσπερ is used only twice by Luke (17:24; 18:11). In Luke 18:11 ὥσπερ occurs in the parable of the Pharisee and the Tax Collector which is thought by many to be part of Luke's special source material. Therefore, the appearance of ὥσπερ at Luke 17:24 in a parallel unit with Matthew, in a context where there is evidence of copying, provides strong proof for the position that Luke, at this point, is using a source.

[32]Goulder, *Midrash and Lection*, 78, is responsible for this terminology. Besides Matt 24:27, 37, 38-39, Goulder also observes similar formulaic statements in Matt 6:21, 18:20, and 24:28. However, that is questionable, since the ὥσπερ/οὕτως formulation is absent in these latter verses. Goulder does not mention Matt 13:40.

Matthew 12:40	Luke 11:30

<table>
<tr><td>

^{40}ὥσπερ γὰρ ἦν <u>Ἰωνᾶς</u>
ἐν τῇ κοιλίᾳ τοῦ κήτους
τρεῖς ἡμέρας καὶ τρεῖς νύκτας,
<u>οὕτως ἔσται</u>
<u>ὁ υἱὸς τοῦ ἀνθρώπου</u>

</td><td>

^{30}<u>καθὼς</u> γὰρ ἐγένετο <u>Ἰωνᾶς</u>
τοῖς Νινευίταις σημεῖον,

<u>οὕτως ἔσται</u> καὶ
<u>ὁ υἱὸς τοῦ ἀνθρώπου</u>
τῇ γενεᾷ ταύτῃ.

</td></tr>
</table>

Matthew 13:40	No parallel in Luke

ὥσπερ οὖν συλλέγεται τὰ ζιζάνια
καὶ πυρὶ κατακαίεται
<u>οὕτως ἔσται</u>
ἐν τῇ συντελείᾳ τοῦ αἰῶνος

Formally, one could argue that the basic features of this literary structure may be either derived from Matthean source material, or are Matthean composition. However, as already noted, ὥσπερ is a linguistic characteristic of the text of Matthew. The repetition of the particular collocation of linguistic items (ὥσπερ γὰρ . . . οὕτως ἔσται ἡ παρουσία τοῦ υἱοῦ ἀνθρώπου), that are strikingly similar in Matthew 24:27, 37, 38-39,[33] could be an indication that they come from the hand of a single author.[34] And, the fact that this specific construction is limited to Matthew 24, can also suggest that a single author may have been the composer of this phraseology. Was this single author the composer of Matthew?

It is now time to account for the appearance of the word παρουσία in this text as well as the other two units in Matt 24:37, 38-39. We have shown in the previous chapter that Matthew may well have found παρουσία in source material utilized by the author of 2 Thessalonians in 2 Thessalonians 2:1 (cf. 1 Thess 2:19; 3:13; 4:15; 5:23; 2 Thess 2:8, 9); and this may well have been a decisive factor for the use of this word in the composition of Matthew 24:3b. Having used παρουσία in Matt 24:3, Matthew may well have used it in his composition of the statement on the coming of the Son of Man in 24:27 as well as 37 and 39, but, we must note, it was not in 24:44, which retains the form of an original Son of Man saying. This explanation has merit. The fact that the Son of Man saying

---

[33]The only significant difference is in Matt 24:38 where Matthew has ὡς instead of ὥσπερ. But ὥσπερ may well be the correct reading. It is supported by the uncials DEFGKY, Codex Petropolitanus, W, and Family 13 and 28.

[34]Tevis, *Words and Phrases of Matthew*, #404 on p. 253, states this with reference to the phraseology, "Thus will be the parousia of the Son of Man."

in Matthew 24:44 does not have παρουσία supports this conclusion. Thus, Matthew having found παρουσία in his source material (either in the Pauline letters or most likely in the tradition behind 2 Thessalonians 2) would then use it four times in one chapter, but nowhere else, to describe the advent of the Son of Man at the end of the age.

The source utilized by Matthew drew a comparison between the appearance of light overcoming darkness and the coming of the Son of Man. It is noticeable that in the New Testament ἀστραπή not only means lightning, but it can also mean a bright ray of light (cf. Lk 11:34). We suggest that in Matthew's source tradition, the *Coming of the Son of Man* was compared with the suddenness and deliberate certainty of the movement of light from east to west early in the morning. Matthew, through his usage of the ὥσπερ / οὕτως formula and παρουσία, has incorporated this tradition into his composition to highlight the theme of the universality (from east to west) of the impact of the coming of the Son of Man.[35]

Matthew 24:37-39 // Luke 17:26-27 (28-30)

In the minds of some commentators the double use of the comparison formula ὥσπερ (ὡς) . . . οὕτως by Matthew in 24:37 and 38a, 39b is a clear indicator that Matthew, along with Luke, has similar knowledge of a common source which compares the coming of the Son of Man with both the times of Noah and Lot and, in so doing, Matthew used a version of this double formula (cf. Luke 17:26, 28a, 30b).[36] As a corollary to this thesis, it is argued that Matthew then omitted the Lot statement (found in Luke 17:28-29), and subsequently had on his hands two formulas of comparison, which he placed clumsily at the beginning and ending of his source material on Noah (24:37-39).[37]

We believe that this view leaves several major questions unanswered. The central issue revolves around the supposed Matthean omission of the Lot material. If, as it is alleged, that Matthew knew the Lot saying, and chose to omit it, it is unlikely that he would enter the same comparison formula into a composition that was supposed to frame the saying which was rejected (Lk 17:28a, 30b).[38]

---

[35]It is possible that φαίνεται (24:27) is a Matthean anticipation of his description of the sign of the Son of Man in 24:30.

[36]C. M. Tuckett, *The Revival of the Griesbach Hypothesis: An Analysis and Appraisal*, SNTSMS 44 (Cambridge: Cambridge University Press, 1983) 169.

[37]Ibid.

[38]The comparison between Lot and Noah has a well-established exegetical connection in both Jewish and Early Christian literature. Given this connection it could just as well have been added by Luke to the Matthean source as have been utilized from a common

It is granted that the twofold use of the comparison formula in Matthew 24:37, 38-39 is somewhat awkward; but another explanation for its compositional structure can be put forward that does not entail reckoning with the difficulties implicit in the view that Matthew and Luke were using a common source. This explanation presumes acceptance of the hypothesis that Matthew 24:27, 37, 38-39, and perhaps 44 was a single source of either three or four sayings about the coming of the Son of Man. All of these sayings generally stressed the theme of the sudden and unexpected nature of the coming of the Son of Man. Matthew, finding these sayings in source material utilized them in the composition of the Olivet Discourse with a change of focus. Instead of an emphasis, just on the suddenness and unexpectedness of the coming of the Son of Man, Matthew wished to use them to stress the very serious consequences of the end and its accompanying Judgment—a theme that will pervade the entire last part of the Eschatological Discourse (cf. Matt 24:40-41, 50-51; 25:10-12, 28-30, 41).

Given this insight, the basic compositional method of Matthew now becomes clear. The second saying on the parousia of the Son of Man (24:37) serves as a thesis sentence to the whole of the last part of the Eschatological Discourse (24:37–25:46). It shifts the focus from the concerns of Matthew 24:32-36 (certain resolution of the eschatological events in that generation) to the gravity of the time of the end of the age itself—especially with respect to the unprepared. Matthew 24:37, in the form of a gnomic statement, sets forth the thesis, "As it was in the days of Noah, so it will be at the time of the parousia of the Son of Man." That is, the unprepared will suffer a terrible fate.

Then follows the third saying of 24:38-39 with its stress on the terrible flood. When the flood came so many were found to be unprepared.

Immediately following, at Matthew 24:40-41, the author has inserted additional material on the theme of the separation at the end ("one shall be taken and one left behind").[39]

Finally, after inserting material from the unit on the Thief in the Night (also utilized by Paul in 1 Thess 5:2) for the composition of 24:42-43, the composer of Matthew may have incorporated the fourth saying from his source on the *Coming of the Son of Man* (24:44) into the final composition. This saying stresses the

---

source by both Matthew and Luke. Cf. M. D. Goulder, *Luke: A New Paradigm*, vol. 2, JSNTSS 20 (Sheffield: JSOT Press, 1989) 651-52; McNicol, *Composition of the Synoptic Eschatological Discourse*, 171.

[39]Although it cannot be proven, perhaps a version of Matt 24:37a, was in Matthew's source immediately preceding the text of Matt 24:40a, and the present Matt 24:37b came at the end of Matt 24:41. In that case all of Matt 24:37-41 would have constituted the special source. At any rate, the terminology of one taken and the other left (Matt 24:40-41) appears to be fully in keeping with the Matthean theological emphasis which highlights the final separation which takes place at the parousia.

need to be prepared for the end of the age, which in the latter part of the Eschatological Discourse, is the regnant theme in the Matthean composition.[40]

Summary

Our source-critical study of Matthew 24 has revealed positive results. It has brought forth evidence that Matthew may have utilized two identifiable source traditions as the basis for the fundamental structural arrangement of this unit. First, there would have been a source on the *Final Crisis of the Era* (Matt 24:4b-6, 10-12, 14-15, 21-24, 29-31). This source appears to have been known and echoed by the author of 2 Thessalonians 2:1-12. Second, on this reconstruction, Matthew also utilized a source on the *Coming of the Son of Man* that served as the basis for the composition of Matthew 24:27, 37, 38-39, [44].[41] This source is not echoed in the writings attributed to Paul. This is not particularly surprising since Son of Man is not Pauline terminology. However, the simile of the Thief in the Night, which we have shown in an earlier chapter was echoed by Paul (1 Thess 5:3), was utilized by Matthew (Matt 24:42-43). As we have noted, in this case, it was our conclusion that this suggests independent use of a common tradition by these two writers.

It is *not* the purpose of this study to argue that these two sources, or the use of a simile on the Thief at Night, were drawn from collections of the genuine sayings of the earthly Jesus, nor is it the purpose of this study to trace the tradition history of how these collections were brought into being. Suffice it to say that, as best as we can determine the function of these formulaic statements, with their emphasis on the need to be prepared for an impending final crisis which will be resolved by the appearance of the Son of Man and the themes that characterize them, are congruent with what we know as a major emphasis of the esoteric teaching of the earthly Jesus to his disciples. However, it *is* our purpose to discuss how this source material may have been used by Matthew in the composition of the Eschatological Discourse. To this issue we now turn.

---

[40]Other differences in composition of Lk 17:26-30, 34-35 from Matthew can be accounted for by Lukan redaction. A number of these have been noted by McNicol, *Composition of the Eschatological Discourse*, 171-72; also Goulder, *Luke: A New Paradigm*, 2:652-58.

[41]It is possible that the source behind Matt 24:27, 37, 38-39, [44] could also have included the parable of the Chief Servant and Slaves (Matt 24:45-51). However, there is little evidence to warrant this as a firm conclusion. There is no formulaic saying on the coming of the Son of Man as we find in the rest of the source. And, the common use of μεθύειν in Matt 24:49 and 1 Thess 5:7, is hardly enough evidence to build a connection between 1 Thess 5:7 (or a source behind it) and Matt 24:45-51 (contra Goulder, *Midrash and Lection*, 437).

The Matthean Setting for 24:3–25:46 and Its Structure

Focus and Setting

As already noted above, the immediate setting for the Olivet Discourse is found in Matthew 24:1-3. In 24:1 Jesus had left the temple precincts in an emphatic manner. This is indicated both by the use of the participle ἐξελθών ("and after he left") and the verb ἐπορεύετο ("he began to proceed"). This definitive move away from the temple is the final result of Jesus having declared the temple forsaken and spiritually desolate (23:38).[42] The presupposition is that Jerusalem and her leadership will remain in such a condition until she hails her Messiah (23:39). In the narrative world of the composer of Matthew this will be at the end of the age.

The determined exit of Jesus from the temple is balanced in Matthew with two approaches to Jesus by the disciples. First, the disciples focus his attention on the impressive building (24:1b). Jesus' response is that it will be destroyed (24:2). The impact of this prediction is heightened by the formulaic statement ἀμὴν λέγω ὑμῖν ("truly I say to you") which is also found in 23:36, 24:34, 24:47. The saying about the temple's destruction falls in the wake of Jesus' decision to leave the temple.

This leads to the second approach of the disciples in the form of the question of 24:3. Matthew constructs 24:3 very carefully. While Jesus was seated on the Mount of Olives the disciples approached Jesus directly.[43] The composition is highlighted by the use of the construction προσῆλθον αὐτῷ ("they came to him"). Προσέρχεσθαι appears more than fifty times in Matthew and is followed by the dative at least twenty-five times.[44] The word occurs much less frequently in Luke and Mark (only six times, and only twice in the dative) and thus appears to be a linguistic preference of Matthew. In Matthew, it often is used to describe others coming to Jesus with an esoteric inquiry (5:1-2; 18:1; 24:1). Earlier the word was used in the LXX frequently to describe the cultic approach to God. All

---

[42]Matt 23:38 seems to reflect an exegetical tradition dependent upon Jer 12:7 and 22:5 (LXX). There the Lord has abandoned his house (i.e., the Davidic leadership in Jer 22:5). The apparent use of this exegetical tradition by Matthew weighs in favor of our accepting ἔρημος as stemming from the work of the composer of the first gospel and not a later addition due to the end of Jerusalem. At the very least, what is being argued here is that the divine blessings are no longer upon the Jerusalem leadership of Matthew's time.

[43]As we have noted above, Tevis, *Words and Phrases*, #46 on p. 72 indicates that καθημένου δὲ αὐτοῦ ἐπὶ τοῦ + Noun + verb + pronoun + noun + participle of λέγω also occurs at Matt 27:19 but nowhere else in the N.T. This stands as literary evidence of the hand of a single author; and as noted earlier, we are strongly of the view that this single author was the composer of Matthew.

[44]Tevis, *Words and Phrases*, #20 on pp. 43-44.

of this is consonant with the view that the disciples drew near to their Lord privately endeavoring to learn some esoteric secrets about the end of the age (cf. 14:23; 17:1, 19; 20:17).

The esoteric question of Matthew 24:3 addressed to Jesus is, "When will these things be and what will be the sign of the parousia and end of the age?"

There is no doubt that the first part of the question, "When will all these things be? (πότε ταῦτα ἔσται) refers back to Matt 24:2, the harsh announcement of the destruction of the entire temple complex (ταῦτα πάντα).

The rest of the composition of Matthew 24:3 is based on the fundamental presupposition that the actual destruction of the temple (ταῦτα) and the end of the age are coterminous events. The disciples ask, "When will these things (i.e., the previously discussed destruction of the temple), *and at the same time* (καί), what will be the sign of your parousia and the end of the age?" (24:3b).[45] The

---

[45]Our translation presumes that the first καί (πότε ταῦτα ἔσται καὶ τί τὸ σημεῖον) functions epexegetically and not as a conjunction. Burnett, *The Testament of Jesus*, 207, argues strongly for this understanding of the use of καί although his exegesis of the passage then moves off on a very different direction than our own. The position that the author of Matthew argues that the temple will be destroyed at the parousia of the Son of Man, which will take place at the end of the age, is very compatible with the view that this work was composed in the late 60s of the first century, perhaps after the commencement of the revolt against Rome. The Matthean Jesus anticipates a final crisis at the temple (24:15-21). This is labelled in 24:21 as the "Great Tribulation." For this to happen, by definition, the temple is still standing at the time of composition. Then, immediately after the anticipated crisis of the Tribulation in 24:29a (εὐθέως), comes the parousia of the Son of Man (24:29-31). Presumably, at this time, the temple is to be destroyed (and re-built?) and the Son of Man is revealed in his glory (cf. 19:28; 25:31-46).

The alternative view (often dictated by the presumed priority of the Markan version of the Discourse) is that Matthew was composed sometime after 70 CE. This inevitably leads the interpreter into a maze of painful exegetical choices, none of which have been found to be widely convincing in the academy. For example, those who take the position that, after Matt 24:2, a major caesura takes place with respect to this verse being the end of discussion about the temple (it is now presumed destroyed) and 24:3-31 refers entirely to post 70 events, have to explain why Matthew included 24:15-16 in his composition. The suggestion of Burnett, *The Testament of Jesus*, 315-38, that this is a cryptic reference to apostasy in the church has, to my knowledge, not gained widespread support. Without question, as the post-70 Jewish apocalypse 4 Ezra makes us well aware, the destruction of the temple sent shock waves among the Jewish community throughout the Eastern Mediterranean. It is very difficult to conceive that in the environment of post-70 Greater Syria the words of Matt 24:15-22 could have been written and read without some connection to the Fall of Jerusalem (24:1-2?) being made. But, even if Burnett's exegesis is granted, and Matthew was composed some years after 70, this position still faces the difficulty of explaining the use of εὐθέως in 24:29. After what set of events does the parousia immediately follow? Finally, the other major alternative position in favor of post-70 authorship is that the parousia of the Son of Man of Matt 24:3 is the destruction of Jerusalem (24:29-31). Cf. S. Brown, "The Matthean Apocalypse," 13; R. T. France,

answer is given definitively in Matthew 24:4-31. Thus, the destruction of the temple, as coterminous with the end of the age, provides narrative continuity for the entire unit.

We have already noted that Matthew has carefully crafted the composition of 24:3.[46] However, something more should be said about the reference to τὸ σημεῖον ("the sign"). We have argued that perhaps this is Matthean composition in Matthew 24:3 and functions as an anticipation of the phraseology of "the sign of the Son of Man" in Matthew 24:30. But what precisely is Matthew's point in using τὸ σημεῖον in these places?

In our view the use of τὸ σημεῖον in both 24:3 and 24:30 provides not only general boundary markers for the answer to the question in 24:3 but also the clue for understanding the focus to the first segment of the Discourse (24:4-31). In these verses Matthew is deeply concerned that his readers be aware of the grave danger of the various signs (σημεῖα) and wonders (τέρατα) and other misleading claims of the false prophets (Matt 24:4b-5, 11, 23-24). In some cases they even claim that these workers re-present the presence and word of the Messiah. Such people are a clear and present danger to Matthew's community.

The Gospel According to Matthew (Grand Rapids: Eerdmans, 1985) 343-46. This certainly solves the problem of the appearance of εὐθέως ("immediately") in 24:29; but it leaves very serious issues concerning the interpretation of 24:29-31. These problems are as follows: In 24:3 there is a direct linkage in the disciples' questions to Jesus between the parousia and the end of the age. The συντελείας τοῦ αἰῶνος in Matt 13:43, 49 clearly refers to the end of linear history in the Matthean narrative (cf. 28:20). Likewise, in 24:37, 39, the reference to the parousia refers definitely to a similar time. Matt 24:29-31 (which has a close linkage through use of the same tradition to Paul's description of the end-time events in 1 Thess 4:15-17) is the culmination of Jesus' response to the disciples' questions in 24:3. The end will take place only after the appearance of cosmic signs, and it will involve a gathering of the elect from the ends of the earth. It will cause mourning among the tribes of the earth. Even allowing for the pictorial nature of this language it is clear that an event of universal proportions is being discussed here. The tribes of the earth, by and large, were not grieved that Jerusalem was levelled by the Romans. At the Judgment, in Matthean terms, they have every reason for concern. Thus, the identification of Matt 24:29-31 with the Fall of Jerusalem is impossible. Therefore, the best alternative is to understand Matthew as being composed immediately before 70 CE. In 24:3, the disciples anticipating the profanation of the temple, and being under the presumption that it will be destroyed at the time of the parousia, ask for a sign for these events. The Matthean Jesus then gives a response. This dating would be affirmed further if the reference to "Zechariah, the son of Barachiah" in Matt 23:35b is a reference to the Zechariah whom Josephus (*Jewish War* 4.334-44) argued was killed in the Temple in 67-68 CE (cf. Brown, "The Matthean Apocalypse," 5-6).

[46]We have concluded above that both the use of παρουσία and συντελείας τοῦ αἰῶνος probably represents the compositional activity of the final author of Matthew.

Perhaps Matthew is suggesting that even the disciples themselves as trans-parencies of the leaders of the Matthean community are succumbing to the danger of requesting the definitive sign of the end with their question to Jesus in 24:3. At any rate, the Matthean Jesus responds to the situation. The appropri-ate information about the end of the age is not dependent on the basis of a con-temporary prophet's interpretation of current events. But, based on the word of Jesus alone, the definitive sign will come with the cosmic appearance of the Son of Man in his parousia (24:30). No one will be able to miss it (24:27-28; 30-31; cf. 37-41). Its occurrence is not to be connected with rumors of the Messiah being in hiding, or signs on earth, but only on the word of the Son who is subject to the Father (cf. 24:36).

Thus the focus of the first part of the Discourse comes into play. In the setting of the hallowed Mount of Olives, in an intimate talk with his disciples, Matthew has Jesus respond to their concerns about the future. In 24:4-31 the Matthean Jesus will set forth a careful picture of the days after he has gone which will culminate with the parousia of the Son of Man. In many ways this is a conventional first century Palestinian scenario for the end involving a great crisis in Judea, apostasy, tribulation, and shortly thereafter, the last Judgment. But above all, the focus is on the need to be humbly obedient to Jesus' word and not to be led away by various prophets with their false signs and fantastic calcula-tions.[47] Having given this warning, in a brief parenthesis (24:32-36) the author of Matthew reinforces his belief in the sure and certain outworking of these events. Then, in the second part of the Discourse, because these momentous eschatological events would culminate with the final judgment of the Son of Man, given the all important significance of this terrible event, the disciples are exhorted to spend the intervening time in faithful service to their Lord (24:37–25:46). It will be terrible not to be prepared when this day comes.

The Structure of the Matthean Eschatological Discourse

Structurally, it is the goal of Matthew to pull together the two major sources, several similes, parables, and isolated sayings into a coherent order to construct 24:4-25:46. The Discourse falls into five distinct units.[48]

1. *Turbulence during the Current Era of Mission to the Gentiles (24:4-14).* Matthew describes the turbulent current era of the first generation Christian-Jewish community and its witness to the nations (24:14). In the world of

---

[47]Cf. J. Dupont, *Les Trois Apocalypses Synoptiques Marc 13; Matthieu 24-25; Luc 21,* Lectio Divina 121 (Paris: Cerf, 1985) 52-53.

[48]The five-part outline is similar in a number of respects to V. K. Agbanou, *Le Dis-cours Eschatologique de Matthieu 24-25; Tradition et Rédaction* (Paris: J. Gabalda, 1983) 225-28, although our understanding of the origin of the source tradition is vastly different.

Matthew, at the last day, all peoples will be judged by the Son of Man (Matt 25:31-32). In order to hold them accountable the testimony of the gospel must first be brought to them (24:14a). But this proclamation of the message will not be easy. Hostility and persecution will accompany the proclamation of the gospel every step of the way. This is recounted in 24:4-14.

2. *The Appearance of the Horrible Desecration (24:15-28)*. This unit falls into two sections. First, in 24:15-22 Matthew describes the climactic events of the era culminating in the Horrible Desecration he thought was about to take place in Jerusalem. Matthew, however, is careful not to say that this specifically is the sign of the end even though it is a period of great tribulation. Second, in 24:23-28 Matthew adds a brief parenthesis warning the community not to accept the false claims of many that they know the Messiah is secretly present in the world. There is no esoteric sign of the end given to a privileged group. When the parousia of the Son of Man comes it will be universal and visible to all (cf. 24:27-28).

3. *The Parousia of the Son of Man (24:29-36)*. Matthew describes the parousia and the end of the age. In keeping with current apocalyptic ideas, the end will come shortly after the tribulation and period of final crisis (24:29). The sign of the Son of Man is the parousia of the exalted Jesus himself. Again, as with the previous unit, Matthew ends the unit with a brief parenthesis (24:32-36). In contrast to the false prohets who claim that the Messiah is present, Matthew argues that the scenario set forth by the word of the Son of Man himself is the only sure guide on the end.

4. *Vigilance is Demanded While the End-Time is Delayed (24:37-25:30)*. As the end is delayed, the disciples are not to become weary and quit. The Son of Man will return in due course and will judge harshly those who are not prepared for his coming. Seven parables of warning are given to accentuate the need to be prepared.

5. *The Judgment of the Nations (25:31-46)*. At the end all nations will be judged. The major basis of the judgment will be how they have reacted to the mission of the disciples.

Summary

The basic structure of this section can be reduced to the following outline.

A   Witness to the Nations before the End (24:4-14).
    B   The Horrible Desecration calls for Vigilance (24:15-22).
        C   A Parenthesis: Heed not the false prophets
           that the End is Here (24:23-28).
           D   The Parousia of the Son of Man
              before the Tribes or Nations of the Earth (24:29-31).
        C'   A Parenthesis: Heed the Son of Man
           that the End is Near (24:32-36).

B′   The Delay calls for Vigilance (24:37-25:30).
A′   The Judgment of the Nations at the End (25:31-46).

The Matthean Composition of 24:4–25:46

We will now follow the Matthean work of composition systematically through the five thought units of 24:4–25:46.

Witness to the Nations before the End (24:4-14)

Overview of 24:4-14. The unit 24:4-14 may be broken into four separate thought units which follow an A B A′ B′ structure. In 24:4-6 and 9-13 the focus is upon the effect on the believing community from outside hostile forces during the period of delay before the appearance of the Son of Man. There is great concern that this time will be marked by lack of committment and even apostasy within the Matthean community. In 24:7-9, 14, Matthew has highlighted the role of the nations; especially as they cause turmoil or interact with the gospel message. It is worthwhile to note that the subject of the nations not only reappears later in another mountain speech (28:16-20), but also surfaces in the last unit of the extended Discourse (25:31-46). As we have noted, for 24:4b-6 and 10(-13)-14, Matthew may have drawn on a source, *On the Final Crisis of the Era*. In 24:4a, 7-8, 9, 13, we believe we find either Matthean redaction or Sondergut.

A key structural feature of the unit is found in the use of τέλος ("end") and its cognates and synonyms. The whole unit has already been set up in Matthew 24:3 with the inquiry of the disciples as to the end of the age. The use of συντέλεια ("end") at this point, is especially noticeable.

In response, in 24:4b-7, the disciples are told about some things that will take place before the end; although Matthew does not designate these events specifically as signs. However, the disciples are told in 24:6 explicitly that the appearance of wars and similar things are not the end (τέλος). But these things (πάντα) are the beginning of the birthpangs of the end (24:8). All of this gives an indication that Matthew is speaking of a time that has already passed for his readers. By use of τότε (24:9a) Matthew prepares to bring his readers into the contemporary situation of the time of his composition.

The unit of 24:9-13 continues to be addressed directly to the disciples who appear to be a transparency of the leaders of the believing community. With its combination of warnings both about the hostility of the Gentiles and of internal conflict, the description seems to reflect the current situation of Matthew's church.[49] This view is given credence in that it fits the Matthean pattern which presumes a witness had been inaugurated among the Gentiles but was still to be fully realized in the future (24:14a; cf. 28:18-20). Only when that mission was accomplished would the end come (24:14b). Thus, in this unit, from the perspective of the author of Matthew, some of Jesus' predictions of the future were realized (24:4b-8), some are being realized (9-13), and others are yet to be fully realized. As the disciples await the end (τέλος in 24:13), they come to fulfill the mission of preaching to the whole of creation. Only then will the end come (24:14b). Thus we see that τὸ τέλος is the last word of the unit. We now turn to the specifics of the text.

Analysis of 24:4-14. Matthew 24:4a is characteristic terminology for the composer of Matthew. The collocation of an aorist participle, plus the noun, plus the verb of saying is congruent with Matthean compositional style (cf. 14:28; 15:15; 17:4; 26:23).[50] Here it functions as part of the connective structure composed by Matthew to bring in the source commencing with βλέπετε μὴ ("take heed lest") in 24:4b. The source (4b-6) is then carefully entered by Matthew into the Discourse. A major concern of the author is that the community (i.e., under the nom de plume of the disciples) not be led astray. The word πλανεῖν ("to deceive"), a characteristic of the source 24:4, 5, 11, 24, may have originally referred primarily to the work of the man of lawlessness; but now it was applied to the danger of internal apostasy within the community. Some apparently representing themselves with the authority of the risen Christ (ἐπὶ τῷ ὀνόματί μου) were causing grave concern (24:5).[51] It is not possible in this work to pursue an extensive study on the effect false prophets had upon the Matthean community.[52] Clearly, as a community that operated to some degree within wider Israel, Matthew's church had many contacts and interconnections with them. Most likely they were from the same circles as those mentioned in Matthew 7:21 and 13:41.[53]

---

[49]W. G. Thompson, "An Historical Perspective on the Gospel of Matthew," *Journal of Biblical Literature* 93 (1974: 248. However, contra Thompson, I consider that 24:7-8 stands primarily in the past.

[50]Luz, *Matthew 1-7*, 55; for similar constructions see Tevis #200, pp. 139-40; #202, pp. 143-44; #232, p. 176.

[51]Tevis, *Words and Phrases*, #336 on p. 235 notes that the phrase ἐπὶ τῷ ὀνόματί μου ("by my authority") occurs only twice in the N.T. in Matt 18:5 and 24:5 with Synoptic parallels. He concludes it is a linguistic characteristic of one writer. The phrase may have been added in 24:5 to his source by the final composer of Matthew.

[52]Burnett, *The Testament of Jesus*, 234-41 sets forth the major features of the discussion and gives relevant references to the secondary literature.

[53]The fact that some of these prophets call themselves ὁ χριστός may underscore their attempt to claim that the spirit of the Christ has incarnated itself again in them. cf. Beare, "Synoptic Apocalypse," 125. But it is unclear whether these are deviant leaders

There is a slight disjunction between 24:5 and 6 as the subject changes abruptly from false prophets to the problem of wars. False prophets and disturbed political conditions are part and parcel of the standard picture of a first century Jewish view of the end time crisis. The community is warned not to be disturbed unnecessarily by the turbulent political conditions of the era. Echoing Daniel 2:28, it is explained that these things were part of the necessary course of things in the last days, but, of course, it is not the end. The use of ὅρατε μή ("take heed not to") may be Matthean redaction.[54] But, even if this is the case, it does not account for anything more than a stylistic preference of the composer to emphasize the call to be alert. The statement that it is not the end is neatly balanced with the statement in 24:8 that it is only "the beginning of the birthpangs of the new age."

Matthew 24:7-8 was not identified on the basis of unusual linguistic characteristics as a source. We are unable to tell whether it is an extension of the source used in 24:5b-6 or is Sondergut. At any rate, the causal particle γάρ ("for") in 24:7 explains further why it is not the end. The reference to conflict among the Gentiles must have been a familiar part of the current landscape for Matthew's readers. In our view, this situation fits well with a date of compostion in the late sixties: the turbulent last days of Nero's rule and its immediate aftermath.[55] Nevertheless, during this era the strife among the Gentiles will be balanced by a proclamation of the gospel of Christ to them (cf. 24:14).

The analogy between the birth pains (24:8) and the "last days" is well known in eschatological writings and appears elsewhere in the Jesus tradition (1 Thess 5:3; cf. our later analysis of Lk 21:35). This is an important verse because it allows us to situate definitively the historical perspective of the author of Matthew. It is his belief that the world is entering the period of the horrors of its last crisis. The current strife among the Gentiles (24:7) will be an active precipitating factor in bringing this horrible time to pass.

With 24:9-13 we have arrived at the time when Matthew was writing. Resumptive τότε ("then") in 24:9 alerts us to the reality that the Gentiles were harassing the believing community. Matthew 24:9 is either Matthean repetition or a doublet of Matthew 10:17b, 21b-22. It was in the mission to Israel that Jesus of Nazareth encountered bitter opposition; Matthew restates the wording of

---

within Matthew's own believing Christian community or that these prophets come from within other groups within Judaism. Probably the distinction would not have that much relevance for the author of Matthew.

[54]Tevis,*Words and Phrases*, #214 on p. 152. This construction occurs four times in Matthew and has synoptic parallels twice. The only other place that ὁράω followed by the negative μή occurs in the N.T. is at 1 Thess 5:13!

[55]M. Hengel, "Studies in the Gospel of Mark," 22-28, documents copiously the effect that the death of Nero had in causing turmoil in the eastern part of the Roman Empire.

10:17b and 21b-22 to show that, in similar fashion, the mission to the Gentiles, not surprisingly, can expect to encounter the same type of opposition. As Jesus would be handed over by his own, and killed by the Gentiles (Matt 27:2), a similar situation could be expected to happen to his followers.

Matthew 10:17, 21, 22a	Matthew 24:9
¹⁷προσέχετε δὲ ἀπὸ τῶν ἀνθρώπων. <u>παραδώσουσιν</u> γὰρ <u>ὑμᾶς</u> εἰς συνέδρια, καὶ ἐν ταῖς συναγωγαῖς αὐτῶν μαστιγώσουσιν ὑμᾶς. ²¹παραδώσει δὲ ἀδελφὸς ἀδελφὸν εἰς θάνατον καὶ πατὴρ τέκνον, καὶ ἐπαναστήσονται τέκνα ἐπὶ γονεῖς καὶ θανατώσουσιν αὐτούς.	⁹τότε <u>παραδώσουσιν ὑμᾶς</u> εἰς θλῖψιν
	καὶ ἀποκτενοῦσιν ὑμᾶς. (both refer to martyrdom)
^{22a}<u>καὶ ἔσεσθε μισούμενοι</u> <u>ὑπὸ πάντων</u> <u>διὰ τὸ ὄνομά μου.</u>	<u>καὶ ἔσεσθε μισούμενοι</u> <u>ὑπὸ πάντων</u> τῶν ἐθνῶν <u>διὰ τὸ ὄνομά μου.</u>

The display indicates how Matthew has composed with an anticipation of the crisis that arises during the time of the mission to the Gentiles in mind. The earlier reference to the handing over of disciples to the Jewish courts and the disposition of the synagogues characteristic of the mission to Israel is omitted. Now betrayal to the Gentiles takes place in the time of eschatological crisis (θλῖψιν). Hatred now stems specifically from the Gentiles (24:9).

At 24:10 Matthew resumes following his source *On the Final Crisis of the Era*. Matthew follows very closely the paratactical construction of the source in order to describe the internal situation of the church during the current era. After the resumptive καὶ τότε, Matthew has a number of successive clauses all beginning with καί detailing the grim conditions of this period.

The outer hostility of the Gentiles promotes disunity and lack of morale within the church. Many are offended (i.e., they are in danger of quitting; cf. 18:6a). They betray and hate one another. The increase of ἀνομία ("lawlessness") burgeons as the false prophets have a field day.[56] Usually for Matthew,

---

[56]Hawkins, *Horae Synopticae*, 4, lists ἀνομία as a Matthean linguistic characteristic. If this is the case, then we understand this as Matthean redaction of the source *On the Final Crisis of the Era*. However, note 2 Thess 2:3 and a disputed reading of Dan 9:24 (LXX). The latter is quite significant as the text of Daniel is echoed strongly throughout this source tradition. This may be one case where the statistical evidence would lead one

ἀνομία refers to a failure to make Jesus' interpretation of the commandments the norm for obedience and faithful following of the new righteousness (13:41; cf. 5:17-20; 22:34-40). This failure to maintain the essence of God's demands causes the love of many to grow cold and die (24:12). In this grim eschatological situation, all one can do is to urge faithfulness until the end (24:13). This is what Matthew does through a hortatory exhortation in 24:13, which, drawn from a repetition of the mission to Israel in 10:22b, he adds to his source which he used for the composition of 24:10-12.

Finally, we are brought into the immediate future in 24:14a. The mission to the Gentiles, already under way, must continue in the immediate future until its completion. According to Jeremias, a version of Matthew 24:14 goes back to Jesus himself, albeit with the different idea of the universal proclamation of the triumph of God at the last days (perhaps by an angel) to the Gentiles.[57]

Adding additional force to this conclusion, our analysis of 2 Thessalonians 2:1-12 has revealed that in the body of authoritative tradition used by that author, there may well have been material asserting that a mission to the nations would take place before the end.[58] Since we have identified that body of authoritative tradition as the source *On the Final Crisis of the Era*, which also stands behind much of Matthew 24, we may hypothecate that just as Matthew has utilized this source in 24:10-12, he also utilized a version of the same source in the composition of 24:14.

We take this position notwithstanding there is considerable evidence that the author's editorial activity is pervasive in this verse. The phraseology καὶ κηρυχ-θήσεται τοῦτο τὸ εὐαγγέλιον τῆς βασιλείας ("This gospel of the Kingdom shall be proclaimed") has close parallels elsewhere in Matthew leading one to conclude that this particular wording is the work of a single author.[59] Moreover, the phraseology εἰς μαρτύριον . . . τοῖς ἔθνεσιν occurs else-where in Matthew at 8:4 and 10:18. It appears that this phrase comes from the hand of a single writer.[60] Perhaps, as Matthew has repeated 10:17 at 24:9, he

---

to conclude this is redaction; but the source history leading to a different result is stronger and could overrule the statistical evidence. For further helpful exposition on these verses, see Justin Taylor, "'The Love of Many Will Grow Cold': Matt 24:9-13 and the Neronian Persecution," *Revue Biblique* 96 (1989): 352-57.

[57]Jeremias, *Jesus' Promise to the Nations*, 22-23.

[58]Ibid.

[59]Tevis, *Words and Phrases*, #7 on p. 28 argues that the specific phraseology of καί + κηρύσσω + (τοῦτο) τὸ εὐαγγέλιον τῆς βασιλείας occurs in 24:14, as well as in 4:23, 9:35, and 26:13 without βασιλείας but does not occur elsewhere in the New Testament. For Tevis, this suggests that this phraseology all comes from the same writer. Since Matt 4:23-25 and 9:35 function redactionally there is a strong possibility that the phrase comes from the composer of the text of Matthew.

[60]Tevis, *Words and Phrases*, #101 on p. 87-88.

paraphrases 10:18, and combines it with his source tradition in 24:14 to highlight the view that, in the future, the original mission to Israel in Matthew 10 will be expanded to the Gentiles.

Thus, in light of this widespread evidence for redaction, we can only conclude that Matthew has thoroughly transformed his source on a crucial mission to the nations before the end. As we have noted, Matthew 24:14 is an anticipation of the important scene in the final unit of the Discourse in 25:32, when all of the nations (πάντα τὰ ἔθνη) are gathered in the presence of the Son of Man. For Matthew the mission to the Gentiles is the necessary precondition for the end. Thus, Matthew gives the careful editorial phraseology καὶ τότε ἥξει τὸ τέλος ("and then the end will come") at the close of 24:14.

It is in this situation of a church both engaged in an expanding mission and, at the same time, under duress from the Gentiles that Matthew concludes this unit of the Olivet Discourse. There is nothing there that would even hint of a lengthy protracted period before the end of the age (cf. 24:32-34). The author of Matthew writes at the beginning of the labor pains signalling the end of the period of the old era and the coming of the new world (cf. 24:8). For Matthew, the world stands at the edge of the final crisis or tribulation before the end of the old era and the beginning of the age to come.

The Horrible Desecration Calls for Vigilance (24:15-22)

Matthew begins the unit by continuing to follow closely the source, *On the Final Crisis of the Era* for the composition of 24:15. As we observed in our earlier discussion on 2 Thess 2:1-12, this implies that the final crisis would be in Jerusalem and would be marked by great opposition toward God embodied in the appearance of the man of lawlessness. Matthew does not go into specifics with reference to this situation. The emphasis is more on the expectation that a critical event will take place shortly in the temple, and the believing community ought to know what to do about it when it happens. It is important to note that nothing specifically is said or hinted that this event involved the destruction of the temple; on the contrary, the continued existence of the temple is a necessary presupposition to make sense out of the narrative account.

This unit opens in 24:15 with the use of ὅταν ("whenever") in association with οὖν ("therefore") used inferentially to pick up the flow of the response to the disciples' question starting in 24:4. In the time frame of the author of Matthew, the reader has now reached the future. (cf. 24:14). Thus it is time to discuss the precipitating factors leading up to the parousia and the end of the age (cf. 24:3 and 24:14). Matthew will lead into this discussion with a description of the circumstances surrounding the appearance of the Horrible Desecration.

The author of 2 Thessalonians had argued that the parousia had not come because the final crisis of the appearance of the man of lawlessness in the temple had not happened. Matthew also presumes that this crisis is in the future. However, it is necessary for Matthew's readers to prepare for the crisis. Therefore, they must be given explicit instructions as to what to do when it happens. This is important even though all of Matthew's readers may not live in Jerusalem. The point is that when the crisis occurs in Jerusalem, then, since this has eschatological implications, it is time for the entire Christian community to take drastic action.

This final crisis is marked by the appearance of the Horrible Desecration (τὸ βδέλυγμα τῆς ἐρημώσεως) in the temple (24:15). This phraseology is different from Paul's description of the man of lawlessness in 2 Thess 2:3b-4. It is directly dependent upon the text of the Greek Bible.[61] Essentially, in its biblical contexts, it refers to the state of a temple being profaned or desecrated by idolatry or sacrifices to pagan gods.[62]

Matthew states that this is a result of the prediction of Daniel the prophet.[63] Daniel was listed among the prophets in some collections of the Scripture. Since in Daniel the locale of the Horrible Desecration is said to be in the temple of Jerusalem and, for Matthew, this is prophecy, the logical conclusion is that the reference to ἐν τόπῳ ἁγίῳ ("in the holy place") in 24:15 is to the Jerusalem temple.

By highlighting the appearance of the Horrible Desecration, Matthew is clearly supposing that his readers have a close familiarity with the prophecy of Daniel. In Daniel 9:27 (LXX and Theodotian) we are told that when the Horrible Desecration appears at the temple the impact of this event will continue until the end (ἕως συντελείας). In Daniel, the mark of the end is the arrival of the kingdom of God.[64] A corresponding idea with similar terminology is seen in Daniel 12:11-13 (LXX). Clearly, what Matthew wishes the reader to infer, in keeping with the scriptural promise of Daniel, and confirmed by the word of Jesus, is that the Horrible Desecration in the temple must precede the coming of the Son of Man (cf. 24:29).

Matthew appears to have had the presumption that his readers would be able to identify the Horrible Desecration when it occurred. Since it was common knowledge that the temple in previous times had been profaned by Gentiles (Antiochus Epiphanes, Pompey, Gaius's attempt in 40-41 CE to compel Jews to do obeisance before Roman standards), it would seem natural in the political turmoil

---

[61]Dan 9:27 (Theodotian A), 11:31, 12:11; cf. 1 Macc 1:54.

[62]Burnett, *The Testament of Jesus*, 304.

[63]This is certainly Matthean composition. Tevis, *Words and Phrases*, #17 on pp. 39-40, notes that the formula τὸ ῥηθέν (ὁ ῥηθείς) + διὰ + prophet's name + τοῦ προφήτου is well distributed throughout Matthew and is most likely redaction. Outside of Matthew, τὸ ῥηθέν does not occur elsewhere in the N.T.

[64]Dan 2:44. cf. M. Hengel, *Studies in the Gospel of Mark*, 131.

of the late 60s that Matthew could conceive of something similar happening again at the instigation of the Romans.[65]

Thus, an event in Judea would have eschatological significance for the entire church in greater Syria and, in an eschatological sense, for the world. Therefore, in order to prepare for this horrible time, there existed a rationale for Matthew to give a more detailed description of the horrors before the final crisis in 24:16-20. This description was probably drawn from Matthean source material other than the source *On the Final Crisis of the Era* since there are few identifiable vocabulary items in common with this latter source.[66]

First, the situation would become so bad that the people were to head for the hills (24:16). This repeats a pattern of responses to crisis in Judea existing from the earliest history of the people of God (Genesis 19:17) to that of more recent times (2 Maccabees 2:28). The mountains were the logical place that could furnish a degree of safety from the horrors of the great tribulation.

Second, the crisis would be so great that the flight was of the utmost urgency and must be in great haste (24:17-18). The reference about not going into the house to pick up one's outer traveling garment also accentuates this point.

Third, in 24:19, Matthew adds another metaphor about the stress of those times. Pregnant women and mothers with infants dependent upon their breasts are always among the most vulnerable in society. In these times they will suffer terribly because of the duress.

Finally, because of the crisis (24:20), one may even have to travel on the Sabbath despite the obvious difficulties this may present in Palestine. They were to pray to be spared this horror.

Again, the point is to highlight the sense of urgency of crisis that will occur at the appearance of the Horrible Desecration. When that happened it was more than the beginnings of the birthpangs of the end (cf. Matt 24:8). It was the real

----

[65]The cryptic addition in Matt 24:15 of ὁ ἀναγινώσκων νοείτω is a call to Matthew's readers to understand that when such a Horrible Desecration takes place at the temple, Daniel's prophecy will have been fulfilled. The net result is the same if we understand that the reader is studying either Daniel or Matthew.

[66]Also, there are hardly any linguistic characteristics of Matthew in 24:16-20. However, the collocation ἐν γαστρί + ἔχω occurs at 1:18, 23, as well as 24:19. Of these three instances, only 24:19 is paralleled in the Synoptic tradition. Tevis, *Words and Phrases*, #248 on p. 292, identifies it as a phrase from a single writer. We cannot tell for sure whether it is from the composer of Matthew. The linguistic evidence indicates that 24:16-20 is stock traditional terminology of a time of crisis. Much of it could well have circulated as part of the Jesus tradition on the general theme of impending Judgment. Most likely it was Matthew who attached this terminology to the source *On the Final Crisis of the Era*, although we cannot be absolutely sure that it was not in the received source.

thing! To mix and extend the metaphor: the old age would be in full labor giving birth to the new time.

Matthew brings his discussion about the Horrible Desecration to an end in 24:21-22 by resuming the use of his source *On the Final Crisis of the Era*. This is a period of great tribulation (24:21; cf. 24:9).

Procedurally, he accomplishes this goal through the use of resumptive τότε to highlight the fact that the climax of the age of horrors has arrived. Perhaps he adds μεγάλη ("great") to stress the intensity of the time of tribulation. The wording consciously resembles that of Daniel 12:1 which may be echoed in the source. The construction οἵα οὐ γέγονεν . . . ἕως τοῦ νῦν ("which sort has not happened . . . until now") is evidence for that position as well. However, similar phraseology with ἀπ᾽ ἀρχῆς ("from the beginning") appears in Matthew 19:8 and is without a parallel elsewhere in the Synoptics. This seems to be evidence of composition by a single writer.[67] The point of Matthew 24:21 is quite evident. The world has entered its darkest hour before the dawn of the new age. The Matthean community will have to take every precaution to survive.

Then in 24:22, there seems to be a word of grace. Matthew shows very little concern to change the wording of his source that is heavily dependent on traditional apocalyptic terminology on the shortening of the end (cf. 1 Enoch 80:2; Syriac Baruch 20:1; 83:1; Greek Baruch 9:7). The promise is that for the sake of the elect (the church) the time of the age of horrors will be short (cf. 24:34). This is in complete fulfillment of the Danielic word that this time period is very limited (cf. Daniel 9:27). The time of the parousia has arrived.

A Parenthetical Warning (24:23-28)

Before the author gives the description of the parousia (24:29-31), Matthew inserts a brief parenthesis which serves as a further warning to the community not to be deceived by the false prophets and teachers at work in this era. The presupposition, apparently, is that the false prophets are a clear and present danger; and in the future chaotic period of the great tribulation, the evil influence of these teachers will be extremely pervasive and insidious.[68]

Structurally, this warning takes the form of two present general conditional sentences in 24:23, 26.

ἐάν τις ὑμῖν εἴπῃ . . . μὴ πιστεύσητε (24:23)
ἐὰν οὖν εἴπωσιν ὑμῖν . . . μὴ πιστεύσητε (24:26)

---

[67]Tevis, *Words and Phrases*, #237 on p. 181, claims that the phraseology ἀπ᾽ ἀρχῆς + οὐ γέγονεν in Matt 19:8 and 24:21 comes from a single writer. However, it is impossible to say whether this is from the source or the final composer.

[68]As noted by the minor inclusio of 24:4b-5 and 23-24.

On the basis of linguistic characteristics, we have identified 24:24 as a continuation of the use of the source *On the Final Crisis of the Era*. To complete the parenthesis, Matthew either composes or uses source material to give two warnings that the Messiah has not come in secret (24:23, 26). Matt 24:25 is Matthean composition; and 24:27 is drawn from the source on *The Coming of the Son of Man*. The parenthesis accentuates the view that the Messiah is not secretly present in the world, but his future coming will be an event of universal import.

In 24:23, Matthew opens the parenthesis characteristically with resumptive τότε. During these times the community is warned not to believe any claim that the Messiah is secretly present to certain followers during the great tribulation. The warning is emphatic: μὴ πιστεύσητε! ("do not believe!").

In Matthew 24:24 the mood is very somber. Twice the stem ψευδο- is introduced to create a duplicate expression as a means of intensifying the gravity of the situation. The signs and wonders of the false teachers are said to be great, in keeping with the eschatological magnitude of the era. As already noted, the author composes 24:25 to accentuate the warning.

In 24:26-28 Matthew completes the parenthesis. Matthew, by introducing inferential οὖν, is careful not to bring in anything new temporally, but merely to sum up the eschatological situation to this point (cf. 24:15). The disciples are warned not to believe the claims of the false prophets that the Messiah is in some secret earthly place, either in the country or the city, waiting to be revealed. In contrast, the final appearance of the Son of Man will not be in secret but visible to all—as a flash of light across the sky; or as the added isolated saying (24:28) attests, just as the vultures in the sky serve as a signal to all of a certain reality (i.e., dead carcasses), so the coming of the Son of Man (24:27), also something visible to all, will signify the universal reality (cf. 24:29-31) that the last Judgment has come.

Matthew has now finished his description of the Horrible Desecration and its attendant circumstances. One fact becomes very clear. Matthew is interested, above all, in preparing his readers for this time. When the Horrible Desecration comes, the believers are to understand that the time before the end is very short. They are to hasten to make quick preparations for the end. For their sakes the terrible era will be shortened. The false prophets, who constituted a problem in the past (24:4b-5), and in the present (24:11-12), will carry out an even more intensive work at the time of the end (24:23-26). Yet, despite what they say, they work only false signs. The only true sign of the parousia will be the reappearance of the exalted Lord himself.

The Parousia of the Son of Man (24:29-31)

For the description of the parousia itself (24:29-31) Matthew has utilized the major source *On the Final Crisis of the Era*. In our second chapter we produced evidence that this source was echoed by Paul as the authority for his claims on the resurrection in 1 Thess 4:16-17.

Our initial reconstruction of the source based on a comparison of Matthew and Paul described four features of the parousia.

1. The coming of the Son of Man on the clouds.
2. With power and great glory.
3. The angels go forth.
4. With the sound of a great trumpet.

Revelation 1:7, which echoes Zechariah 12:10, indicates the possible presence of a fifth feature of the coming of the Son of Man: the mourning of the tribes on earth. This is also a feature of Matt 24:30.[69] In addition, since the description of the sun, moon, stars, and powers in 24:29b, a typical description of cosmic occurrences in the LXX (cf. Isa. 13:10; 34:4), functions as part of the integral framework for the parousia, probably this verse should also be reckoned to be from the same source that Matthew uses as the basic framework for the Olivet Discourse.

Compositionally, two major features of redaction are apparent in the unit. First, in 24:29a Matthew introduces the source with the important εὐθέως ("immediately" or "at once"). After the appearance of the Horrible Desecration (24:15) and the Tribulation (24:9, 21) there will follow very soon the parousia of the Son of Man.[70] As we have noted repeatedly, this is in keeping with the Matthean view that this time of tribulation would be short (24:22) and events would come to full culmination within a generation from the time of the Olivet Discourse (24:34).

Second, there is the oddness in the order of the threefold καὶ τότε . . . καὶ τότε . . . καὶ ὄψονται construction of 24:30. The natural expectation of the reader would be to understand that the mourning of the tribes of the earth would take place *after* the appearance of the Son of Man. This is the case in Revelation 1:7.[71] But Matthew has placed the account of the mourning of the tribes of the earth between the appearance of the sign in heaven and the actual coming of the Son of Man on the clouds. Thus, there is an issue whether the order of Matt 24:30 was the order of Matthew's source.

---

[69]Our position already stated is that the Didache 16, parallel to Matt 24:30, is dependent upon the text of Matthew.

[70]The tortuous attempts to say that εὐθέως does not mean immediately or soon in a temporal sense are well documented by T. Donaldson, *Jesus on the Mountain: A Study in Matthean Theology*, JSNTSS 8 (Sheffield: JSOT Press, 1985) 162-65. However, after a fine analysis on this point, we cannot concur with his view that εὐθέως serves nontemporally as an indication of the suddeness or unexpectedness of what is to follow, as in a new stage of affairs.

[71]Cf. Didache 16.

It may be that Matthew did not desire to place two Son of Man sayings in his source material together. In this case, however, one would suspect that Matthew could simply omit one and thus solve the problem. More likely, there is another compositional solution for the present order of Matthew 24:30. We suggest that this solution appears to involve the attempt to highlight structurally the answer to the disciples' question in 24:3 as to the time of the parousia and end of the age.

We have concluded that Matthew received from his tradition the saying that the Son of Man would appear on the clouds and, most likely, this included the account of the mourning of the tribes of the earth (Rev 1:7). The two sayings placed together constitute a fine wordplay. The tribes will see the appearance (ὄψονται) of the Son of Man and show remorse (κόψονται; cf. Rev 1:7).[72] However, we have no direct evidence that Matthew had the saying on the sign of the Son of Man (24:30a) in his source *On the Final Crisis of the Era*. Indeed, we have argued that the reference to the disciples asking for the sign in 24:3 was probably Matthean redaction. Similarly, the answer in 24:30a may also be Matthean redaction.[73] That is, in contrast to the ambiguous signs of the end given by the false prophets (24:24), the true sign of the end will occur with the appearance of the Son of Man. This will be the universal sign given to all. When it occurs, as is typical in Matthew's theology, it will not only be an indicator of the vindication of the elect, but it will be a cause for dismay among the various tribes of the earth (24:30).[74] Thus, it was for these compositional reasons that the author of Matthew placed the saying of the sign of the Son of Man into 24:30a, and then to avoid the Son of Man references being placed side by side, reversed the order in the original source of the "seeing" of the Son of Man and "mourning" of the tribes of the earth.

---

[72]Gundry, *Matthew*, 488.

[73]Hawkins, *Horae Synopticae*, 8, 34 identifies φαίνεσθαι (Matt 24:27, 30) as a characteristic word of Matthew. We have already noted τὸ σημεῖον is probably Matthean redaction. See above.

[74]The exegetical issue as to whether Matt 24:30 has a temporal sequence of, first, the sign, then, the mourning of the tribes, and finally the appearance of the Son of Man is a point we have not the space to develop in this chapter. Clearly the author of the Didache (chap. 16) saw a temporal sequence and interpreted the sign to be a cleavage in heaven. In the history of exegesis the writer of the Didache has had many imitators who have speculated wildly about the nature of the sign. If Matt 24:30a is making the point that the sign will not occur until the end, then the rest of the verse may well be epexegetical in nature. Clearly, there is nothing in the text that would indicate that upon the appearance of the sign the opponents of the Son of Man will have an opportunity to change their minds and repent before the end. On the contrary, for all but the righteous (24:31), the appearance of the sign of the son of Man spells doom.

Again, it is noticeable that not a word is said about the destruction of the temple in Jerusalem. For Matthew, the definitive word on the end of the temple was given in 24:2. In 24:15-22 the temple was the locale for the Horrible Desecration. But, most likely that is a reference to a terrible occurrence there, not its destruction. Matthew simply assumes the temple will last until the end of the age. Then, in keeping with early Jewish-Christian theology, he probably held either that it would be replaced by the presence of the Messiah with his people (cf. Rev 21:22-23) or be destroyed and rebuilt in keeping with earlier promises in the prophets and other esoteric writings. If this exegesis is correct, it is unproven and, indeed, highly unlikely that the first gospel was composed after the destruction of the temple in the year 70 of our era.

A Second Parenthesis 24:32-36

Having given a description of the climactic end of the eschatological events of the era, culminating in the parousia of Christ, Matthew now adds a brief parenthetical statement emphasizing his conviction on the nearness of the end.

The unit opens with the parable of the fig tree which Matthew apparently found in source material (24:32-33). Then Matthew adds three chreia, perhaps compiled from Sondergut, which serve as an appeal to take seriously the view that end-time closure was at hand (24:34, 35, 36).

The parable of the fig tree features two grammatical constructions having the indefinite particle ὅταν ("whenever") and the present imperative γινώσκετε ("know") with the adverb ἐγγύς ("near") in 24:32, 33. Whenever the fig tree buds the disciples are to know that the θέρος ("the summer harvest") is near (24:32).[75] Whenever the disciples see all these things come to pass, the disciples are to know the time is near (24:33).[76] Both constructions appear to be parallel.

The main exegetical issue is to determine specifically what is meant by these ὅταν references. Specifically, what is meant by ὅταν ἴδητε πάντα ταῦτα ("whenever you see all these things") in 24:33? It is very important to note that a similar construction (ὅταν . . . ἴδητε) is found in Matthew 24:15 where the referent is the appearance of the Horrible Desecration and the onslaught of the Great Tribulation. This is congruent with Matthew's point in the parable of the fig tree. In the near future, when the final crisis in Jerusalem comes, then "all these things," (i.e., the events surrounding the Horrible Desecration) will quickly

---

[75]William R. Telford, *The Barren Temple and the Withered Tree: A Redaction—Critical Analysis of the Cursing of the Fig Tree Pericope in Mark's Gospel and Its Relation to the Cleansing of the Temple Tradition*, JSNTSS 1 (Sheffield: JSOT Press, 1980) 242.

[76]For our purposes it is not important to determine whether ἐγγύς ἐστιν ἐπὶ θύραις should be understood impersonally (it is near at the doors) or personally (he is near at the door). In both cases the reference is to the parousia.

initiate a course of events leading to the end. It can be compared with the simile of the fig tree—a quick move from bud to final harvest (i.e., the parousia).[77]

Again, it should be noted that there is nothing said here about the destruction of the temple. It is assumed that will take place in connection with the parousia and final judgment.

The first chreia of 24:34 states that "this generation will not pass away until all these things take place." The chreia was probably included at this point to accent as repeated language πάντα ταῦτα ("all these things") in 24:33. The solemn use of ἀμήν ("truly") is characteristic of Matthew.[78] Likewise, the use of the construction ἕως ἄν is characteristic of the author of Matthew (24:34).[79] The reference to generation is almost surely a temporal reference (the contemporary era) and not a qualitative one (this kind of people).[80] The solemn declaration is that the πάντα ταῦτα (the entire eschatological scenario until the parousia) will take place within a generation. This is in keeping with the Matthean view about the nearness of the end propounded elsewhere in the Gospel (10:23; 16:28).

The second chreia that Jesus' words will last forever fortifies the claims of the first (24:35). The solemn claim of assurance from the Lord of the church states that this word has absolute status.

The third chreia that no one knows the day except the father is transitional (24:36).[81] On the one hand, it continues the theme of the very close proximity of the end of the age with the slight modification that the precise day and hour cannot be known by humans. Even when one sees the shadow of the coming of the Horrible Desecration one cannot calculate the precise time of the parousia. Thus, a bridge is built to the issue that is addressed in 24:37–25:30; namely, the need to remain continually prepared in faithful service in light of the terrible consequences of the last judgment at the parousia. Therefore, as one moves into the next section, the emphasis on preparation for the time continues.[82]

With the identity of the nature of the true sign of the end followed by subsequent assurances that this is the word of the Lord, Matthew has now

---

[77]It should be remembered that "all these things" cannot refer to the event of the parousia itself (24:29-31) for the simple reason that the parousia *is* the end. The whole point of the warning given to the disciples is to say that when they see "these things" (i.e., the Horrible Desecration) *preceding* the end, then they are to know it is near.

[78]Matthew has many more usages of ἀμήν than Mark or Luke (31/14/6).

[79]Luz, *Matthew*, 59.

[80]A. J. McNicol, "The Lesson of the Fig Tree in Mark 13:28-31," *Restoration Quarterly* 27/4 (1984): 202.

[81]Lambrecht, "Parousia Discourse," 325.

[82]Note the number of temporal references here: hour (24:36, 44); day(s) (24:37-38, 42, 50); watch (24:43); time (24:45); day and hour (25:13).

finished the answer to the question of the disciples in 24:3. To finish his account of the Last Discourse, Matthew will include an additional discussion on the need to be ready for the climatic events of the end.

The Delay Calls for Vigilance (24:37-25:30)

In this unit, Matthew, as the basis of his composition, uses material drawn from his source on *The Coming of the Son of Man* (24:37-39, [44]), the similes on working in the field and the mill (24:40-41), the parable of the Thief in the Night (24:42-43), and additional parables (24:45-25:30).[83] The unit of 24:37-25:30 is highlighted by the urgent call to be vigilant and prepared for the end. The final scene of the Discourse which follows is hardly a parable but an apocalyptic description of the Judgment at the coming of the Son of Man. As such, it balances with the description of the parousia given in the center of the Discourse in 24:29-31 and the initial reference to parousia in 24:3. The entire unit of 24:37-25:30 presses home the theme of the terrible consequences for those who would come under the Judgment of the Son of Man at the end of the age. The pronouncements of doom upon the representatives of the old order, the leaders of Jerusalem, were given in 23:34-39. Now the people of the new order are warned not to repeat the same mistake. The whole unit of 23:1-25:46 resonates with the call to be faithful in view of the intense importance of the appearance of the Son of Man. Many of the leaders of Jerusalem will be unprepared and their temple will be destroyed (23:1-24:2). The Olivet Discourse opens with a call for Jesus' disciples (a transparency of the church) to be ready as well (24:4-36); it then offers a stern warning on the consequences for the church as to what will happen if it also is not ready (24:37-25:30).

Since we have identified the unit of 24:37-25:30 as having four major units of material, we will now note briefly the editorial highlights of their Matthean composition.

The first unit consists of several similes of warnings to be prepared for the parousia of the Son of Man (24:37-44). The simile on Noah is designed to underscore the terrible fate that awaits the unprepared. At the flood, a cataclysm (Gen 6:16 LXX) came and all perished. Thus, it will be at the coming of the Son of Man (24:39). The flood is a prototype of the last Judgment. Similarly, in 24:40-41 Matthew adds, through use of the resumptive τότε, again, the terrible nature of the Judgment. At the Judgment there will be a terrible separation among humankind. Two men working in the field will be separated forever. Two women laboring at an ancient stone mill will be separated forever. Here we have an

---

[83]The parables of the Chief Servant and Slaves (24:45-51); the Wise and Foolish Virgins (25:1-13); and the Talents (25:14-30).

example from the composer of Matthew of an inclusive address: one for men, one for women. In both cases the idea is that one of the two will undergo Judgment. Presumably the other (the one left?) will be blessed.

As in the case of 24:36, Matthew 24:42 is transitional. Matthew connects back to 24:37-41 by use of the word "day" (24:37-38). Also, the use of γρηγορεῖν ("to watch") in 24:42, 43 is the link forward to the simile on the Thief in the Night. The phraseology of 24:42 is γρηγορεῖτε οὖν ὅτι οὐκ οἴδατε ποίᾳ ἡμέρᾳ ὁ κύριος ὑμῶν ἔρχεται ("Watch therefore, because you do not know in what day your Lord comes"). This terminology links one over to similar terminology in 25:13, the end of the parable of the Wise and Foolish Virgins.[84] The point in the Matthean redaction is that if one is not ready for the coming of the Son of Man, he or she will suffer the same fate as the householder who was not ready for the coming of the thief.

The second unit is the parable of the Chief Servant and Slaves (24:45-51). Matthew continues to emphasize the all encompassing significance of the Last Judgment and the need to be prepared for it. When the Lord finally comes the lax servant receives a terrible punishment; he is hacked to pieces (24:51). He is consigned to a fate μετὰ τῶν ὑποκριτῶν ("with the hypocrites")—a Matthean redactional term for the reprobates.[85] Finally, Matthew 24:51b ends with the Matthean formula "There will be weeping and gnashing of teeth." The latter phrase (ὁ κλαυθμὸς καὶ ὁ βρυγμὸς τῶν ὀδόντων) is certain Matthean composition.[86]

The third block of material that Matthew inserts into this composition is the parable of the Wise and Foolish Virgins (25:1-13). As one may expect, Matthean editorial activity is mainly confined to the seams. This unit begins with resumptive τότε (25:1). It ends in 25:13 with the plaintive statement on "watching" which, we have seen, (note 84), Matthew utilized previously (24:42) on the basis of his remembrance of Jesus tradition. Again, there is an emphasis on the vindication of the prepared (cf. ἕτοιμοι in 24:44 and 25:10). These are contrasted to

---

[84]Tevis, *Words and Phrases*, #229 on p. 173, considers this phraseology to be the work of a single author. Since the phraseology is echoed in 1 Thess 5:2, it probably comes from source tradition rather than the final composer of Matthew.

[85]Cf. Luz, *Matthew*, 70. The Greek word for hypocrite occurs fourteen times in Matthew, only once in Mark, and three times in Luke. Besides being almost certainly Matthean redaction, it also serves as analogue to the Matthean polemic against the leaders of Israel (22:18; 23:13, 14, 15). Without change the self-satisfied people of God, whether they be the traditional leaders of Israel or Matthew's Christian-Jewish church, face imminent danger.

[86]Tevis, *Words and Phrases*, #206 on p. 149 notes that this phrase (8:12; 13:42; 13:50; 22:13; 24:51; 25:30) almost certainly comes from a single writer. We would claim that this writer was the final composer of Matthew.

those who receive the terrible fate reserved for the ones who are shut out because of lack of adequate preparation (25:10).

Similarly, the final unit on The Talents reveals editorial activity around the seams. This time Matthew uses ὥσπερ ("as") to resume the narrative (25:14).[87] Matthew concludes the unit with his characteristic phraseology on the weeping and gnashing of teeth, which we have identified (note 86) as a certain linguistic usage of the final composer of (25:30b). This follows the immediately preceding statement that the worthless servant would be cast into outer darkness on account of his failure to show resourcefulness while his master was absent (25:30a).

The emphasis of the whole unit has been on vigilance. The great difference between reward and punishment mandates that the disciples live fruitfully and resourcefully as they await the coming of the Son of Man.

The Judgment of the Nations at the End (25:31-46)

Finally, the Olivet Discourse is concluded with Matthew's description of the last Judgment (25:31-46). Again, there is evidence of redactional activity at the seams. The unit opens with the statement, "Whenever the Son of Man comes in his glory and all the angels with him, then he will sit upon his throne of glory." Embedded in this verse is the construction ὅταν + ὁ υἱὸς τοῦ ἀνθρώπου + καθίζω + ἐπὶ θρόνου δόξης αὐτοῦ, which occurs also at Matthew 19:28 (cf. 16:27). Since this phrase does not occur elsewhere in the New Testament, Tevis considers it a linguistic characteristic of a single writer.[88] We consider that, likely, this is the phraseology of the author of Matthew. The end of the narrative is clearly delineated by 26:1—the fifth and final appearance of Matthew's famous marker, "When Jesus finished all these words. . . . " Throughout the narrative there is some Matthean characteristic vocabulary.[89] However, this is not so widespread as to lead us to the conclusion that the entire unit was the creation of Matthew.[90]

Since Matthew 24:37, the major emphasis of Jesus' words has been on the certainties of rewards and punishments on the last day for the disciples of Jesus. There is no doubt that they will have to give an answer for their stewardship at the Judgment. Thus, it is appropriate that the Discourse ends with a description of the last Judgment. Here again we encounter the existence of a great gulf

---

[87]As noted earlier, Hawkins, *Horae Synopticae*, 8, identifies ὥσπερ as a certain linguistic characteristic of Matthew.

[88]Tevis, *Words and Phrases*, #225 on p. 105.

[89]O. Lamar Cope, "Matthew XXV:31-46 'The Sheep and the Goats' Reinterpreted," *Novum Testamentum* 11 (1969): 36; Goulder. *Midrash and Lection*, 443-44.

[90]Contra Cope, "The Sheep and the Goats," 43.

between those who were blessed and those who were punished. Here, also, there is a strong emphasis on the severity of the punishment (25:41, 46).

But there is also a major difference from the other units. At this scene the focus is upon *all the nations of the earth* who are gathered for judgment; the believers in Jesus stand at the margins only to serve as a basic criterion for this Judgment.[91] Specifically, it is the conduct of the nations that is under scrutiny—not that of the church. Matthew argues that the work of the disciples as they take the gospel to the nations has universal implications (24:14). Those peoples (nations) who give hospitality and refuge to the marginalized followers of Jesus will, sometimes to their complete surprise, be rewarded at the last day. Others, who thwarted the mission, will be punished severely.[92] In Matthew 24:37-25:30 faithfulness and persistence under persecution until the parousia is urged upon the Matthean church. It will be rewarded at the final judgment. Those in the wider human community who welcomed Jesus in the faithfulness of the disciples and treated them well, will also be rewarded at the end (25:31-46). Thus the theme of the obedience of the nations, a major theme of the book of Revelation, already begins to emerge in Matthew.

Summary and Conclusion

Before one can begin to unlock the secrets of the Matthean version of Jesus' Last Discourse (24:4b–25:46), one must appreciate its function in the wider context of Matthew. The Matthean view of reality emerges within the five great teaching discourses of the Gospel which are placed strategically around the crucial unit where Jesus explicitly founds a new community (Matt 16:13-20).

The Sermon on the Mount states the norms for this new community. The real origin of this community was in the Mission to the lost sheep of Israel. The Parable Discourse places this mission in the context of the critical eschatological events of the time. Upon the official announcement of the founding of the

---

[91]The reference to πάντα τὰ ἔθνη in 25:32 most likely is an inclusive term that means "all peoples," including Israel (24:9, 14, and 28:19). This is to be distinguished from the reference to τὰ ἔθνη which usually, in Matthew, refers only to the Gentiles (cf. 4:15; 6:32; 10:5, 18; 12:18, 21; 20:19, 25). The case for this view is argued against other positions by Allan McNicol, "Discipleship as Mission: A Missing Dimension in Contemporary Discussion on Matt 28:18-20," *Christian Studies* 10 (1989): 47. On the other hand, the reference to the least of my brethren (24:40, 45), as the marginalized early Christian community is widely accepted amongst contemporary exegetes. (cf. Lambrecht, "Parousia Discourse," 335-36).

[92]Cope, "The Sheep and the Goats," 40-42 shows well the close connection with how this scene both points back to the mission to Israel (10:40-42) and forward to the mission to all peoples in 28:16-20.

community (16:13-20) the rules for its discipline are stated in the Community Discourse. Finally, as the community has made the transition from a mission only to Israel to a mission to all nations (Matt 28:16-20), the focus shifts to a preview of the ultimate destiny of both Israel and the nations. Israel and all other nations are called to be prepared decisively for the all important appearance of the parousia of the Son of Man at the end of the era.

Logically, the fate of the mission to Israel is the subtext of 23:7-24:2. The message to Israel is grim. The contemporary leadership in Jerusalem has forfeited any claim to legitimacy. In 23:37-39 the leadership in Israel is pronounced as desolate. The disciples now function as the nucleus of the leadership of the people of God in the last days.

Yet, they need not be complacent. The disciples (a transparency for the church) are charged with a mission to the nations (24:14). This mission has crucial eschatological ramifications for the human community. The sequence of the Eschatological Discourse (24:3-25:46) revolves around the course of this mission. The future course of history down until the pen-ultimate events of the end, signalled by the emergence of the Horrible Sacrilege (24:15-22), culminates in the mission to the nations (cf. 24:14). The coming of the Son of Man at the parousia will be a matter of concern to the nations (24:31). At the final Judgment the nations will be judged on how they received the ambassadors of the mission (25:31-46). Thus Matt 23:1–25:46 is deeply anchored within the framework of biblical salvation history.

Yet, as programmatic as the word is for both Israel and the Gentiles, the central focus of the Discourse remains on the future fortunes of the disciples (i.e. the church). The church faces dangers from without and within. Utilizing two major sources, *On the Final Crisis of the Era* (24:4b-6, 10-12, 14-15, 21-24, 29-31) and *The Coming of the Son of Man* (24:27, 37-39, 44), to which he adds seven parables or similes (one drawn from a tradition known by Paul) and other source tradition, Matthew composes a coherent statement to address the situation.

The Discourse is precipitated by the key question of the disciples, "What will be the sign of your parousia and the end of the world?" The query comes against a background where false messiahs and prophets are gaining a hearing through the putatative performance of various signs and wonders. In contrast to these deceivers, the Matthean Jesus claims that the only sign of the end will be the appearance of the Son of Man himself in his parousia. Therefore, the church should be alert to the dangers posed by these false prophets.

But there is another danger as well. In the subsequent days, as a result of its mission, the early Christian community would be marginalized both in Israel and among the Gentiles. There is the very live and real danger that the church will lose heart, especially during the period of the Horrible Desecration. Thus the Discourse skillfully combines both exhortations to remain faithful (cf. 24:13, 42) and a word of hope that, although they will have to go through tough times, they will be vindicated (24:21-22, 46-47; 25:10). The coming of the Son of Man is the great reality before which Israel, the Gentiles, and the church must live. What is called for is vigilance and disciplined living in order that one will be rewarded when he appears.

5.
The Lukan Version
of the Eschatological Discourse

In the previous chapter we set forth the view that the Gospel of Matthew was written, probably in the Roman province of Greater Syria, in the turbulent era between 68 and 70 CE. Part of that composition involved the working together of various source traditions into a united discourse given by Jesus on the Mount of Olives. Upon the composition of the Matthean version of the Olivet Discourse, a body of Jesus tradition had been transformed from a collection of verbal materials on eschatological matters into an organized composition that had its own narrative integrity in Matthew's biography of Jesus' life. Similar to the last speeches attributed to Jacob, Joshua, Moses, or David in the Old Testament, the Last Discourse may have functioned as a kind of last will and testament of Jesus.[1]

On our source hypothesis, when Luke began to compose a narrative account of the life of Jesus he had access to Matthew. Luke actually composed three units of Jesus' teachings on eschatological matters using mostly material from the major source of Matthew 24:1–25:46 (Lk 12:35-48; 17:20-37; and 21:5-36).[2] The first two units have no direct contextual parallel in the text of Matthew. However, Luke 21:5-36 is roughly parallel in setting and context to the Matthean Olivet Discourse.

Yet, Matthew and Luke produced their own versions of Jesus' last Eschatological Discourse under quite different historical circumstances. Matthew expected the temple to remain until the end of the age. This was not the presupposition of Luke. Indeed, our analysis of Luke 21:5-36 will indicate that Luke wrote in a time after 70 CE when the Jerusalem temple had been destroyed. Luke very carefully, in 19:45–21:38 provided a setting in Jesus' ministry where he prophetically anticipated this eventuality. The writer of Luke still anticipated the future coming of the Son of Man; but with the temple in ruins, Luke must now write primarily for a readership that needed instruction regarding how to live in the intervening time before the full realization of redemption. In Luke 21:5-36,

---

[1]Hence the title of Burnett's book, *The Testament of Jesus-Sophia*.

[2]An earlier analysis of how Luke composed these three units on eschatological matters based on Matt 24:1–25:46 has been set forth in detail in McNicol, "Composition of the Synoptic Eschatological Discourse," 160-82.

a full theological agenda is set forth that both presupposes the fall of Jerusalem and addresses the new situation.

The Genre and Structure of Luke

The title "Gospel according to Luke" may have been found as a heading for copies of the third Gospel as early as the second century.[3] Its point of focus— after the destruction of the holy city—seems to cohere with the need of the early Christian movement to establish its identity as it grew and expanded within a pervasive Hellenistic cultural setting. In the Greco-Roman world there were many who admired Judaism because it appeared to be a strong venerable faith system that went back into antiquity. Luke seems to base his literary work within an ethos that presumed this positive view toward Judaism. Jesus of Nazareth, a Jew, had incorporated the most worthwhile and admired aspects of Judaism (from a Hellenistic perspective) into a new universal faith system that did not demand that Gentile converts keep food laws, circumcision, or the Sabbath which earlier had served as badges of identity for the people of God. To accept Christianity was to receive the idea that the ancient promises of the God of Abraham, Isaac, and David to redeem the nations had come to fulfillment in Christ.

Luke is part of a two-volume work (Luke-Acts).[4] In the first volume Luke sets the story of Jesus within the ethos of traditional Judaism in Galilee and Judea. Jesus commences his mission in his hometown of Nazareth in Galilee where already the contours of the final outcome of his mission become clear (4:16-30). There he is rejected by many of his own people; but there is a positive thrust towards the Gentiles. This tendency continues throughout Luke-Acts. At the end of the two-volume work the Christian message has spread to Rome. By now the growth of the Jesus movement has developed into a well-established community with its own history and traditions. Peter and Paul, two of its major practitioners who are dominant figures in Acts, are models of the best in traditional Jewish piety. But they also come to the full acceptance of Gentiles into the new community on the basis of faith. Throughout both Luke and Acts this development is represented as being both the fulfillment of the promises of Scripture and the working out of the will and purpose of God in the contemporary era.[5]

---

[3] Hengel, *Studies in Mark*, 66.

[4] We assume the unity of Luke-Acts as a literary composition as a basic presupposition of our work. The issue of the dating of Acts, vis-à-vis the composition of Luke, a point that has been reopened in modern discussion, is not directly relevant to the purposes of this monograph. As noted above, a reading of the Gospel of Luke as coming after 70 CE makes sense on the basis of our analysis of Luke 21. We presume that the same could be said with reference to Acts.

[5] Paul Schubert, "The Structure and Significance of Luke 24," in *Neutestamentliche*

The Issue of Genre

We understand that Luke-Acts was composed as a version of apologetic historiography to explain programatically to its readers the grounds for the claim that the Christian movement was built on secure foundations.[6]

Contemporary discussion on issues of genre in Luke-Acts may well be considered to have begun with the work of Charles Talbert. Specifically, Talbert argued that Luke-Acts was a version of Greco-Roman writing that presented both an account of the life of a founder of a community and the biographical history of the founder's successors; such an account functioned as a norm for maintaining the memory and tradition of the founder in the later community of followers.[7] Such authoritative works on the founding and development of the community provide a basis for its legitimacy. As such, it functioned as a kind of succession history. Thus, a basic aim of Luke-Acts was to give the narrative story of the founder of Christianity (Jesus), and to argue that the true tradition about him was passed on through the twelve, to Paul, and ultimately to the Ephesian elders, who, in the perspective of the author (Acts 20), inherited the Pauline legacy.[8]

Such a view has some distinct advantages. Besides being able to give a reason for the writing of the Lukan biography of Jesus, it also was able to give a rationale for the focus on historical narrative in Acts. On face value, Luke appears to fall into some version of the genre of Greco-Roman biography while Acts appears to be some form of ancient history. But in Talbert's account both works (Luke on Jesus and Acts on Peter and Paul) were biographical accounts of the founder of the community and his successors. This enabled scholars to see a way beyond the old debate as to whether Luke-Acts was history or theology. It was neither. Primarily, it was a series of theological biographies which created the founding story of the community.

Studien für Rudolf Bultmann, BZNW 21, ed. W. Eltester (Berlin: Alfred Töpelmann, 1954) 176; idem, "The Final Cycle of Speeches in the Book of Acts," *Journal of Biblical Literature* 87 (1968): 2-3.

[6]Cf. Lk 1:4; the term apologetic historiography is that used by Gregory E. Sterling, *Historiography and Self-Definition: Josephos, Luke-Acts, and Apologetic Historiography*, NovTSup 64 (Leiden: E. J. Brill, 1992) 16-19; 315-21. Essentially apologetic historiography as a specific type of writing is an attempt to tell the story of a subgroup of people in a specific culture in prose narrative for an audience outside that particular subgroup.

[7]Charles H. Talbert, *Literary Paterns, Theological Themes, and the Genre of Luke-Acts*, SBLMS 20 (Missoula MT: Scholars Press, 1974) 125-36; also by the same author, *What Is a Gospel? The Genre of the Canonical Gospels*, ROSE 9 (Macon GA: Mercer University Press, 1985 = Philadelphia: Fortress Press, 1977) 92-98, 134.

[8]C. H. Talbert, *Reading Luke: A Literary and Theological Commentary on the Third Gospel* (New York: Crossroad Publishing Company, 1982) 3.

A major criticism of Talbert focuses on the primary textual evidence for the models on which he based his claims. Talbert found his basic model in Diogenes Laertius, *Lives of Eminent Philosophers*, a mid-third century CE work; and even there, the model was only remotely connected with the important issue of the legitimacy of the community and its successors.[9]

Talbert could respond that his analysis is not totally dependent on Diogenes Laertius. There are other examples of this kind of writing that antedate the New Testament. A far more problematical point, however, is the determination of how this model for understanding the genre of Luke connects with the reality of its compositional structure.

Specifically, any model of compositional structure must make sense of the all-important preface of Luke 1:1-4, which, in turn, is crucial for understanding the basic structure of the entire narrative. This is where an appreciation of Luke-Acts as apologetic historiography makes better sense of this literary work than Talbert's model. Even without detailed analysis of Luke 1:1-4, it is quite easy to see that the author begins this work by making a fundamental point of comparison between the past and the present. In Luke 1:1-2 we are told that *in the past* many have produced narrative accounts of the matters that had already been fulfilled (in keeping with the promises of Scripture) along the lines that the eyewitnesses of these things had stated.[10] Then, in 1:3-4, the author claims that he has conducted a very detailed review of these accounts and, on the basis of this research, writes accurately and in appropriate chronological order (ἀκριβῶς καθεξῆς) for a literary work of historiography in order that the readers may have complete confidence in these matters.[11]

This is more than an account of the story of the founder of the community who, in due time, hands over its leadership to successors; it is an attempt to make a defense, based on the use of historical sources, and an acceptable way of writing a historical treatise for the validity of the very existence of the Christian community.[12] This existence was anchored in the hopes and promises for re-

---

[9]Cf. Aune, *The New Testament in Its Literary Environment*, 79.

[10]On the Two Gospel Hypothesis this would include the Gospel of Matthew and other special sources used by Luke (*Sonderquellen*).

[11]Sterling, *Historiography and Self-Definition*, 341-46, has an analysis of Lk 1:1-4. The analysis is judicious but suffers somewhat on account of dogmatic acceptance, without sufficient recognition that there are alternative perspectives, of the view that Mark was one of the narrative accounts utilized by Luke. Sufficient recognition is not given to alternative perspectives of looking at the evidence.

[12]N. T. Wright, *Christian Origins and the Question of God*, vol. 1 of *The New Testament and the People of God* (Minneapolis: Fortress, 1992) 373-78, has noted a number of illuminating parallels between Luke's historical defence of the Christian movement and that of Josephus in the *Jewish War*. Among the most striking are: (1) the attempt to prove that Israel's history had a most unexpected fulfillment. In the case of

demption of ancient Israel. The author utilizes the traditional rhetorical techniques of the Greco-Roman literary historian (e.g., acknowledgment of divine purpose, journeys, speeches) to attain the result of convincing the reader that Christianity has emerged and developed at the appointed time, in keeping with the divine purpose to fulfill these hopes. The structure of Luke fits such an agenda.

Structure of Luke

Structurally, it is helpful to examine the compositional organization of Luke in light of Acts. We see quickly that the basic principle of organization in Acts is found in 1:8 where the early believers are told that they will be witnesses in Judea, Samaria, and to the end of the earth. It is generally accepted that this is an anticipation of the basic organizational structure of Acts which selectively tells of the progress of the gospel in Jerusalem (1:1–8:3), greater Judea, and Samaria (8:4–12:25), and to Rome (13:1–28:31). Retrospectively, Acts 1:1 provides an analogous principle of organization for Luke when the author states that in the first book he has presented a statement on all "that Jesus began both to do and teach until the time when he was taken up."[13] Following the account of the birth and infancy of Jesus and John (1:5–2:52), and how these respective figures began their ministry (3:1–4:13), Luke gives an account of what Jesus began to do (4:14–9:50), teach (9:51–19:28), and carry out until the time he was taken up (19:29–24:53).[14] This general organizational principle of Luke is sufficient for our purposes.

The one major point of contention among critics on the issue of the Lukan outline is the determination of where the travel narrative ends. The older view that the travel narrative ended at 18:30, as Tyson has pointed out, was based on the presupposition that Luke, at this point, departed from his Markan source.[15]

Josephus, Israel's God had abandoned the temple and gone over to Rome. For Luke, Israel's God had appointed Jesus of Nazareth crucified by the Romans as the Lord of history. (2) The attempt by both Luke and Josephus to support their respective arguments by the use of prophecy. (3) Both Luke and Josephus attempt, through use of the genre of Hellenistic historiography, to place their respective constituencies in the most favorable light before responsible people who accept the Flavian dynasty. At the very minimum, Wright's observations reveal that Luke falls very easily into the category of Hellenistic Jewish historiography.

[13]Bernard Orchard and Harold Riley, *The Order of the Synoptics: Why Three Synoptic Gospels?* (Macon GA: Mercer University Press, 1987) 51.

[14]Ibid. We differ from Orchard and Riley by ending the travel narrative at 19:27. Strangely for advocates of the Griesbach Hypothesis, they prefer to end it at 18:30 (see ibid., 63).

[15]Joseph B. Tyson, *The Death of Jesus in Luke-Acts* (Columbia: University of South

But, if this source presupposition is not accepted, such a division in the last stage of the travel narrative is artificial. As Tyson has also noted, the view that the travel narrative ends at 19:27 can be questioned, because Jesus does not enter the temple precincts until 19:45, and thus can be considered to be still on his journey until 19:45.[16] However, 19:28-44, takes place around the Mount of Olives and functions as a critique of Jerusalem. This is a major theme of 19:45–21:38, and is echoed further in the Passion Narrative. Consequently, we have decided to include it in the last section of Luke's account. With this explanation in view, we propose a fivefold division of the birth and infancy of John and Jesus, their early ministry, and successive accounts of the deeds, extended teaching, and the death and exaltation of Jesus. Supplemented with the account of Acts, the two volumes explain how Christianity has grown from obscure beginnings in a remote part of the empire (Galilee), to Jerusalem in fulfillment of the venerated Scriptures of the Jews, and on to Rome, the center of power among the Gentiles. This providential growth and expansion of the Christian message functions as evidence for Luke's sustained proposal to undergird the validity of the Christian enterprise.

The Scope and Setting of the Lukan Version
of Jesus' Last Eschatological Discourse

There is no debate over where Luke's version of the last speech of Jesus begins and ends. We find it in Luke 21:8-36. However, the setting for the Discourse is different than that given in the Matthean account. Unlike Matthew, who has Jesus leave the temple and speak on the Mount of Olives, Luke has Jesus deliver the speech on the temple premises (Matt 24:1-3; Lk 21:5).

In Luke 19:28-44 Jesus makes his way down the Mount of Olives to the city. Then, in 19:45-47 Jesus, after arriving at the edge of the holy city, enters into the temple and begins to teach in its precincts. In Luke 19:45–21:38 Luke stucturally arranges Jesus' teachings so that he goes into the temple precincts during the day (19:45-47; 20:1, 37) and at night returns to the Mount of Olives (21:37; cf. 22:39). So, in Luke 20:1, in keeping with this procedure, Jesus enters the temple and teaches publicly. This sequence continues until the end of the Eschatological Discourse when, at 21:37, Jesus returns to the Mount of Olives. Indeed, the whole of Luke 20:1–21:36 may have been intended by the author to reflect a typical day's teaching following this pattern of activity. The framing of Luke 20:1–21:36 with references to Jesus' teaching is Luke's compositional way of providing a place to house what he considers the most significant aspects of the activities of Jesus between the entry into Jerusalem and the account of the Passion.

Carolina Press, 1986) 28.
   [16]Ibid.

The account opens with a series of dialogues between Jesus and the chief priests, scribes, and Sadducees which takes place in the presence of the people (20:1, 19, 27). Starting from 19:41, Luke had already made it clear that Jesus had predicted the destruction of the temple (cf. 19:41-46); then, after his final critique of the Jewish leaders, artfully placed in juxtaposition with the contrasting example of the poor widow (20:45–21:4), Jesus returns again to speak of the temple (21:5-6). At the end of Luke 21, the author makes another direct reference to the temple (21:37). In between, Luke has Jesus discuss coming eschatological events which, unlike the account in Matthew, will involve considerable discussion about the ultimate destruction of the city with its temple and the relationship of this event to the end.

The Source Tradition behind Luke 21:5-36

Toward the end of a recent survey on the present state of source criticism on the Gospel of Luke, Joseph Tyson makes an acute observation.[17]

We, therefore, stand at a time at which it must be said that we have no dependable knowledge about the sources of Luke.

Such a statement may be contrasted with the more confident assertions made in the earlier part of our century. For example, the comment of F. C. Burkitt is quite well known:[18]

It is assumed that the author of the third gospel used the Gospel of Mark practically in its extant form, and also that where he does thus follow Mark he had no other source available.

More than fifty years has elapsed between the respective published statements of Burkitt and Tyson. The consensus on the priority of Mark no longer exists. In this section we will argue that Luke has used Matthew 24:1-42 as the major source for this unit and that Luke did not use Mark. Later in this chapter, we will argue that Luke used another source, which we called earlier in chapter 2 of this study *The Sudden Calamity of the End*, in the composition of Luke 21:34-36. This latter source was also echoed by Paul in 1 Thessalonians 5:3.

---

[17]Joseph B. Tyson, "Source Criticism of the Gospel of Luke," *Perspectives on Luke-Acts*, ed. Charles Talbert (Edinburgh: T. & T. Clark, 1978) 36; cf. David Tiede, *Prophecy and History in Luke-Acts* (Philadelphia: Fortress Press, 1980) 22. The focus of the latter author is to say that too often Luke's theological perspective has been traced on the presupposition that he is slavishly following Mark.

[18]F. C. Burkitt, "The Use of Mark in the Gospel according to Luke," *The Beginnings of Christianity*, pt. 1, vol. 2, ed. F. J. Foakes Jackson and Kirsopp Lake (London: Macmillan, 1922) 106-15.

Finally, we also note that Luke used Matthew 10:17-22 and some isolated sayings to complete the composition.

As literary grounds for our argument, we will utilize the evidence of common sequence of the pericopes in Luke with the major source (Matthew), the occurrence of several Matthean linguistic characteristics in parallel texts of the same context in Luke; and we will show evidence of massive Lukan compositional activity in keeping with Luke's known literary tendencies and theological purposes in places where source tradition is not followed. This evidence will serve as the basis for our claim that Luke used Matthew as his major source. We believe this constitutes a reasonable hypothesis to account for the composition of Luke 21:5-36.

Besides our claim that the major source for the composition of Luke 21 is Matthew 24 and not Mark 13, we need to take into consideration that there are some who have argued that behind Luke 21 stands another major source that is *neither* in Matthew 24 nor Mark 13. Such a theory goes back to the work of B. H. Streeter.

In his magnum opus on the *Four Gospels*, published in 1924, Streeter put forward in considerable detail a theory of the composition of Luke.[19] He argued that the Gospel of Luke was composed in two drafts. The first draft was a combination of Q and special Lukan material (L). The latter was a source of great authority for Luke. Into this outline, Luke is supposed to have incorporated blocks of material (much of Lk 4:31–6:19; 8:4–9:50; 18:15-43; and much of 19:28–22:13) from the Gospel of Mark to form the second and final draft of the Gospel. The net effect of the work of Streeter was to make the claim that the first draft—Proto-Luke, as it was called—was foundational to the structure of Luke. Mark, although very important, was a secondary source.

A considerable body of scholarship, especially in the Anglo-Saxon world, taking the Proto-Luke thesis as a starting point, expanded the scope of this source. So, in their own ways, Vincent Taylor,[20] and T. W. Manson,[21] both argued that Luke, in 21:5-36, actually utilized a source tradition other than Mark 13 as the authoritative basis for the composition. In their case this source tradition was not necessarily Streeter's Proto-Luke; nevertheless, it was clearly something like it. This position continues to have its advocates.[22]

---

[19]B. H. Streeter, *The Four Gospels. A Study of Origins: Treating of the Manuscripts Tradition, Sources, Authorship, and Dates* (London: Macmillan, [1]1924) 199-222.

[20]Vincent Taylor, *Behind the Third Gospel: A Study of the Proto-Luke Hypothesis* (Oxford Clarendon Press, 1926) 101-25.

[21]T. W. Manson, *The Sayings of Jesus as Recorded in the Gospels according to St. Matthew and St. Luke Arranged with Introduction and Commentary*, repr. of pt. 2 of *The Mission and Message of Jesus* (1937) (London: SCM Press, 1971) 325.

[22]L. Gaston, *No Stone on Another*, 355-65.

Essentially the argument is that Luke used as the framework for Luke 21 a source *On the End of Jerusalem*. Gaston has argued that the source originally existed in the order of our present Luke 19:37-48, 21:5-7; 20-24; 10-11, 25-28, 37-38.[23] However, the order was rearranged by Luke and material from Mark was integrated with this source to form the present Luke 19:37-48 and 21:5-36.[24] Given his unique understanding of the use of multiple sources utilized by the Synoptic authors, a somewhat similar position was taken by Boismard.[25]

The major argument for the existence of these various "Proto-Lukes" is that there exists a certain thematic coherence in the reconstructed material on the subject of "The End of Jerusalem." This argument may be supplemented by the observation that some vocabulary in this material is said to differ markedly from the usual Lukan vocabulary. However, for this position to hold, it must provide convincing literary evidence that the portions of Luke 21 not paralleled in Matthew or Paul are not Lukan redaction or a combination of redaction and isolated Sondergut.[26] Otherwise, the latter solution, which argues that Luke composed freely based on Matthew and which does not hypothecate an unknown source, must carry the day.

In our judgment the case that Luke in chapters 19 and 21 has utilized a special segment of "Proto-Luke" on *The End of Jerusalem*, cannot be sustained. A coherent theme is one criterion for proof of the existence of a source. But, in and of itself, this does not necessarily prove the existence and use of a source; it only proves that Luke needed to place the prediction of the destruction of Jerusalem in his narrative account of Jesus' life, presumably because Jesus' making these predictions, which echo strongly the wording of the earlier biblical prophets, was considered to be one of the precipitating factors that led to his arrest as a false king.

The crux of the argument for an independent source turns on the issue of vocabulary. Here two points must be addressed. First, the issue of linguistic characteristics; can certain linguistic characteristics peculiar to this material be identified? Second, there is the issue of language heavily echoing the text of the Septuagint.

---

[23]Ibid., 355-56.

[24]Ibid.

[25]M.-É Boismard, "Réponse Aux Deux Autres Hypothèses," in *The Interrelations of the Gospels*, 283-87. Boismard sees the beginning of the source as commencing at Lk 19:41-44 rather that Gaston's 19:37. With reference to Lk 21, only verses 20, 21b-22, 23b-25, and 28 come from Boismard's Proto-Luke.

[26]Goulder, *Luke—A New Paradigm II*, 702-704, following the Austin Farrer hypothesis, seems to regard all the non-Mark-Mathew material as redaction. He dismisses other positions that allow for a combination of redaction and isolated sayings as being too equivocal.

With regard to the former, there is no doubt that there is *some* highly un-usual vocabulary for Luke in 21:20, 21b-22, 23b-25, and 28.[27] The usual argu-ment is that such vocabulary about the fate of Jerusalem comes from Proto-Luke.[28] But caution is necessary. In order for this particular position, on its face, to be received with certainty, it would be necessary for us to know the linguistic characteristics of Proto-Luke. Then, if this unusual vocabulary matched Proto-Luke, the argument that these particular verses in Luke 21 (especially 21:20-28) came from Proto-Luke would be sustained. No such list of linguistic characteris-tics of Proto-Luke exists. Boismard has been quoted as saying that it is almost impossible to distinguish between such a source and Lukan redaction.[29]

If one gives up on Proto-Luke (an entailment of a particular source theory?), it could still be possible to say that just as Matthew 24 utilized a major source in his composition, Luke utilized a source on *The End of Jerusalem*. But, as far as we know, in this instance, this is not done. In any case, without having inde-pendent evidence for the existence of another source as, for exanple, we do have for Matthew 24 with the use of 2 Thessalonians 2:1-12, it would seem better to accept the position that the non-Matthean material in Luke 21:20-28 is Lukan composition. This is especially the case since we have some evidence of the hand of the final redactor in this part of Luke's Gospel.

Furthermore, the question of the appearance of frequent use of language drawn from the Septuagint in this material must be raised briefly.[30] We will not go into the matter in detail. Rather we will formulate a thesis to be demonstrated in the section on compositional analysis later in the chapter. This is the thesis. The existence of Luke's use of vocabulary heavily dependent upon the Greek Bible in Luke 21:20-28 is evidence of a consistent theme shown throughout this Gospel that in the Christ event God's purposes for Israel, revealed in the ancient prophets, have come to fulfillment. In particular, Luke composed 21:20-28 with the understanding that Jesus was a prophet who brought to *completion* the words of the earlier prophets on the siege and defeat of Jerusalem on account of her apostasy. This phenomenon of echoing directly the LXX, which is characteristic of Luke, provides a sufficient reason to account for Luke's unusual vocabulary in Luke 21:20-28. In composing Luke 21:20-28, Luke is freely redacting the text of Matthew in keeping with his theological intention to have Jesus' message of

---

[27]Thus Vincent Taylor, "A Cry from the Siege: A Suggestion regarding a Non-Marcan Oracle embedded in Lk 21:20-36," *Journal of Theological Studies* 26 (1925): 136-44; Boismard, *Response*, 284-87. Taylor, in particular, gives a list of the relevant vocabulary.

[28]Gaston, *No Stone on Another*, 355-56.

[29]Frans Neirynck, "Response to the Multiple-Stage Hypothesis: The Eschatological Discourse, "*The Interrelations of the Gospels*, 115.

[30]As noted by C. H. Dodd, "The Fall of Jerusalem and the 'Abomination of Desolation'," in *More New Testament Studies*, 69-84.

doom comport with the word of the earlier prophets. Furthermore, the vocabulary for siege and military conquest is very technical and there is no reason to expect to see it in many other places in Luke. To account for Luke 21:20-28 as the redaction of Luke's major source of Matthew 24, thus seems to be at least as plausible a position to take as the view that it is a combination of Mark and special source material of Luke.

We conclude that Luke in 21:5-33 is using only Matthew as a major source. In our compositional analysis we will show how Luke, in a different *Sitz im Leben* from that of Matthew 24, redacted Matthew's version of Jesus' Last Eschatological Discourse to account for the Fall of Jerusalem as an event in God's prophetic purpose leading up to the coming of the Son of Man. Besides the use of Matthew the only other use of a source tradition by Luke in chapter 21 was in the composition of 21:34-36. In these verses he used the special source also known to Paul, on the *Sudden Calamity of the End*. How he utilized this source will be shown in the analysis later in the chapter.

The Lukan Composition of 21:5-36: The General Context

The Concern about Jerusalem

It is a presupposition of our study that when Luke began to compose his version of Jesus' Last Eschatological Discourse the revolt of the Jews against Rome had been crushed and the temple in Jerusalem lay in ruins.

Echoes of Luke's perception of this fact emerge at Luke 19:28, the unit that begins the account of Jesus' arrival at the city. Upon his arrival at the edge of the city Jesus descends the Mount of Olives; and in language heavily dependent upon Jeremiah (LXX) he announces that the city will fall to its enemies (19:41-44). The divine ἐκδίκησις ("vengeance") promised in the ancient Hebrew prophecies was about to come to final fulfillment (cf. 21:22). Luke's account of the "cleansing" of the temple was abbreviated (19:45-46) because any further account of Jesus' actions in this place were unnecessary; Jesus had already uttered a prophecy against the city (cf. 19:41-44; 13:34-35).

The dialogues on the temple premises give additional confirmation of the recalcitrance of the established Jerusalem leadership (19:47–20:44, cf. in particular, 19:47 and 20:19). This critique of the leaders comes to a climax in 19:45–21:4 where the actions of the scribes are treated pejoratively in contrast to those of the poor widow. And it comes as no surprise that at 21:5-6 Luke has appended a version of the saying that the temple will be destroyed which Luke found in Matthew 24:1-2.

However, in taking over as his main source Matthew's account of Jesus' Last Discourse, which presumes that the temple will last until the end, Luke faced several compositional problems. Luke must now distinguish between the time of the destruction of Jerusalem and the appearance of the Son of Man at the end. This intervening period is the very time in which Luke was composed. Thus, in the use of his source, Luke must reflect this changed situation. Already in the disciples' response to Jesus in 21:7, Luke begins to prepare readers for this distinction. In this regard, the composition of the whole pericope of Luke 21:5-7 is worthy of close scrutiny.

The End of the Temple and Call for a Sign

Matthew 24:1-3	Luke 21:5-7
¹<u>καὶ</u> ἐξελθὼν ὁ Ἰησοῦς ἀπὸ τοῦ ἱεροῦ ἐπορεύετο, καὶ προσῆλθον οἱ μαθηταὶ αὐτοῦ ἐπιδεῖξαι αὐτῷ τὰς οἰκοδομὰς <u>τοῦ ἱεροῦ</u>.	⁵<u>καὶ</u>
	τινων λεγόντων περὶ <u>τοῦ ἱεροῦ</u>, ὅτι λίθοις καλοῖς καὶ ἀναθήμασιν κεκόσμηται,
²ὁ δὲ ἀποκριθεὶς <u>εἶπεν</u> αὐτοῖς οὐ βλέπετε <u>ταῦτα</u> πάντα; ἀμὴν λέγω ὑμῖν, οὐ μὴ ἀφεθῇ ὧδε <u>λίθος ἐπὶ λίθον</u> <u>ὃς οὐ καταλυθήσεται</u>.	<u>εἶπεν</u>, ⁶<u>ταῦτα</u> ἃ θεωρεῖτε ἐλεύσονται ἡμέραι ἐν αἷς οὐκ ἀφεθήσεται <u>λίθος ἐπὶ λίθῳ</u> <u>ὃς οὐ καταλυθήσεται</u>.
³καθημένου δὲ αὐτοῦ ἐπὶ τοῦ ὄρους τῶν ἐλαιῶν προσῆλθον αὐτῷ οἱ μαθηταὶ κατ' ἰδίαν <u>λέγοντες</u>, εἰπὲ ἡμῖν πότε ταῦτα ἔσται, <u>καὶ τί τὸ σημεῖον</u> τῆς σῆς παρουσίας καὶ συντελείας τοῦ αἰῶνος.	⁷Ἐπηρώτησαν δὲ αὐτὸν <u>λέγοντες</u>, Διδάσκαλε, πότε οὖν ταῦτα ἔσται, <u>καὶ τί τὸ σημεῖον</u> ὅταν μέλλῃ ταῦτα γίνεσθαι;

Luke's account of Jesus' announcement of the destruction of the temple has some material similarity to that of Matthew, especially in the actual wording of Jesus' saying, and the response of the disciples. However, as we have noted earlier, for compositional purposes the respective setting of the two accounts are somewhat different. In Matthew, Jesus leaves the temple and goes in the direction of the Mount of Olives (24:3). On the Mount of Olives, a traditional site of eschatological activity, Jesus responds to a question from the disciples. The emphasis in Matthew is to connect Jesus' leaving the temple with his pronouncement of doom upon it. In Luke, the setting is more general. Jesus is on the temple premises and receives a question from certain unidentified people. However, the movement away from the concrete Matthean compositional setting (an esoteric discussion between Jesus and disciples) to the more general setting which encompasses the crowd, is not in itself unusual for Luke. Luke does this regularly throughout his narrative, and it is suggested by Goulder that this change in setting may be merely a characteristic of style rather than a direct reflection of a theological strategy.[31]

Nevertheless, there is evidence that Luke uses this pericope to provide the basis for giving a definitive statement on his eschatological perspective. For Luke (unlike Matthew where the destruction of the temple and the end of the present age is coterminous) the destruction of the city of Jerusalem/temple will be set forth as a major happening in the progress of events as they move towards the end. But its destruction must clearly be distinguished from the end itself. In this light, the composition of Luke 21:6 makes sense. Jesus announces that the destruction of the temple will take place in the coming days.

This brings us to Luke 21:7. In response to Jesus' announcement in 21:6 of the end of the temple, the bystanders respond in terms reminiscent of Matthew's formulation (Matt 24:3). But there are some key differences.[32] Unlike Matthew, Luke does not have the bystanders ask Jesus either about his parousia or the end of the age.[33] Instead they ask obliquely

πότε οὖν ταῦτα ἔσται, καὶ	("Therefore, when will these things be and
τί τὸ σημεῖον ὅταν μέλλῃ	what will be the sign when
ταῦτα γίνεσθαι;	these things are about to come to pass?")

That is, in response to the saying against the temple in 21:6, Jesus is asked when will the destruction of the temple take place? And, in addition, through the use of conjunctive καί, what will be the sign when such an event will take place? In short, the question is on the end of the temple—nothing less, nothing more.[34] Yet, for the reader, the end of the temple has to be placed into some context. How is the end of the temple to be viewed in connection with other pivotal events in the eschaton? This is the reason for the discourse.

Specifically, the end of the temple will be placed into a sequence of several occurrences beginning with 21:8 and ending with 21:28.[35] The end of the temple per se (21:20-26) is a crucial stage before the end, a kind of a "red alert," but not

---

[31]Goulder, *Luke: A New Paradigm II*, 704.

[32]It is often argued that Luke has taken his use of διδάσκαλος from Mk 13:1. However, the collocation of καί/δέ + ἐπερωτάω + 3rd person pronoun + a participle of λέγω + the vocative διδάσκαλε is noted by Collison, "Linguistic Usages in the Gospel of Luke" (Ann Arbor MI: University Microfilms, 1977) 149, as peculiarly Lukan. This indicates that Luke 21:7a is Lukan redaction.

[33]Luke does not use the word παρουσία in his literary corpus to describe the return of Jesus; neither does Luke ever use the noun συντέλεια.

[34]Fitzmyer, *Luke (X–XXIV)*, 1331, notes commendably that Luke 21:7 refers directly to the destruction of the temple.

[35]Luke 21:8-11, 12-19, 20-26; 27-(28); cf. I. H. Marshall, *Commentary on Luke*, 753, whose reconstruction is somewhat similar.

the end of history. After that event, (καὶ τότέ) the Son of Man will appear in great power and glory (21:27). Only then (probably in Luke's view a relatively short span of time) will final redemption be realized (21:28).

With this theological outline in mind, the whole composition of Luke 21:5-36 becomes intelligible. The thrust of Luke 21:5-7 is to have representatives of a general audience ask when the destruction of the temple will take place? Luke places the answer to that question within the framework of a wider response with respect to the total eschatological scheme of things.

The Structure of the Lukan Eschatological Discourse

Luke arranged into four overlaping areas Jesus' discussion about the future (Luke 21:8-11; 12-19; 20-26; 27-28). There are two striking divergencies in Luke from the main source of Matthew 24. First, Luke has omitted Matthew's description of the Horrible Desecration of the temple and its aftermath (Matt 24:15-20). In its place Luke has a unit on being sustained through persecution (Lk 21:12-19) that has little material connection in content to Matthew 24:15-20. Second, in Luke 21:20-26, Luke has Jesus make an extended reference to the siege and fall of Jerusalem. Here the Lukan Jesus echoes both the terminology and predictive power of the Old Testament prophets in this polemic against Jerusalem. Thus Luke has no account of the Horrible Desecration. In its place Luke has attempted to show that the destruction of Jerusalem was a visitation of divine vengeance in keeping with the word of the Old Testament prophets. For Luke, the former dwelling place of the God of Israel is trodden down by Gentiles until the time of redemption (Lk 21:22, 28). It is important to understand that the time of the Lukan composition is the period shortly after the destruction of Jerusalem. What Luke undertakes in the Discourse is to place into a scenario of eschatological events the full sequence of dramatic occurrences which pertain to the end time that are to take place from the Temple Speech until the return of the Son of Man (21:7, 36). Luke accomplishes this in five identifiable pericopes (21:8-11; 12-19; 20-26; 27-28; 29-36).

1. *The Horrors Leading up to the End (21:8-11)*. In this unit Luke set out the basic features of a pattern of disintegration that will come in Eastern Mediterranean society prior to the fall of Jerusalem. This pattern of disintegration involves three major elements. First, there will be the appearance of false messianic pretenders (Lk 21:8). Second, there will be tremendous civil strife (21:9). Third, this civil strife will intensify with earthquakes and cosmic omens (21:10-11). When these latter signs appear the destruction of Jerusalem is at hand.

2. *On Being Sustained through Persecutions (21:12-19)*. Two major themes highlight this unit. Now the focus is not sociopolitical events but the conduct of

the disciples. Before the defining event of the Fall of Jerusalem, Jesus' followers are told that they will experience persecution (Lk 21:12-13; 16-17). This persecution may invoke even the internal betrayal by one's own family (21:16). Yet, there will be another dynamic at work as well. Christ will be with the community of believers and will sustain them through this terrible time of persecution (21:14-15; 18-19). This divine presence will enable them to explain their faith before the authorities and bring them protection. These two promises of a coming sustained persecution and divine sustenance stand in tension. Perhaps the best commentary on Luke 21:12-19 is the book of Acts. There, despite ferocious persecution and hostility, the earliest Christian community continues to be sustained and becomes solidified (cf. Acts 14:22).

3. *Jerusalem Is Destroyed and the Times of the Gentiles Are Inaugurated (21:20-26).* In Luke 21:20, the author continues with a description of the series of eschatological events that were begun in 21:8-11 and were interrupted by the interlude in 21:12-19. The cosmic signs and omens of Lk 21:11 were indicators of the Fall of Jerusalem. This Fall is fully described in Luke 21:20-26.

4. *The Coming of the Son of Man (21:27-28).* After the times of the Gentiles, Luke anticipates the coming of the Son of Man (Luke 21:27). The readers are to view this event as the culmination of the process of redemption. The call is to maintain hope in the reality of final redemption.

5. *The Final Exhortation to Vigilance (21:29-36).* Having constructed a scenario of eschatological events from Jesus' last week in Jerusalem until the time of redemption, Luke now has Jesus furnish three exhortations for his followers to maintain full vigilance until the end.

The parable of the fig tree and other trees (21:29-31) indicates that the eschatological events, commencing with the death of Jesus, which have run their course so quickly, are like trees in Spring giving promise of the final harvest. In "this generation" all things will be resolved (21:32-33). Since the eschatological time clock is counting down, the community of believers should not lose heart and be burdened down with the cares of the time; rather it should wait patiently for the coming of the Son of Man (21:34-36).

**An Analysis of Luke's Version
of Jesus' Last Eschatological Discourse
(Luke 21:8-36)**

The Horrors Leading up to the End (Luke 21:8-11)

Matthew 24:4-7	Luke 21:8-11

⁴Καὶ ἀποκριθεὶς ὁ Ἰησοῦς <u>εἶπεν</u>
αὐτοῖς βλέπετε μή τις ὑμᾶς <u>πλανήσῃ</u>

⁸ὁ δὲ <u>εἶπεν</u>
βλέπετε μὴ <u>πλανηθῆτε</u>

⁵πολλοὶ γὰρ ἐλεύσονται   πολλοὶ γὰρ ἐλεύσονται
ἐπὶ τῷ ὀνόματί   ἐπὶ τῷ ὀνόματί
μου λέγοντες· ἐγώ εἰμι ὁ Χριστός,   μου λέγοντες· ἐγώ εἰμι,
καὶ   καί· ὁ καιρὸς ἤγγικεν·
πολλοὺς πλανήσουσιν.   μὴ πορευθῆτε ὀπίσω αὐτῶν.
⁶μελλήσετε δὲ ἀκούειν   ⁹ὅταν δὲ ἀκούσητε
πολέμους καὶ ἀκοὰς πολέμων·   πολέμους καὶ ἀκαταστασίας,
ὁρᾶτε μὴ θροεῖσθε·   μὴ πτοηθῆτε·
δεῖ γὰρ γενέσθαι,   δεῖ γὰρ ταῦτα γενέσθαι πρῶτον,
ἀλλ᾽ οὔπω ἐστὶν τὸ τέλος.   ἀλλ᾽ οὐκ εὐθέως τὸ τέλος.
                                 ¹⁰Τότε ἔλεγεν αὐτοῖς·
⁷ἐγερθήσεται γὰρ ἔθνος ἐπὶ ἔθνος   ἐγερθήσεται ἔθνος ἐπ᾽ ἔθνος
καὶ βασιλεία ἐπὶ βασιλείαν   καὶ βασιλεία ἐπὶ βασιλείαν,
καὶ ἔσονται λιμοὶ
καὶ σεισμοὶ κατὰ τόπους·   ¹¹σεισμοί τε μεγάλοι καὶ κατὰ τόπους
                                 λιμοὶ καὶ λοιμοὶ ἔσονται,
                                 φόβητρά τε καὶ ἀπ᾽ οὐρανοῦ
                                 σημεῖα μεγάλα ἔσται.

Luke follows Matthew fairly closely in this unit which describes the emergence and development of the horrors before the end. The focus of the unit is on the process of disintegration that develops with increasing intensity.

First, in Luke 21:8, a warning is given about deceivers. Luke exhorts the readers not to follow those deceivers who claim that ὁ καιρὸς ἤγγικεν ("the time has come"). Luke has added this phraseology to the source found in Matthew 24:4-5.[36] The point is that one should take positive steps not to be deceived by any premature announcement of the end before the full number of eschatological events have run their course.

The appearance of the deceivers is followed by the coming of serious civil disorders (21:9). As with Matthew, Luke may have had in mind the terrible civil wars that shook the Roman Empire in 68–69 CE after the death of Nero. However, the text is not expansive enough to allow us to make such an interpretation with strong confidence. What is noticeable is that Luke again warns that these events do not in themselves constitute necessarily the end. Luke emphasizes this point by adding πρῶτον to the Matthean source (Lk 21:9 ‖ Matt 24:6) in order

---

[36]The terminology of ὁ καιρός is often used by Luke (19:44; 21:36; Acts 1:8; 3:19) to refer to the critical point of time with respect to the emergence of the final eschatological events. Also, Luke uses ἐγγίζειν over twenty times in his gospel and Collison, "Usages in Luke," 46, regards this as a Lukan linguistic usage. Finally, πλανᾶν is found only here in the text of Luke. Since it occurs a number of times in Matthew, four times in Matthew 24 alone, this constitutes linguistic evidence in favor of the view that Luke had copied the text of Matthew.

to claim that these political upheavals are precursors to the actual final redemption; not its very appearance.[37]

Luke opens 21:10 with a resumptive-inceptive statement: τότε ἔλεγεν αὐτοῖς ("then, he began to say to them").[38] This phraseology serves to introduce a prediction of a series of disasters which intensifies and accentuates the deepening process of disintegration that must take place before the end. First, the process of civil strife, already described in the previous verse, intensifies and moves into a deeper level (21:10). Furthermore, strife in the human community spreads to the cosmos itself (21:11). Here Luke expands his source which he found in Matthew 24:7. The use of λιμοὶ καὶ λοιμοὶ ("famines and plagues") improves Matthew's style and, in Greek, reflects alliteration.

Then, aside from famines and pestilences on earth, even more ominously, there appear dreadful portents and signs in the heavens (21:11). This reference to σημεῖα ("signs") is clearly an anticipation of Luke 21:25 that, we will argue, functions as a vivid metaphor for the terrors of the Fall of Jerusalem (Luke 21:20-26).[39] It is noticeable that Luke has moved the references to σημεῖα in Matthew, which refer to the parousia (24:3, 30, cf. 24), to the destruction of the holy city. Thus Luke 21:8-11 functions as a general description of the horrors that take the reader from the time of Jesus up until the time immediately prior to the destruction of Jerusalem (cf. Luke 21:20-26). But before Luke develops this line of thinking farther in Luke 21:20-28, he must give attention to what this means to the situation of believers. He signals this interest in them with his use of the statement πρὸ δὲ τούτων πάντων ("before all these things") in 21:12a.

---

[37]The change of οὔπω in Matt 24:6 to οὐκ εὐθέως in Lk 21:9 also adds emphasis to the Lukan contention that what is described in Lk 21:8-11 is not the end. Has Luke drawn εὐθέως from Matt 24:29 and made it function in an argument for the delay of the end? Also the echo of ἃ δεῖ γενέσθαι in Dan 2:28 (LXX) is fully in keeping with this claim.

[38]Collison, "Usages in Luke," 55, notes that ἔλεγεν/ἔλεγον occurs 23 times in Luke. He regards it as a linguistic usage of Luke and thus it serves here as Lukan redaction.

[39]It has been noticed by a number of commentators (viz., Marshall, *Commentary on Luke*, 765) that the descriptions by Josephus, *Jewish War* 6:288-315, of the carnage surrounding the Fall of Jerusalem in 70 CE, tells of a surfeit of omens and heavenly signs interpreted by various prophets. The claim then follows that Luke, in 21:11, is doing something similar in his discussion. It is noticeable that the author of Luke-Acts is remarkably reserved in using apocalyptic terminology (as compared to Matthew and Paul) in the description of the return of Christ. This probably explains why Luke omitted Matt 24:8 with its reference to the beginning of the birthpangs (of the new age).

On Being Sustained through Persecutions (Lk 21:12-19)

Matthew 10:17-22	Matthew 24:8-13	Luke 21:12-19

⁸πάντα δὲ <u>ταῦτα</u>
ἀρχὴ ὠδίνων.

⁹τότε <u>παραδώσουσιν</u>
ὑμᾶς εἰς θλῖψιν

¹⁷Προσέχετε δὲ ἀπὸ τῶν
ἀνθρώπων <u>παραδώσουσιν</u>
γὰρ ὑμᾶς εἰς συνέδρια
καὶ ἐν <u>ταῖς συναγωγαῖς</u>
αὐτῶν μαστιγώσουσιν
ὑμᾶς·
¹⁸καὶ <u>ἐπὶ ἡγεμόνας</u> δὲ
<u>καὶ βασιλεῖς</u> ἀχθήσεσθε
<u>ἕνεκεν ἐμοῦ εἰς</u>
<u>μαρτύριον</u> αὐτοῖς
καὶ τοῖς ἔθνεσιν.

¹⁹<u>ὅταν δε</u> παραδῶσιν
ὑμᾶς,
<u>μὴ μεριμνήσητε πῶς</u>
<u>ἢ τί</u> λαλήσητε· δοθήσεται
γὰρ <u>ὑμῖν ἐν</u> ἐκείνῃ
<u>τῇ ὥρᾳ</u> τί λαλήσητε·
²⁰οὐ γὰρ ὑμεῖς ἐστε οἱ
λαλοῦντες ἀλλὰ τὸ πνεῦ-
μα τοῦ πατρὸς ὑμῶν
τὸ λαλοῦν ἐν ὑμῖν.
²¹<u>παραδώσει δε</u> ἀδελφὸς
<u>ἀδελφὸν</u> εἰς θάνατον
<u>καὶ</u> πατὴρ τέκνον, <u>καὶ</u>
ἐπαναστήσονται τέκνα
ἐπὶ γονεῖς <u>καὶ θανατώ-</u>
<u>σουσιν</u> αὐτούς.
²²<u>καὶ ἔσεσθε μισούμενοι</u>
<u>ὑπὸ πάντων</u>
<u>διὰ τὸ ὄνομά μου·</u>

¹²πρὸ δὲ <u>τούτων πάντων</u>
ἐπιβαλοῦσιν ἐφ' ὑμᾶς
τὰς χεῖρας αὐτῶν καὶ
διώξουσιν, <u>παραδιδόντες</u>

εἰς <u>τὰς συναγωγὰς</u> καὶ
φυλακάς, ἀπαγομένους

ἐπὶ <u>βασιλεῖς καὶ ἡγε</u>
<u>μόνας</u>
<u>ἕνεκεν</u> τοῦ ὀνόματός
μου·
¹³ἀποβήσεται ὑμῖν
εἰς <u>μαρτύριον.</u>
¹⁴θέτε οὖν
ἐν ταῖς καρδίαις ὑμῶν
μὴ προμελετᾶν
ἀπολογηθῆναι·
¹⁵ἐγὼ γὰρ δώσω ὑμῖν
στόμα καὶ σοφίαν ᾗ οὐ
δυνήσονται ἀντιστῆναι ἢ
ἀντειπεῖν ἅπαντες οἱ
ἀντικείμενοι ὑμῖν.

¹⁶<u>παραδοθήσεσθε δὲ καὶ</u>
ὑπὸ <u>γονέων</u>
καὶ <u>ἀδελφῶν</u>
καὶ συγγενῶν καὶ φίλων,
καὶ <u>θανατώσουσιν</u>
ἐξ <u>ὑμῶν,</u>
¹⁷<u>καὶ ἔσεσθε μισούμενοι</u>
<u>ὑπὸ πάντων</u>
<u>διὰ τὸ ὄνομά μου.</u>

<u>καὶ</u> ἀποκτενοῦσιν <u>ὑμᾶς,</u>
<u>καὶ ἔσεσθε μισούμενοι</u>
<u>ὑπὸ πάντων</u> τῶν ἐθνῶν
<u>διὰ τὸ ὄνομα μου.</u>

¹⁰καὶ τότε σκανδαλισθήσον-
ται πολλοὶ καὶ ἀλλήλους
παραδώσουσιν καὶ μισή-
σουσιν ἀλλήλους·
¹¹καὶ πολλοὶ ψευδοπροφῆται
ἐγερθήσονται καὶ πλανή-
σουσιν πολλούς·
¹²καὶ διὰ τὸ πληθυνθῆναι
τὴν ἀνομίαν ψυγήσεται
ἡ ἀγάπη τῶν πολλῶν.

¹⁸καὶ θρὶξ ἐκ τῆς κεφαλῆς
ὑμῶν οὐ μὴ ἀπόληται.

ὁ δὲ ὑπομείνας εἰς   ¹³ὁ δὲ ὑπομείνας εἰς   ¹⁹ἐν τῇ ὑπομονῇ ὑμῶν
τέλος οὗτος σωθήσεται.   τέλος οὗτος σωθήσεται.   κτήσασθε τὰς ψυχὰς
ὑμῶν.

The material in Luke 21:12-19 is a compilation of various logia which have been organized into a basic A B A' B' structure. The first logia in 21:12-13 is a prediction that the followers of Jesus will be handed over to various administrative authorities for punishment. But, conversely, even under these terrible circumstances, by going before the political authorities, unique opportunities will be provided for Jesus' followers to testify to his power.

Corresponding to Luke 21:12-13, in 21:16-17, the followers of Jesus are told that they will be "handed over" to the authorities on account of their allegiance to his name (cf. the repeated use of παραδίδοναι, "to hand over," in 21:12, 16, and τὸ ὄνομά μου, "my name," in 21:12, 17). Only in these verses the sense of betrayal is deepened. The "handing over" will be done by family and friends. The final result for some of these believers will be death (Lk 21:16).

Balanced opposite the two units on persecution (Luke 21:12b-13; 16-17) are two units (B and B') that promise a sustaining divine power to the disciples while they undergo these terrible events (Lk 21:14-15; 18-19). The two separate bodies of material stand together in some form of tension. Thus, in Luke 21:16, we are told that some of the followers of Jesus will be put to death; but, on the other hand, in 21:18 they are assured that "not a hair of your head will be destroyed."[40] Yet, despite this tension, the overall point is clear. The life of faithfulness and service in mission within the messianic community goes forward despite individual cases of harassment and persecution. Indeed, as noted earlier, Luke 21:12-19 may be viewed as an anticipation of much of the story line of Acts. There, although the church faces crisis after crisis, it continues to grow and expand due to the sustaining power of the Holy Spirit.

---

[40]Goulder, *Luke: A New Paradigm II*, 709, views this as further proof of his contention that Luke is "a confirmed muddler." In our view, Goulder has missed the paradox of divine sustenance in persecution that Luke is attempting to convey.

Compositionally, Luke has juxtaposed these two blocks of material together in a manner fully in keeping with the compositional procedure used throughout this work. Luke frequently breaks up the major Matthean speech units and incorporates smaller units into his narrative framework. With respect to the Mission Discourse, Luke has used Matthew 9:35–10:16 for the two accounts of the Mission of the Twelve and the Seventy (Lk 9:1-6; 10:1-16). Similarly, Matthew 10:19-20 and 26-33 was used in the composition of Luke 12:1b-12; Matthew 10:34-37 for Luke 12:49-53; and Matthew 10:37-39 for Luke 14:25-33. Matthew 10:24-25 is echoed in Luke 6:37-42. Thus, up until this point Luke had not used Matthew 10:17-18 or 21-23 in his composition. By use of the recurrent word παραδίδοναι, which Luke found in his source at Matthew 24:9, Luke, following the lead of the author of Matthew 24 who repeats terminology found in Matthew 10, returns to Matthew 10 and incorporates Matthew 10:17-18 and 21-22 (with the exception of Matt 10:23, the only verses of the Mission Discourse not used) into his composition to describe the persecution of the church.[41]

Luke prefaces the composition of 21:12-19 by composing 21:12a. The collocation πρὸ δὲ τούτων ("before these things") is shown elsewhere to be from the hand of Luke (Acts 5:36).[42] The phraseology ἐπιβάλλειν τὰς χεῖρας ("they will lay hands upon [you]") is Lukan (Luke 9:62; 20:19; Acts 4:3; 5:18; 12:1; 21:27). Luke's point is that before the ultimate sign of the end of Jerusalem, the followers of Jesus would have to undergo a sustained period of persecution. Luke 21:12b-13, utilizing Matthew 10:17-18, drives home this point.[43]

At 21:14-15, Luke places the first of his two statements of assurance of sustenance in persecution which are given in this unit. Specifically, Jesus' hearers are promised the gift of wisdom that will allow them to confound their opponents. Since Luke has utilized Matthew 10:19-20 for the composition of Luke 12:11-12, to avoid a doublet, he omits using these verses again. So Luke

---

[41]Perhaps the Travel Narrative itself (Lk 9:51–19:27) is the Lukan version of Matt 10:23? We cannot be fully certain why Luke preferred to omit Matt 24:10-12, 14. The whole issue is discussed by McNicol, "The Eschatological Discourse," 177. The simplest reason may be that Luke preferred to use Matthew 10 because of a preference for its content that focused on persecution primarily from the synagogue. Luke is not averse to using some of the material from Matt 24:10f. He seems to echo 24:14 (οἰκουμένη) at Lk 21:26.

[42]Also in Acts 21:38 we find ὁ πρὸ τούτων τῶν ἡμερῶν.

[43]Luke has made several changes from Matt 10:17-18 for his Hellenistic audience. Luke has φυλακάς (21:12) for the more Palestinian συνέδρια (Matt 10:17). Luke has omitted the Matthean reference to the persecution of the Gentiles (Matt 10:18), as Luke apparently read this as an unduly gratuitous reference for his mainly Hellenistic audience. Also, the motif of acting on account of the name of Jesus which is highlighted here is a central theological motif in Acts (2:21, 38; 3:16; 4:10, 12).

composes 21:14-15 which now functions as a paraphrase of the material he found in Matthew 10:19-20.[44]

Having completed units on both the prospect of persecution and of being sustained in it, for emphasis, Luke now gives further material again on these two themes. For the composition of Luke 21:16-17, Luke uses Matthew 10:21-22 as his source. As is characteristic of his composition, Luke highlights the dispensability of loyalty to parents as a condition of discipleship. Luke has developed this idea before (cf. 18:29). In this case the parents are guilty of treachery.[45] Yet in this terrible situation there is still hope that the cause will be sustained. The all encompassing promise of martyrdom in Matthew 10:21 is qualified by Luke 21:16; only some will die, although the Christian community will be hated by all.

This theme of being sustained in persecution continues in the final section of the pericope in Luke 21:18-19. Luke 21:18 is possibly a logion that Luke has composed. Interestingly enough, Luke has placed similar words in the mouth of Paul in Acts 27:34. This continued theological outlook is maintained by Luke's rewriting of Matthew 10:22b in Luke 21:19. By being faithful Jesus promises the inheritance of eternal life.

In incorporating Matthew 10:17-18, 21-22 into Luke 21:12-19, Luke has overlapped Matthean duplicate expressions in Matthew 24 (Matt 24:9b || Lk 21:16b-17; Matt 24:13 || Lk 21:19). Then, Luke omits Matthew 24:14 although, as we have noticed, it is echoed at Luke 21:26. At this point, Luke again resumes following the text of Matthew as the major source of the composition (Matthew 24:15 || Luke 21:20). In the next unit, we will set forth how Luke utilized this source for his compositional purposes.

---

[44]Cf. Farmer, *The Synoptic Problem: A Critical Analysis* (corr. repr. Dillsboro NC: Western North Carolina Press; Macon GA: Mercer University Press, 1976) 271. Evidence of Lukan composition is the use in Lk 21:14 of θέτε οὖν ἐν ταῖς καρδίαις ὑμῶν, featuring the imperative of τίθημι with a prepositional phrase which Collison, "Usages in Luke," 222, has identified as a general linguistic usage of Luke (Lk 9:44; cf 1:66; Acts 5:4; 19:21); the use of ἀπολογεῖσθαι in Lk 21:14 echoes ἀπολογεῖσθαι in the corresponding pericope in Lk 12:11 (cf. Acts 19:33; 24:10; 25:8; 26:1,2,24). In addition, with respect to Lk 21:15, Goulder, *Luke: A New Paradigm II*, 701, has noted that ἐγωγάρ has six usages in Luke-Acts and none in Matthew and Mark; ἅπας, σοφία, and ἀντειπεῖν are all words that qualify for Goulder's table of Lukan vocabulary (cf. Goulder, *Luke: A New Paradigm II*, 801, 808). Finally, οἱ ἀντικείμενοι only also in Luke 13:17 is found nowhere else in the Synoptic Tradition.

[45]The phraseology συγγενῶν καὶ φίλων is overwhelmingly Lukan. Luke-Acts has forms of συγγενής or a cognate 9 times as opposed to only one usage in Matthew or Mark; and φίλος appears in Luke-Acts 18 times as opposed to no usages in Mark and once in Matthew.

Jerusalem Is Destroyed and the Times of the Gentiles Are Inaugurated (Luke 21:20-26)

Matthew 24:15-22, 29	Luke 21:20-26
¹⁵Ὅταν οὖν <u>ἴδητε</u>	²⁰<u>Ὅταν</u> δὲ <u>ἴδητε</u> κυκλουμένην ὑπὸ στρα-
τὸ βδέλυγμα <u>τῆς ἐρημώσεως</u>	τοπέδων Ἰερουσαλήμ, τότε γνῶτε ὅτι
τὸ ῥηθὲν διὰ Δανιὴλ τοῦ προφήτου	ἤγγικεν <u>ἡ ἐρήμωσις</u> αὐτῆς.
ἑστὸς ἐν τόπῳ ἁγίῳ,	
ὁ ἀναγινώσκων νοείτω,	
¹⁶<u>τότε οἱ ἐν τῇ Ἰουδαίᾳ φευγέτωσαν</u>	²¹<u>τότε οἱ ἐν τῇ Ἰουδαίᾳ φευγέτωσαν</u>
<u>εἰς τὰ ὄρη,</u>	<u>εἰς τὰ ὄρη</u> καὶ οἱ ἐν μέσῳ αὐτῆς
¹⁷ὁ ἐπὶ τοῦ δώματος μὴ καταβάτω	
ἆραι τὰ ἐκ τῆς οἰκίας αὐτοῦ,	
¹⁸<u>καὶ ὁ ἐν</u> τῷ ἀγρῷ	ἐκχωρείτωσαν <u>καὶ οἱ ἐν</u> ταῖς χώραις
<u>μὴ</u> ἐπιστρεψάτω ὀπίσω	<u>μὴ</u> εἰσερχέσθωσαν εἰς αὐτήν.
ἆραι τὸ ἱμάτιον αὐτοῦ.	²²ὅτι ἡμέραι ἐκδικήσεως αὗταί εἰσιν
	τοῦ πλησθῆναι πάντα τὰ γεγραμμένα.
¹⁹<u>οὐαὶ δὲ ταῖς ἐν γαστρὶ ἐχούσαις</u>	²³<u>οὐαὶ ταῖς ἐν γαστρὶ ἐχούσαις</u>
<u>καὶ ταῖς θηλαζούσαις ἐν ἐκείναις</u>	<u>καὶ ταῖς θηλαζούσαις ἐν ἐκείναις</u>
<u>ταῖς ἡμέραις.</u>	<u>ταῖς ἡμέραις·</u>
²⁰προσεύχεσθε δὲ ἵνα μὴ γένηται ἡ	
φυγὴ ὑμῶν χειμῶνος μηδὲ σαββάτῳ.	
²¹<u>ἔσται γὰρ</u> τότε θλῖψις <u>μεγάλη</u>	<u>ἔσται γὰρ</u> ἀνάγκη <u>μεγάλη</u> ἐπὶ
	τῆς γῆς καὶ ὀργὴ τῷ λαῷ τούτῳ,
	²⁴καὶ πεσοῦνται στόματι μαχαίρης καὶ
	αἰχμαλωτισθήσονται εἰς τὰ ἔθνη πάν-
	τα, καὶ Ἰερουσαλήμ ἔσται πατουμένη
	ὑπὸ ἐθνῶν, ἄχρι οὗ πληρωθῶσιν καιροὶ
οἷα οὐ γέγονεν ἀπ' ἀρχῆς κόσμου	ἐθνῶν.
ἕως τοῦ νῦν οὐδ' οὐ μὴ γένηται.	
²²καὶ εἰ μὴ ἐκολοβώθησαν αἱ ἡμέραι	
ἐκεῖναι,οὐκ ἂν ἐσώθη πᾶσα σάρξ·	
διὰ δὲ τοὺς ἐκλεκτοὺς κολοβωθήσονται	
αἱ ἡμέραι ἐκεῖναι.	
²⁹Εὐθέως δὲ μετὰ τὴν θλῖψιν τῶν	
ἡμερῶν ἐκείνων ὁ <u>ἥλιος</u> σκοτισθήσε-	²⁵Καὶ ἔσονται σημεῖα ἐν <u>ἡλίῳ</u>
ται, <u>καὶ ἡ σελήνη</u> οὐ δώσει τὸ φέγγος	<u>καὶ σελήνῃ</u>
αὐτῆς, <u>καὶ οἱ ἀστέρες</u> πεσοῦνται	<u>καὶ ἄστροις,</u>
ἀπὸ τοῦ οὐρανοῦ,	καὶ ἐπὶ τῆς γῆς συνοχὴ ἐθνῶν ἐν
	ἀπορίᾳ ἤχους θαλάσσης καὶ σάλου,
	²⁶ἀποψυχόντων ἀνθρώπων ἀπὸ φόβου
	καὶ προσδοκίας τῶν ἐπερχομένων τῇ
καὶ <u>αἱ δυνάμεις</u>	οἰκουμένῃ, <u>αἱ γὰρ δυνάμεις</u>
<u>τῶν οὐρανῶν σαλευθήσονται.</u>	<u>τῶν οὐρανῶν σαλευθήσονται.</u>

Luke has described with considerable literary skill the growing intensity of the eschatological events as they move towards closure. Commencing with the appearance of false teachers, moving through the coming of civil wars, and culminating with catastrophic disturbances on earth, the impression is created that history is moving to a major climax (Lk 21:8-11). However, before the reader arrives at the final climactic events (21:12a), Luke provides a parenthetical interlude whereby one is allowed to see the effects this process had upon believers living in the world (Lk 21:12-19). In a time of persecution believers will be sustained by the Holy Spirit (21:15). In Luke 21:20-26 the interlude introduced in 21:12a is over and, with the description of the destruction of Jerusalem, Luke begins to bring the narrative description of the eschatological events to its climax.

For the basis of his composition Luke commences with Matthew's account of the appearance of the Horrible Desecration in the Temple as the major source (cf. Matt 24:15-16, 19-22, 29). However, since at the time of the composition of Luke the temple had been destroyed, Luke's account has reoriented the focus of Matthew's discussion. Instead of viewing the Horrible Desecration as an action taking place in the temple initiating the parousia of the Son of Man who will come in the final Judgment, Luke focuses on the destruction of the holy city itself as the penultimate event that sets the stage for his future appearance. Luke thus freely composes, on the basis of Matthew 24:15-16, 19-22, 29, adding considerable phraseology that echoes prophetic passages in the Septuagint, to reinforce the argument that this horrendous event predicted by Jesus was taking place in fulfillment of the divine purpose shown throughout Scripture (cf. Luke 24:25-27; 32).

An alternative perspective on the composition of this passage is that Luke has used a special source in 21:20, 21b-22, 23b-24, 25b-26a to supplement his major source in Matthew or Mark. In an earlier section of this chapter we set forth the reasons why we do not favor the latter position. Now in our analysis, we will set forth the reasons why we concluded that these additions to the Matthean material constitute Lukan composition. We will argue that Luke composed 21:20-26 to show that the destruction of Jerusalem did not usher in the coming of the Son of Man, but inaugurated an era (a brief unspecified amount of time) of Gentile dominance over fallen Jerusalem which was to last until the time of final redemption.

We start in Luke 21:20. First, as indicated in the display, with the use of ὅταν δὲ ἴδητε Luke appears to have resumed following the text of Matthew (cf. Matthew 24:15). This presupposition is also indicated by Luke's use of ἐρήμωσις ("desolation") which also appears in the text of Matthew 24:15.[46] Here, unlike Matthew, ἐρήμωσις is made to refer to the actual destruction of

---

[46]This is the only use of ἐρήμωσις in the whole synoptic tradition (Matt 24:15 ‖ Mk 13:14 ‖ Lk 21:20). On the Two Gospel Hypothesis it would mean that Luke has echoed Matt 24:15 at this point.

Jesus' Directions for the Future

the city of Jerusalem and not to the actual appearance of the Horrible Desecration in the temple [of the city].[47]

From 21:20 to 26, Luke will expand the Matthean reference to the ἐρήμωσις with a number of echoes of prophetic phraseology found in the text of Daniel 9:26 and various places in Jeremiah on this devastation (cf. Jer 4:7; 7:34; 22:5; 32:4; 51:6, 22 LXX).[48] Specifically, with respect to the terminology we find in Luke 21:20, it is noteworthy that the text of Jeremiah (40:1 LXX) describes Nebuchednezzar and the whole of his στρατόπεδον ("army") making war against Jerusalem (cf. Jeremiah 48:12). In so doing we learn also from Jeremiah 52:7 that this army surrounded Jerusalem in a κύκλῳ ("circle").[49] Thus Luke has used terminology drawn from Old Testament descriptions of the sieges of Jerusalem in Daniel and Jeremiah to describe the Fall of Jerusalem. For Luke, such terminology constituted a fair representation of the prophecies of Scripture now restated by Jesus the prophet (cf. 19:41-44).[50]

Having set the scene for the description of the end of Jerusalem in 21:20, Luke utilizes the next verse of the major source (Matt 24:16) as his basis for a description of a detailed warning given to the people in the city prior to its collapse (Lk 21:21-23a). The epexegetical explanation of the time of Horrible Sacrilege in Matthew 24:17-18 is omitted; it was used by Luke in 17:30-32 in connection with the call to remember Lot's wife. In its place Luke gives a series of prepositional phrases functioning as substantives to accentuate the point that one should leave the doomed place.[51] The first phrase, οἱ ἐν τῇ Ἰουδαίᾳ

---

[47] Marshall, *Commentary on Luke,* 770-72.

[48] We are indebted to C. H. Dodd, "The Fall of Jerusalem and the 'Abomination of Desolation'," in *More New Testament Studies*, 73, for these references.

[49] Goulder, *Luke: A New Paradigm II*, 711.

[50] The important point for Luke is not to give historically accurate descriptions of what happened in 70 CE at Jerusalem, but to stress that the events that happened then must be viewed through the prism of the divine purpose of God revealed in Scripture. Thus to quibble over whether Luke's description of the Fall does not always dovetail with Josephus's account is to miss the point. For Luke the language of Scripture was a far more accurate gauge for understanding what happened in 70 than the accounts of other contemporaries. The argument of Bo Reicke, "Synoptic prophecies on the Destruction of Jerusalem," *Studies in New Testament and Early Christian Literature: Essays in Honor of Allen P. Wikgren*, NovTSup 33, ed. D. E. Aune (Leiden: E. J. Brill, 1972) 121-34, that the special Lukan language of Lk 21:20-28 can be accounted for from biblical terminology is correct. Reicke believed that this was an argument for the view that Luke was written before the Fall of Jerusalem. As noted above, we believe there are more cogent ways of explaining the evidence.

[51] The fact that by the use of οἱ ἐν μέσῳ αὐτῆς, Luke appears to have shifted to refer to Jerusalem from the more general reference to Judea earlier in the verse, has been used by many as evidence for the view that this is Lukan conflation of two sources. Although we would not exactly call it a prominent feature of his compositional style,

("those in Judea"), Luke found in Matthew 24:16. The others he apparently composed.[52]

The reason for leaving the doomed city is now given. We are told that these days of vengeance are a fulfillment of things written, presumably in Scripture (Lk 21:22). The reference to αἱ ἡμέραι ("days") in an eschatological context echoes Jesus' terminology in Luke 19:42, 43, 21:6, and ultimately Jeremiah 26:10 (LXX). All of these texts functioned to predict the doom of Jerusalem and the temple. The destruction of Jerusalem was a terrible time and the Matthean woe was utilized by Luke to describe its horrors (Matthew 24:19 || Luke 21:24).[53]

The next segment of this pericope is Luke 21:23b-24. As C. H. Dodd has shown, the text again is replete with terminology drawn from certain prophetic passages in the Septuagint.[54] This catena of texts from the Septuagint was constructed by Luke to show that the destruction of Jerusalem in 70 CE was indeed in keeping with divine purposes shown in the Scripture. For Luke, the fact that Jerusalem is in ruins is not only the present reality in which he composes; but it is a situation that should be viewed as wholly consistent with the full purposes of God. It is the penultimate event which shows that Jesus truly was God's prophet and thus provides a foundation for belief in his return.[55]

Luke will often expand from his sources bringing in additional descriptive points that stand in some tension with what had already appeared in the narrative. A classic case in point is Lk 9:10-12, where we are told that Jesus and the twelve were in Bethsaida; but two verses later, without a change of locale, we learn they are in a desert place. We conclude that Lk 21:21 is probably due to Luke's compositional style rather than serving as an indicator of the creation of a seam between two sources.

[52]Collison, "Usages in Luke," 227, identifies the use of the substantivised prepositional phrase with ἐν used attributively as a general linguistic usage of Luke. It is found in Luke in fourteen instances.

[53]The use of the plural of ἡμέρα (21:22a and 23) provides a brief inclusio highlighting the fate of the city. Also, there may be here an echo of Matt 24:22 which Luke has omitted. Interestingly enough, the phraseology ἐν γαστρὶ ἔχω has been identified by Tevis, *Words and Phrases*, #248 on p. 192, as the work of a single author (cf. Matt 1:18, 23; 24:19). This usage by Luke of a literary characteristic of the text of Matthew is a confirmation that Luke is using the text of Matthew at this point.

[54]Dodd, "The Fall of Jerusalem," 76-79. A synopsis of some of the main texts include: the usages of Zeph 1:15a (ἡμέρα ὀργῆς ... ἡμέρα θλίψεως καὶ ἀνάγκης); καὶ πεσοῦνται ἐν μαχαίρᾳ (Jer 20:4; cf. Jer 21:7, which utilizes στόμα); and θήσομαι τὴν Ἰερουσαλὴμ λίθον καταπατούμενον πᾶσιν τοῖς ἔθνεσιν (Zec 12:3). Only the phraseology ἄχρι οὗ πληρωθῶσιν καιροὶ ἐθνῶν is not found in the Septuagint; but, as Dodd notes well, this may well be Luke's rewriting of Daniel 9:26-27 (cf. Dan 7:25).

[55]The argument of Chance, *Jerusalem*, 35, that there may be a hint in the text of the restoration of Jerusalem, after the times of the Gentiles are complete, seems to stretch the evidence. For Luke 21:25-26, the next great event will be the return of the Son of Man. As far as we can see there is no provision in Lukan theology for the restoration of

The use of terminology that echoes the Septuagint in Luke 21:23b-24 is so pervasive that it is difficult to determine very many traces of Lukan composition. However the use of the periphrastic future ἔσται πατουμένη ("will be trampled") is probably an indicator of Lukan composition (Luke 21:24).[56]

A similar literary pattern remains true with reference to the composition of Luke 21:25-26. In this concluding section of the pericope, Luke finally returns to the reference to omens and signs in the heavens (Luke 21:12). Many commentators tend to presume that these signs and omens are directly associated by Luke with the coming of the Son of Man at the end of the age because that is the case in Matthew and Mark.[57] However, this may not necessarily be the case for Luke. Josephus went into great detail describing various omens and signs in heaven that purportedly took place during the siege and Fall of Jerusalem.[58] Luke, who possibly did not know Josephus, but demonstrably parallels his literary style as a writer to a Hellenistic audience, may well have had a similar understanding of the cosmic signs as an indicator of a calamitous event on earth.[59]

This exegetical suggestion makes excellent sense in light of the composition of Luke 21:5-11. In Luke 21:5-6 Jesus pronounced doom on the temple. Then Jesus is asked what will be the sign (Luke 21:7). Luke rehearses a series of events culminating with the appearance of omens in the sky (21:11). Luke then resumes the description, after a brief interlude ("before these things..." in 21:12-19) on the situation of the disciples in these perilous times, with the account of the Fall of Jerusalem (Luke 21:20-21). Luke 21:25-26 is an epexegetical expansion of Luke 21:11. It stresses the strong connection between these heavenly portents and the catastrophic events, symbolized by the Fall of Jerusalem, which will come to pass on the whole world during the time of the Gentiles (Luke 21:24-26).[60] For Luke, this period of turmoil was the immediate precursor of the final Judgment and the Coming of the Son of Man.

Compositionally, Luke introduced the construction of 21:25-26 by moving up from the main source at Matthew 24:21-24 to Matthew 24:29 and using the latter as the basis of the composition for Luke 21:25a.[61] It is easy to see why

---

Jerusalem before the full coming of the Kingdom of God.

[56]Collison, "Usages in Luke," 75.

[57]Marshall, *Commentary on Luke*, 775; Fitzmyer, *Luke (X–XXIV)*, 1349.

[58]Cf. Josephus, *Jewish War* 6:286-315.

[59]N. T. Wright, *The New Testament and the People of God*, 373-78.

[60]It is odd that Dodd, "The Fall of Jerusalem," does not extend his discussion to Lk 21:25-26. If he did, he would see that Luke utilized a catena of Septuagint passages in a similar way as he did in 21:20-24. For Lk 21:25b-26 terminology has been drawn from passages like Isa 24:15-19 and Ps 88:10 (LXX) to describe this era of terror on the earth.

[61]It is noticeable that Luke has omitted the Matthean εὐθέως (Matt 24:29). For Luke, the era of the times of the Gentiles, after the Fall of Jerusalem, was probably brief

Luke could make such a compositional move. There is the common linguistic link with θλῖψις ("distress") in Matthew 24:21, 29 and, there is repeated linguistic terminology in respect to the use of "those days" in Matthew 24:22 and 29. For Luke, "those days" constitutes the final period of turmoil ushered in by the Fall of Jerusalem leading up until the coming of the Son of Man. Luke echoes Matthew 24:24 with the use of σημεῖα in Luke 21:25. Finally, Luke had used Matthew 24:26-27 at Luke 17:23-24 and Mathew 24:28 at Luke 17:37.[62] Thus it is easy for Luke to link the terminology of Matthew 24:21-24 and 29 together.

Therefore, we conclude that Luke 21:25-26 was used by Luke to frame the prophetic language echoed in the Greek Bible to describe the age of horrors ushered in by the Fall of Jerusalem. With this full description of the Fall of Jerusalem, the question that was posed to Jesus in Luke 21:7 has been answered. He has explained definitively that the events of 70 CE bring to a fulfillment the ancient prophetic oracles against Jerusalem.

The Coming of the Son of Man (Luke 21:27-28)

Matthew 24:30-31	Luke 21:27-28
[30]καὶ τότε φανήσεται τὸ σημεῖον τοῦ υἱοῦ τοῦ ἀνθρώπου ἐν οὐρανῷ καὶ τότε κόψονται πᾶσαι αἱ φυλαὶ τῆς γῆς <u>καὶ ὄψονται τὸν υἱὸν τοῦ ἀνθρώπου</u> <u>ἐρχόμενον</u> ἐπὶ τῶν <u>νεφελῶν</u> τοῦ οὐρανοῦ <u>μετὰ δυνάμεως καὶ δόξης</u> <u>πολλῆς</u> [31]καὶ ἀποστελεῖ τοὺς ἀγγέλους αὐτοῦ μετὰ σάλπιγγος μεγάλης, καὶ ἐπισυνάξουσιν τοὺς ἐκλεκτοὺς αὐτοῦ ἐκ τῶν τεσσάρων ἀνέμων ἀπ' ἄκρων οὐρανῶν ἕως (τῶν) ἄκρων αὐτῶν	[27]<u>καὶ τότε ὄψονται τόν υἱὸν του</u> <u>ἀνθρώπου ἐρχόμενον ἐν νεφέλῃ</u> <u>μετὰ δυνάμεως καὶ δόξης πολλῆς.</u> [28]ἀρχομένων δὲ τούτων γίνεσθαι ἀνακύψατε καὶ ἐπάρατε τὰς κεφαλάς ὑμῶν, διότι ἐγγίζει ἡ ἀπολύτρωσις ὑμῶν.

(cf. The Parable of the Fig Tree in the next verses of 21:29-31). However, Luke could not go so far as to say that the coming of the Son of Man would happen immediately after the Fall of Jerusalem.

[62]McNicol, "Composition of the Eschatological Discourse," 179-80.

This unit, as compared with Matthew 24:29-31, is marked by considerable literary economy. In an almost matter-of-fact way, Luke unpretentiously states that in these times the Son of Man will appear on a cloud with power and much glory (cf. Matt 24:30b and Acts 1:9-11). The great climax of history is almost an anticlimax!

The reference to "when these things begin to come to pass" (Luke 21:28a) is a retrospective reference to the sequence of eschatological events, culminating in the Fall of Jerusalem, which was narrated in Luke 21:8-26. As this sequence of events unfolds, the people of God are to be prepared for the time of their ultimate redemption, which will culminate in the coming of the Son of Man (21:27).

Compositionally, Luke 21:27 omits the puzzling Matthean reference to the sign of the Son of Man in heaven, as well as much of the Matthean apocalyptic terminology. For Luke, *the sign* is the Fall of Jerusalem (Luke 21:7, 25; cf. 21:11). Nevertheless, there is room for some brief parenesis which Luke provides in 21:28. The phraseology of Luke 21:28 is typical of his composition. Luke begins the sentence with a characteristic genitive absolute featuring the use of ἄρχεσθαι ("to begin").[63] Luke has already used ἀνακύπτειν ("to stand erect") at 13:11; Goulder has identified ἐπαίρειν ("to lift up") as characteristic Lukan linguistic terminology.[64] A similar point can be made with reference to ἐγγίζειν ("to draw near") which Collison has identified as a certain linguistic characteristic of Luke.[65] A significant word for Luke in the whole verse is ἀπολύτρωσις ("final deliverance"). As Goulder notes, Luke is quite capable of using words with the λυτ-stem (Luke 1:68; 2:38; 24:22; Acts 7:35); noticeably in these usages the key idea is deliverance.[66] Thus, Luke 21:28 is an exhortation to be faithful in view of a soon anticipated deliverance. This deliverance was to occur upon the return of Jesus.

---

[63]Collison, *Usages in Luke*, 77-78.

[64]Goulder, *Luke: A New Paradigm II*, 803.

[65]Collison, *Usages in Luke*, 46.

[66]Goulder, *Luke: A New Paradigm II*, 714; cf. Robert Maddox, "The Purpose of Luke-Acts," in *Studies of the New Testament and Its World*, ed. John Riches (Edinburgh: T. & T. Clark, 1982) 121-22; 149-50, where Maddox makes a strong case for the position that ἀπολύτρωσις is a functional equivalent for the coming of the kingdom of God. In Lk 2:38 Anna speaks of the redemption of Jerusalem. But for Luke that redemption will come in a way that was unexpected to traditional expectations. First, Jerusalem would be destroyed. Then, a restored Israel, consisting of both Jew and Gentile who have faith in Jesus, would emerge. This community would be the inheritors of the kingdom which would be fully realized at the coming of the Son of Man.

The Final Exhortations to Deliverance (Luke 21:29-36)

1 Thessalonians 5:3	Matthew 24:32-36	Luke 21:29-36

	³²Ἀπὸ δὲ τῆς συκῆς μάθετε τὴν <u>παραβολήν·</u> <u>ὅταν ἤδη</u> ὁ κλάδος αὐτῆς γένηται ἁπαλὸς καὶ τὰ φύλλα ἐκφύῃ, <u>γινώσκετε ὅτι ἐγγὺς</u> <u>τὸ θέρος·</u> ³³<u>οὕτως καὶ ὑμεῖς,</u> <u>ὅταν ἴδητε</u> πάντα <u>ταῦτα</u> <u>γινώσκετε ὅτι</u> <u>ἐγγύς ἐστιν</u> ἐπὶ θύραις. ³⁴<u>ἀμὴν λέγω ὑμῖν ὅτι</u> <u>οὐ μὴ παρέλθῃ ἡ γενεὰ</u> <u>αὕτη ἕως ἂν πάντα</u> ταῦτα <u>γένηται.</u> ³⁵<u>ὁ οὐρανὸς καὶ ἡ γῆ</u> <u>παρελεύσεται,</u> <u>οἱ δὲ λόγοι μου</u> <u>οὐ μὴ παρέλθωσιν.</u> ³⁶Περὶ δὲ τῆς ἡμέρας ἐκείνης καὶ ὥρας οὐ- δεὶς οἶδεν, οὐδὲ οἱ ἄγγελοι τῶν οὐρανῶν οὐδὲ ὁ υἱός, εἰ μὴ ὁ πατήρ μόνος.	²⁹Καὶ εἶπεν <u>παραβολὴν</u> αὐτοῖς· ἴδετε τὴν συκῆν καὶ πάντα τὰ δένδρα· ³⁰<u>ὅταν</u> προβάλωσιν <u>ἤδη,</u> βλέποντες ἀφ' ἑαυτῶν <u>γινώσκετε ὅτι</u> ἤδη <u>ἐγγύς</u> <u>τὸ θέρος</u> ἐστίν ³¹<u>οὕτως καὶ ὑμεῖς,</u> <u>ὅταν ἴδητε ταῦτα</u> γινόμενα, <u>γινώσκετε ὅτι</u> <u>ἐγγύς ἐστιν</u> ἡ βασιλεία τοῦ θεοῦ. ³²<u>ἀμὴν λέγω ὑμῖν ὅτι</u> <u>οὐ μὴ παρέλθῃ ἡ γενεὰ</u> <u>αὕτη ἕως ἂν πάντα</u> <u>γένηται.</u> ³³<u>ὁ οὐρανὸς καὶ ἡ γῆ</u> <u>παρελεύσονται,</u> <u>οἱ δὲ λόγοι μου</u> <u>οὐ μὴ παρελεύσονται.</u> ³⁴Προσέχετε δὲ ἑαυτοῖς μήποτε βαρηθῶσιν ὑμῶν αἱ καρδίαι ἐν κραιπάλῃ καὶ μέθῃ καὶ μερίμναις βιωτικαῖς καὶ ἐπιστῇ ἐφ' ὑμᾶς <u>αἰφνίδιος</u> ἡ ἡμέ- ρα ἐκείνη ³⁵ὡς παγὶς ἐπεισελεύσεται γὰρ ἐπὶ πάντας τοὺς καθημένους ἐπὶ πρόσωπον πάσης τῆς γῆς. ³⁶ἀγρυπνεῖτε δὲ ἐν παντὶ καιρῷ δεόμενοι ἵνα κατισ- χύσητε <u>ἐκφυγεῖν</u> ταῦτα πάντα τὰ μέλλοντα γίνεσθαι καὶ σταθῆναι ἔμπροσθεν τοῦ υἱοῦ τοῦ ἀνθρώπου.
τότε <u>αἰφνίδιος</u> αὐτοῖς ἐφίσταται ὄλεθρος ὥσπερ ἡ ὠδίν . . .		
Καί οὐ μὴ <u>ἐκφύγωσιν</u>	⁴²γρηγορεῖτι οὖν, ὅτι οὐκ οἴδατε ποίᾳ ἡμέρᾳ ὁ κύριος ὑμῶν ἔρχεται.	

We now turn to a set of three parenetical exhortations that Luke used to conclude his version of Jesus' Last Eschatological Discourse.

The first is the parable of the fig tree and all the trees (Lk 21:29-31). Luke 21:28 concluded with an emphatic statement that deliverance was near. The simile of the trees budding in spring is set forth to show that this is a sure sign that the summer harvest is near. So, for Luke, the occurrence of the events described in Luke 21:8-26 constitute just as certain an indicator that deliverance, or its adjunct in apposition, the kingdom of God (21:31), also known as the coming of the Son of Man (21:27, 36), was also assuredly near.

Luke has continued to use as his source the text of Matthew which he follows in order (cf. Matt 24:32-33). In this pericope Luke has made two notable editorial changes to Matthew's text as well as reflecting compositional features in several places in keeping with his literary style.

With respect to the editorial changes, Luke has broadened the Matthean references to a parable about a fig tree into a parable about a fig tree and all the trees. This is a generalizing comment that simply functions to underscore the point that "If spring comes, can summer be far behind?"

Second, since Luke had earlier omitted the Matthean reference to εὐθέως ("immediately," Matt 24:29a ‖ Lk 21:25) in the description of eschatological events, here in 21:31 Luke also omits the modifier of ἐγγύς ("near") ἐπὶ θύραις ("at the doors") which he found in Matt 24:33. In its place Luke has inserted the phrase "the Kingdom of God is near" (Luke 21:31b). For Luke, the Jerusalem leadership had forfeited its role in the kingdom (Lk 14:15-24 and especially 19:11-27). The city would be destroyed (19:41-44; 21:20-26). The king (Lk 19:12, 38) offers the kingdom to others: the restored Israel incorporating the Gentiles (Lk 12:32; 22:28-30; Acts 1:6-9; 13:47-48; 28:23-30). Its full realization (ἀπολύτρωσις = 21:28) will not come until the appearance of the Son of Man (21:27, 36). Thus, for Luke, its complete coming, symbolized by the rapid movement from spring to summer, is near. He does not have to undergird the point with greater specificity.

The only other noteworthy changes in the first exhortation Luke has made to Matthew's text can be accounted for as characteristics of Lukan composition. Thus, in 21:29, Luke opens the pericope with his usage of the construction εἶπεν + δέ/καί + παραβολή ("and he spoke a parable"). Luke has used this construction five times in his Gospel (Lk 6:39; 12:16; 15:3; 18:9; 21:29). This has been identified as characteristic of Luke's compositional method when using a source.[67] Finally the occurrence of βλέποντες ἀπ' ἑαυτῶν ("seeing for yourselves") reinforces the claim of the meaning of the appearance of the trees in leaf (Lk 21:30).[68] Summer is near! For those who understand that the events described in 21:8-26 are leading to an eschatological climax a simple reference to appearance of the leaves as a sign of summer is all that is needed.[69]

---

[67]Collison, "Usages in Luke," 223.

[68]Fitzmyer, *Luke (X–XXIV)*, 1353.

[69]Throughout the Gospel, Luke has placed considerable emphasis on "seeing" as a

The second exhortation to vigilance in Luke 21:32-33 is closely connected with the immediately preceding parable. Here the reader is left in no doubt that Luke considers that the series of eschatological events, which were carefully described, has brought the world to the point of the coming of the kingdom of God. The end will bring ultimate deliverance. Luke states flatly that the coming of this deliverance will take place within a generation.[70]

Compositionally, Luke has utilized Matthew 24:34-35 very closely.[71] But Luke will not use Matthew 24:36. That verse is an equivocal statement about the end. It is Luke's purpose to be unequivocal.

The third and final exhortation to vigilance is found in Luke 21:34-36. The exhortation operates within the perimeters of the usual advice of early Christian exhortations given in an eschatological context. If one is not heedful to God's word and falls into moral laxness the final day comes suddenly and one will receive judgment instead of deliverance; only the faithful will be vindicated at the coming of the Son of Man.

As is indicated by our display, it seems clear that, aside from perhaps a very faint echo of Matt 24:42, Luke has not utilized Matthew as a source for the composition of Luke 21:34-36. Has Luke used another source at this point, or is this almost entirely Lukan composition?

The results of our earlier analysis in chapter 2 can now be brought back into the discussion. In that previous analysis, we showed that Paul utilized a collection of eschatological parenesis attributed to Jesus, the content of which reflected the terminology of Old Testament prophetic texts (LXX), especially that of Isaiah. Here, we intend to show that Luke also had knowledge of, and used this same collection, in the composition of Luke 21:34-36. Earlier we referred to this collection of Jesus tradition utilized by Paul as the *Sudden Calamity of the*

---

way of perceiving the ultimate significance of the Jesus-Event (Lk 8:18; 10:23; 11:33 cf. 21:8).

[70]We take the position that Luke understands this to mean "within the lifetime of the original readers of his composition." This is consistent with the finding of A. J. Mattill, Jr., *Luke and the Last Things: A Perspective for the Understanding of Lukan Thought* (Dillsboro NC: Western North Carolina Press, 1979) 96-103, who has arrived at similar conclusions based on a detailed study of the use of ἡ γενεά in Luke-Acts and the Synoptic tradition; cf. also Maddox, *Purpose of Luke-Acts.* 111-15. Fitzmyer, *Luke (X–XXIV)*, 1353, opts for "the generation of the end sign." From Luke's perspective that was the era in which he wrote (cf. Lk 9:27).

[71]The omission of ταῦτα (Matt 24:34 ‖ Lk 21:32) seems to be only a stylistic preference of Luke. But, in copying Matthew very closely, Luke has incorporated an important Matthean linguistic characteristic, λέγω ὑμίν + οὐ μὴ + subjunctive verb + ἕως + subjunctive verb into his composition (Matt 5:26; 10:23; 16:28; 23:29; 24:34; 26:29) #204 on p. 127. Cf. Tevis, *Analysis of Words and Phrases.* This is strong evidence for Luke's dependence upon Matthew.

End. Now we turn to discuss how that material was incorporated into Luke 21:34-36.

The pericope opens with προσέχετε δὲ ἑαυτοῖς ("take heed") which is Lukan phraseology.[72] This call to "take heed" is supplemented by a warning that hearts not be weighed down with dissipation and earthly cares. The language about hearts being weighed down is probably Lukan composition.[73] Likewise, the reference to the worldly cares.[74] However, the use of κραιπάλη ("intoxication") and μέθη ("drunkenness") to describe the dissipations has strong echoes of Isaiah 24:20 and thus most likely comes from the source tradition on the *Sudden Calamity of the End.*[75] Furthermore, the warning not to let that day sneak up suddenly as a snare likewise comes from the tradition which is heavily dependent upon the wording of Isaiah 24:17-18.[76] Thus, Luke 21:34b (commencing with ἐν κραιπάλῃ) constitutes Luke's use of source tradition. The thought unit commenced in Luke 21:34b is completed in 21:35. Luke continues to make his call for readiness of the coming of the Son of Man utilizing this same source tradition on the *Sudden Calamity of the End.* Here it is emphasized that the Day of the Lord will come upon the whole population of the earth. The stress is on its universal scope. This tradition again is heavily dependent upon the text of Isaiah, especially 24:1.[77]

In 21:36a, the call to vigilance is extended with the exhortation both to ἀγρυπνεῖτε ("to watch") in every season and δεῖσθαι ("to pray"). Again, as at the beginning of Luke 21:34, this is probably Lukan composition. We note δεῖσθαι is found fifteen times in Luke-Acts and surely should be considered to be a characteristic usage of the author of Luke.[78] On the other hand, ἀγρυπ-

---

[72]This phraseology occurs five times in Luke-Acts while being totally absent in Matthew and Mark (Lk 12:1; 17:3; 21:34; Acts 5:35; 20:28).

[73]Luke has used βαρεῖσθαι earlier at 9:32.

[74]Cf. μεριμνῶν . . . καί ἡδονῶν τοῦ βίου in Lk 8:14 as noted by Goulder, *Luke: A New Paradigm II,* 717.

[75]It should be remembered that ὁ μεθύων καὶ κραιπαλῶν is found in Is 24:20, which we identified in chap. 2, above, as the key verse in the catena of texts of the source *On the Sudden Calamity of the End.*

[76]Note again that the verbal from of μέθη echoes Isa 24:20 in 1 Thess 5:7; but there is no reference there to κραιπάλη. Consequently, we have concluded that Luke has not used Paul as his source for this material but that Luke and Paul (viz., 1 Thess 5:3) are dependent on a tradition about events on the end that draws its terminology heavily from Isa 24:1-20.

[77]Note esp. in Isa 24:1, οἰκουμένην (cf. Lk 21:26); τὸ πρόσωπον αὐτῆς and τοὺς ἐνοικοῦντας ἐν αὐτῇ. The reference to the earth, dwellers upon it, or universal habitation is a dominant theme in Isa 24:1-20 (cf. 24:1, 3, 4, 5, 6, 1, 13, 14, 16, 17, 18, 19, 20).

[78]Cf. Collison, "Usages in Luke," 44.

νεῖν ("to watch") is not a Lukan linguistic characteristic. On Markan priority, one could claim that it came from Mark 13:33. But on the Two Gospel Hypothesis, the call to watch ἐν παντὶ καιρῷ ("in every season") probably is Lukan composition based on a reminiscence of Matthew 24:42.[79]

Finally, in Luke 21:36b, Luke reverts again to using the source on the *Sudden Calamity of the End* as the basis for the final exhortation that the hearers may be strong enough to escape the future trials and to stand before the Son of Man. It is noticeable that, again, this passage is heavily dependent upon Isaiah 24:17-20. In these verses we find references to φεύγειν ("to flee"), ἀνιστάναι ("to stand up"), κατισχύειν ("to prevail") in connection with a description of the dissolution of the cosmos on the Day of the Lord. Terminology from this description was incorporated into the source on the *Sudden Calamity of the End* which was echoed by Paul in 1 Thessalonians 5:3.[80] Similarly, Luke used the source to describe the situation at the coming of the Son of Man. Thus we have shown that Luke 21:34b-35, and 36b is an appropriation of the source on the *Sudden Calamity of the End*. The rest of Luke 21:34-36 is redaction.

Having completed his use of the source on the *Sudden Calamity of the End*, Luke brings to an end his version of the Last Eschatological Discourse. As we argued in this chapter, the Final Discourse in 21:8-36 is contained within a massive inclusio in 19:47–21:37 where Jesus gave teaching to the crowds on the temple premises about the fate of Jerusalem and its leadership. After the completion of the inclusio in Luke 21:37-38, Luke continues the narrative with a description of the final events before the Passion (Luke 22:1-71).

Summary and Conclusion

Our analysis has revealed that a central feature of Luke's version of Jesus' Last Eschatological Discourse is a concern to highlight the fate of Jerusalem. At the very center of the discourse (21:20-26) six graphic verses portray its siege and desolation. The destruction of Jerusalem ushers in the "time of the Gentiles"—that final troubled period before the full redemption of God's people is realized. Twice, in his narrative account (12:35-48 and 17:20-37), Luke has used the Matthean version of the Eschatological Discourse as a source for teaching about certain aspects of readiness for the coming of the Son of Man. Then, in Luke 21:5-36, Luke connects the Fall of Jerusalem and its temple to a similar context.

---

[79]Also the phraseology ἐν καιρῷ appears in Matt 24:45 in a context that stresses the call to vigilance.

[80]Particularly noticeable is the use of ἐκφεύγειν.

The fate of Jerusalem was anticipated by Jesus the prophet as he approached the outskirts of the holy city in 19:41-44. After Jesus entered the city, Luke created a major inclusio between 19:47 [20:1] and 21:37, where the whole of the narrative action took place. Jesus stood on the temple premises giving teaching that centers both on the inadequacy of the leadership and the pending destruction of Jerusalem. This is congruent with a wider theme of Luke that the old city of Jerusalem has forfeited its place as the center of the life of the people of God and is to be replaced by a restored Israel which would incorporate the Gentiles in a more inclusive community.[81]

The major inclusio of Jesus' teaching in the temple falls into two major sections: (1) a series of dialogues with the Jerusalem leadership culminating in the announcement that the very place where he stood would one day stand in ruins (20:1–21:6); (2) and a response to a call for a sign when this would take place, which features Jesus giving a speech that delivers the specific answer (21:8-36).

In framing Jesus' answer, Luke uses selected units of Matthew 24:4-36 that were not used in the earlier eschatological units of 12:35-48 and 17:20-37 as the major source for the account.[82] Only in Luke 21:34-36 do we have evidence that Luke used another source, apart from Matthew. In our view this source was known to Paul. We have labelled it the *Sudden Calamity of the End.*

Luke's presentation of Jesus' answer to the direct question about the sign of the end of the temple entailed some significant editorial changes in the main source of Matthew 24. A central focus of Matthew was to contrast the signs of the prophets announcing the coming of the Messiah with the universal sign of the coming of the Son of Man in his parousia. In Luke, the work of the false teachers on the time of the end was relegated to one verse (21:9)—part of the first stage of a series of eschatological events which led up to the Fall of Jerusalem which, in turn, functions as the imminent harbinger of final redemption. Matthew's sign of the coming of the Son of Man (24:30) was omitted by Luke. Possibly the reference to a sign was echoed in the account of the destruction of Jerusalem (Lk 21:25).

Thus we are brought back to the central focus of Luke's concern in giving this version of the Discourse. That focus centers on the end of Jerusalem. Jesus had been asked to give a sign of the destruction of the temple (Lk 21:6-7). He answers that a series of eschatological events will take place in stages culminat-

---

[81]A number of the observations of J. Jervell, *Luke and the People of God: A New Look at Luke-Acts* (Minneapolis: Augsburg Press, 1972) 41-74, are germane at this point.

[82]As we have noted, Luke also utilized a small amount of material from Matthew's Mission Discourse (Matt 10:17-18; 21-22) that he had not used in his narrative account elsewhere. Thus by the time Luke had finished composing Lk 21:8-36, he has used somewhere in his narrative almost all of the Matthean Mission and Eschatological Discourses.

ing in certain signs which have their origin in heaven (21:8-11). Before this matter is developed, a brief interlude on believers being sustained in persecution intervenes as a kind of parenthesis (21:12-19). Then, in no uncertain manner, Jesus answers the question that precipitated the discourse in 21:7: the sign of the fulfillment of this prophecy will be the desolation of Jerusalem. The instrument of this destruction is the Gentiles (20:20-26), although the reality is that this terrible event was an expression of the wrath of God. With the destruction of the city the series of eschatological events precipitated by Jesus' ministry will have come to a climactic point. Following the end of Jerusalem, and the inauguration of the time of the Gentiles, Luke's readers should be prepared to exercise diligence in their preparation for the coming of the Son of Man (21:27-36).

With the fulfillment of these prophecies on the fall of Jerusalem, to Luke's readers, Jesus is shown to be the prophet *par excellence*. His work finally brings to completion the words of the ancient prophets in Israel. On this basis, the reader can be assured that in the events that have come to pass in the founding and establishment of the early Christian community, and with the pending arrival of the new kingdom, the will and purposes of God were being fully realized. It is the essence of the Lukan work of apologetic historiography to lead the reader to this insight.

6.
The Markan Version
of the Last Eschatological Discourse

We have now reached the stage in our discussion where we have accounted for the appearance of the Last Eschatological Discourse of Jesus in two Gospels—Matthew and Luke. On the Two Gospel Hypothesis Mark 13 was composed through use of two similar sources in Matthew 24:1–25:46 and Luke 21:5-36. It is the purpose of this chapter to give a plausible argument as to why, and for what purpose, with two accounts of the Eschatological Discourse in existence, Mark 13:1-37 would supply a third.

The Genre and Structure of Mark

The Issue of Genre

In his handbook *The New Testament in Its Literary Environment*, David Aune makes a key but contestable comment.

> As the first written Gospel it [Mark] does not exhibit ancient literary qualities as obviously as the other Gospels.[1]

This claim is dubious. On all accounts, the position that Mark was the first written Gospel is open to serious question. In this work we assume another view on the matter. But it is not this point, in and of itself, on which we wish to focus. What we would highlight is the conclusion that Aune draws from his dubious premise. He revives the well-worn argument for Markan priority based on the undistinguished style of Mark's Greek and gives it a new twist. His view is that, since it is primitive, Mark is rough and lacks a general literary quality typical of a *biographical writing* of that era. But, as the Gospel tradition developed with the composition of both Matthew and Luke, which increasingly gave evidence of an improved literary quality based on a greater awareness and use of the general conventions of ancient biography, these deficiencies in the literary quality of Mark were overcome. Aune calls this the process of "literaturization."[2]

---

[1]Aune, *New Testament in its Literary Enviroment*, 46.

[2]Ibid., 65. One wonders how one can claim authoritatively that the pagans reacted negatively toward Mark? Clearly, the pagans were bothered by discrepancies between all

As we have said, much of this claim is open to question. If Mark were not the first written Gospel the argument would be invalid. Furthermore, an important monograph in the secondary literature has drawn the conclusion that it is questionable to assume that the direction of composition can be tracked on a scale moving from "primitive" to "more literary" based merely on such matters as improving infelicities in grammar and roughness in compositional style.[3] We can add to this list consistency in adhering to the genre of biography.

Nevertheless, from the perspective of the Two Gospel Hypothesis, there is one point in Aune's comment that should be pursued. Since we agree that Matthew and Luke both show considerable evidence of following certain Greco-Roman conventions of ancient biography and historiography, there is no reason why we must assume that Mark's real interest was in the construction of a biography of Jesus per se. The mold for writing a life of Jesus had been made by the time Mark was written. Based on Matthew and Luke, Mark wished to set forth the now familiar biographical account of Jesus in such a way that the account of the unfolding of his suffering redemptive life given in these earlier Gospels could underscore even more, his normative status for Christian readers.[4] Theology rests at the heart of the Markan agenda.

Such a view is consistent with Mark's statement of purpose in 1:1-3. Here the initial words, "The beginning of the Gospel of Jesus Christ, Son of God," functions as a statement of purpose for the first unit of the account in 1:4-15. It is saying that in fulfillment of the promises of the prophets (1:2-3), John the Baptist (1:4-8), and Jesus (1:9-15) appeared announcing the coming of a new era of salvation to Israel. This Jesus-event is the initial stage of the emergence of the gospel (1:14-15). As the Jesus-story unfolds so does the gospel. The story of Jesus and the gospel is now made synonymous.

There is an issue as to whether the construction εὐαγγελίου Ἰησοῦ Χριστοῦ ("of the Gospel of Jesus Christ") in 1:1 should be thought of as the title of the book, in the sense of being a description of it as a literary work, or whether this phrase should be viewed in a dynamic sense describing the total eschatological act of God which burst forth in the ministry and passion of Jesus.[5] In our judgment, the latter position is correct. The punctuation of the current standard edition of the Greek text would be improved if Mark 1:1-3 were taken

---

three gospels. It is questionable whether they regarded Mark as more vulgar than Matthew and John.

[3]E. P. Sanders, *The Tendencies of the Synoptic Tradition*, SNTSMS 9 (London: Cambridge University Press, 1969).

[4]This seems to be the direction, albeit considerably nuanced, followed by P. Shuler, "The Genre of the Gospels and the Two Gospel Hypothesis," in *Jesus, the Gospels, and the Church*, ed. E. P. Sanders (Macon: Mercer University Press, 1987) 73-74; 84-86.

[5]H. Anderson, *The Gospel of Mark*, NCB (Greenwood SC: Attic Press, 1976) 66.

as one sentence. As noted by Guelich, καθὼς γέγραπται ("just as it stands written") in 1:2 does not begin a new thought in New Testament Greek.[6] Therefore, one should read 1:1-3 as a descriptive statement which announces that the initial stages (ἀρχή) of the Jesus-event are about to emerge. It is saying that the eschatological happening, "the gospel concerning Jesus Christ," having its origin in promise in the prophets, now begins a process of unfolding. The action gets underway in 1:4, and continues on to full emergence when the story of Jesus is fully narrated. Thus, it is grammatically clumsy to designate Mark 1:1 as a title. And it is even a greater mistake to designate εὐαγγέλιον ("Gospel") in 1:1 as a peculiar literary genre.[7]

Considerable effort has been expended by scholars to determine why Mark used εὐαγγέλιον in the opening of his literary account the life of Jesus. Matthew and Luke did not choose to call their works "gospel."[8] Such terminology would not be appropriate for a literary work of Hellenistic biography or historiography. Indeed, Luke does not use εὐαγγέλιον at all in his account of Jesus' life;[9] and Matthew focuses the use of εὐαγγέλιον on Jesus' proclamation of the "Gospel of the Kingdom" (4:23; 9:30). Yet, it is not always noticed that Mark, after the initial unit in 1:1-15, limits the references to "gospel" to the period in Jesus' ministry following the announcement that he would die (8:35; 10:29; 13:10; 14:9). There seems to be some coherence here with the structure of the sermons of Peter and Paul as recalled in their earlier sermons in Acts. In all cases focus on the death, burial, and resurrection of Jesus was at the heart of the proclamation of "the Gospel."

---

[6]R. Guelich, "The Gospel Genre," *The Gospel and the Gospels*, ed. P. Stuhlmacher (Grand Rapids: Eerdmans, 1991) 194-95.

[7]There seems to be a general consensus among scholars that the early church did not designate the biographies of Jesus in the New Testament as "Gospel" until at least the second century. Even in the second century they were called by Justin, at least fifteen times, ἀπομνημονεύματα τῶν ἀποστόλων ("reminiscences of the apostles"). Hengel, *Studies in the Gospel of Mark*, 64-84, has made a case for the view: (1) that the titles placed above the early manuscripts to identify them did include the word (εὐαγγέλιον); (2) but these references to "Gospel" referred not to a book but to the dynamic account of the eschatological salvation brought by Jesus Christ.

[8]Otto Betz, "Jesus' Gospel of the Kingdom," *The Gospel and the Gospels*, ed. P. Stuhlmacher (Grand Rapids: Eerdmans, 1991) 66-74.

[9]However, Luke does use εὐαγγελίζεσθαι ten times in his account of Jesus' life. Some are doubtful that for Luke it means much more than "to announce" or "to proclaim" the kingdom. Cf. Fitzmyer, *Luke (I-IX)*, 148; W. Marxsen, *Mark the Evangelist: Studies on the Redaction History of the Gospel*, trans. James Boyce et al., with Roy Harrisville (Nashville: Abingdon Press, 1969) 143-46. On the other hand, Betz, "Jesus' Gospel," 58, understands it to refer to the distinct self-understanding of Jesus as the eschatological ambassador of Isaiah 52:7 and 61:1. In either case, Luke is interpreted as saying that Jesus' proclamation was primarily associated with the coming of the kingdom.

Only now Mark understands the gospel to be not only the kerygma of the death, burial, and resurrection of Jesus, but it has its inception in the fulfillment of the word of the prophet Isaiah starting with the proclamation of John the Baptist, unfolding in Jesus' ministry, and culminating in the death and burial of Jesus and the account of the empty tomb. For Mark, this narration of Jesus' life is "The Gospel."

The Structure of Mark

Among biblical scholars today there is no agreed-upon principle for determining the structure of Mark. Earlier commentators tended to develop structural outlines along geographical lines;[10] and to some extent this tendency has continued.[11] However, the dominant procedure among recent interpreters is to formulate Mark's structure along thematic or Christological lines.[12] Our procedure will fall within the latter perspective. We will argue that the theme of seeing or knowing was critical for the way that Mark organized his account of Jesus' life.

As we have already noted in the previous section, the first unit of the Gospel is 1:1-15. There we are told that John the Baptist and Jesus have undertaken ministries in fulfillment of ancient promises and have announced the arrival of a new era: the Kingdom of God. In 1:16–3:6 Jesus goes forth on his initial mission, teaching, healing, and doing exorcisms (1:16-45). In so doing, he enters into conflict with the local religious authorities (2:1–3:6). Throughout this unit Jesus is meticulous in attempting to please the Palestinian authorities (1:44, 2:19-22), and responds willingly to reasonable demands for evidence and proof of his claims as a teacher.[13] Nevertheless, his mission of announcing the kingdom is met with scorn and rejection from the contemporary establishment. They do not see any connection between his mission and the coming of the kingdom (3:6).

The initial rejection of Jesus is followed by a carefully constructed series of units in 3:7–8:21. Here Jesus is far less interested in furnishing proofs of his authenticity to those outside his immediate circle. Instead, after a brief transition (3:7-12), Jesus chose the twelve (3:13-19); they are inducted into a new esoteric family that is different from the usual household tied together by blood and kin (3:20-35). Jesus teaches this new family in parable and epigrams (4:1-34). Simi-

---

[10]Vincent Taylor, *The Gospel according to St. Mark: The Greek Text with Introduction, Notes, and Indexes* (London: Macmillan, 1966) 107-11.

[11]P. Vielhauer, *Geschichte der urchristlichen Literatur* (Berlin: W. de Gruyter, 1978) 331-32.

[12]As noted by R. Guelich, *Mark 1–8:26*, WBC 34a (Dallas: Word Books, 1989) xxxvi.

[13]Timothy J. Geddert, *Watchwords: Mark 13 in Markan Eschatology*, JSNTSS 26 (Sheffield: JSOT Press, 1989) 41-42.

lar concerns are expressed in 8:14-21. These two units form an inclusio around the whole unit (4:1–8:21) which may be entitled "On Proper Understanding." By demonstrations of power (4:35–6:6), and by teaching that life in the kingdom is eternal food that satisfies (6:7–8:13), the Markan Jesus shows that God's new world comes powerfully but mysteriously to those with "eyes of faith." Yet the disciples (transparencies of some in the house churches in Rome?), who were inducted into the mysteries of the kingdom (4:11-12), remain almost as blind and recalcitrant as the outsiders in Israel (8:14-21). Something more is needed to be revealed through Jesus' life in order for full understanding to emerge.

This leads to the famous unit where the disciples go with Jesus to Jerusalem (8:27–10:45). This unit is framed by the stories of healings of blind men (8:22-26; 10:46-52). These two men, especially the first with his gradual coming to sight, are figures who serve as models of would-be disciples who are called to follow after Jesus and to share his fate.[14] Anyone who would follow Jesus must take on a distinct cruciform identity apart from the wider circle of those outside who lack any insight into the connection between Jesus' death and the kingdom of God.

This distinction between insiders and outsiders becomes very clear upon the arrival of Jesus in Jerusalem (11:1–16:6). First, Jesus clashes bitterly with the temple leadership. This ensues in Jesus' final rejection of them (12:1-12), and their institutional cult (13:1-2). Although it is the temple authorities and their allies who represent the ones who stand fully outside the circle of understanding about the true mission of Jesus, the disciples, in their own way, also need to grow in their faithfulness to Jesus. Upon watching the demise of the fig tree and the judgment upon the temple, the disciples hear (11:14), see (11:20), and remember (11:21).[15] Yet it is questionable, before the cross and empty tomb, that they did fully see and know what was entailed in fully identifying with Jesus.

The deep division between those who see and understand and those who do not continues in the account of the Passion (14:1–16:6). The temple authorities finally discover a way to put Jesus to death (14:1-2, 5). Ultimately, by the hands of the leadership of his own people, Jesus is given over to the Romans to be crucified. In these circles, according to the Markan storyline, there is a total lack of understanding as to the true import of Jesus' life. The testimony that Jesus is the

---

[14]On the other hand, the partial insights of Peter (8:29-33), and that of Peter, James, and John (9:2-8) into Jesus' true identity do not fully change the misperception of Jesus' identity revealed earlier in 8:14-21. This is seen clearly in 10:35-45. Nevertheless, we understand that the account of the blind man coming gradually to sight in 8:22-26 and the story of Bartimaeus (10:46-52) are metaphors for the proposition that understanding about the true impact of Jesus life comes slowly. To be sure, insight is partial and does not yet include the understanding that disciples may have to undergo martyrdom (cf. 10:35-45).

[15]Geddert, *Watchwords*, 129.

Son of the Blessed One which had been set forth so carefully at the outset (1:1, 11), and now comes on the lips of Jesus (14:62), is categorically rejected by the high priest as blasphemy (14:63-64).

But it is different for others. Temporarily, through lack of faithfulness, the disciples abandon Jesus (14:50). Peter, especially, acts despicably; but later he repents with tears (14:72). The story line of the present accepted text ends with the empty tomb. To a reader a half century after the death of Jesus, things turned out differently for the disciples. They came to deeper understanding and insight about the Jesus-event and assumed the leadership of a restored people of God. Mark's Passion account deliberately accents this transition. Precisely, as Jesus dies, the veil of the temple is torn and Jesus is confessed (by a Gentile) as a (crucified) son of God (15:37-38). The promise of a new era announced as coming to fruition in 1:1-15 now comes into effect. To those who have eyes to see the tearing of the veil marked the beginning of the end of the old temple. Simultaneously, this time also marks the transition to a rule of God, through the vice-regency of Jesus who is now acknowledged by a growing number of Jews and Gentiles as the heavenly king. He is inaugurated into his kingship as Son of God through his death. But this kingship can only be perceived now through the eyes of faith. It is God's secret power whereby his rule can be perceived in a time of persecution and demoralization. This is the understanding to which Mark wished to bring his readers.

Yet, one point has not been addressed. Granted that the fulfillment of ancient promises has been realized and with Jesus a new era has arrived, an issue still remains as to what should be the disposition and conduct of those who await the culmination of these eschatological events with the return of Jesus at the end of history. In light of the momentous events taking place after the time of the earthly Jesus, a question remains whether the Jesus story gives any guidance as to how the community should view reality and conduct itself in the interim before the end. Mark, following earlier precedents in Matthew and Luke, addresses this situation through the medium of the final Eschatological Discourse of Jesus (13:5-37). Jesus sits on the Mount of Olives and carefully enumerates what should be the attitude and conduct of his followers as they prepare for the end. Before we proceed in more detail on this point, we will now turn to discuss the setting of Mark 13 within the Gospel.

The Scope and Setting of Mark 13 within the Gospel

It is crucial for the understanding of Jesus' Discourse in Mark 13 to study carefully its compositional setting within the perimeters of the whole literary work. The Discourse is constituted by verses 5-37. But the setting of the immediately preceding and following units are very important for determining its function in the second Gospel.

In 12:35-37a, Mark brings to an end a unit on controversies between Jesus and the Jewish leadership in Jerusalem (12:13-37). In turn, that unit has followed the parable of the Wicked Tenants of the Vineyard which is clearly directed against the Jeruasalem leadership (12:1-12). This hostility toward the Jerusalem leadership is also a central theme in 12:13-37a. On the Two Gospel Hypothesis, for this entire unit, Mark followed Matthew carefully as a major source with only some minor conflation drawn from the parallels in Luke. It is noticeable that in Mark 12:35-37a the scribes are invoked. This is prepartory for a move to follow Luke, who issues a warning against the scribes, as the major source for the next two pericopes (Luke 20:45–21:4 ‖ Mark 12:37b-44).

In the first of these pericopes, Mark 12:37b-40, Mark delivers a stinging verdict against the scribes. This fits well with the overall theme of the chapter: the failure of the Jerusalem leadership to meet God's demands. Mark, it would seem, has now moved to Luke as his major source. Mark did this for two reasons: (1) the use of certain Lukan terminology about the persecution of widows provided Mark with a good link to what he wished to say about a widow in the 'next unit;' (2) and since Mark tends to omit from Matthew lengthy blocks of Jesus' teaching, he omits the Matthean polemic against the Pharisees (Matt 23:1-39) and uses in its place, Luke 12:37-40, a polemic aginst the scribes. The scribes are pictured as greedy men who practice religion primarily for self-aggrandizement and personal gain (Mk 12:37b-40). They consume the homes of widows (Lk 20:47 ‖ Mk 12:40). These descriptions are congruent with a major Markan compositional theme: a call to remain steadfast in the midst of perfidity.

Following his Lukan source (Lk 21:1-4), Mark proceeds to relate the story of one of these poor widows (12:41-44). In a sense this woman is a tragic victim. She has placed her complete confidence in the temple system and subsequently gave her few meager possessions over to the treasury as a gift to God. But, in reality, her gift is appropriated by the caretakers of this failed system for their personal benefits.[16]

In utilizing freely such gifts the contemptible character of the scribes (transparencies of the temple leadership) was illustrated. However, surely a major point is that here is one, who in the offering of her whole life (12:44), anticipates the martyrdom of Jesus that also takes place in a context of terrible treachery. Our observation of this emphasis on the importance of the sacrificial gift of the widow will be critical for our understanding of the function of Mark 13.

---

[16]A. G. Wright, "The Widow's Mites: Praise or Lament?—A Matter of Context" *Catholic Biblical Quarterly* 44 (1982): 262.

It is also significant, that immediately following this unit, Mark picks up the sequence of both the Matthean (24:1-3) and Lukan sources (21:5-7) by having Jesus sit on the Mount of Olives looking over the valley toward the temple Mount and pronounce doom directly on this edifice (13:3). The faith embodied in the sacrifice of Jesus, foreshadowed by the example of the widow, is what will replace the failed institution of the temple. Indeed, Mark highlights this pronouncement with the phraseology κατέναντι τοῦ ἱεροῦ ("opposite the temple") to emphasize that Jesus stood separate and apart from this institution (13:3).[17]

Therefore, the total unit of Mark 12:38–13:3, with its editorially created contrast between a woman practicing piety and scribes acting deceitfully culminates in an announcement of the end of the Temple.[18] The pericopes in this unit, in some way, are connected with the theme of the end of the old order culminating with the destruction of the temple. This is a perfect setting for Mark to have the disciples ask for a sign when this will take place and in turn to have Jesus initiate a response (13:3b-5).

Furthermore, in this connection, the appearance in 13:5 of βλέπετε ("take heed") is quite significant. It appeared first in a sequence of imperative warnings to "take heed" or "beware" in 12:38 and will occur in 13:5, 9, 13, 33.[19] As the disciples are invited by Jesus to ponder the significance of these things, so the reader of Mark is called upon to give due consideration to this discussion about the end of the Jerusalem leadership and what is to follow.

The literary linkage between an account of a pious woman juxtaposed with men practicing deceit is also seen in the unit that immediately follows the Last Discourse of Jesus (Mark 14:1-11). In this unit the conspiracy against Jesus is launched. But as the reader waits for the inevitable events of the Passion to unfold, the scene shifts to Bethany where, in the house of Simon the leper, Jesus is anointed (for kingship in his death?) with very expensive ointment by a woman. It is significant that Mark (as does Matthew) interprets this action as an anticipation of Jesus' burial (14:8). Events are about to take such a precipitous course that this occasion is the most appropriate time for Jesus' body to be anointed. Thus the focus of the unit is to connect directly the action of this woman with the impending death of Jesus. Indeed both the actions of the woman

---

[17]The full construction καί + a participle of a verb for "sitting" + κατέναντι has been identified by David Peabody, *Mark as Composer*, NGS 1 (Macon GA: Mercer University Press, 1987) 110, as a redactional feature of the text of Mark. Cf. 12:41. The phraseology κατέναντι τοῦ ἱεροῦ does not appear in Matthew and Luke.

[18]Geddert, *Watchwords*, 134.

[19]Peabody, *Mark as Composer*, 75, has a list of usages in Mark of βλέπετε as an imperative to mean "watch" or "beware."

and Judas the betrayer anticipate the Passion events which are narrated immediately thereafter.

Viewed retrospectively, the narrative accounts of the woman who anointed Jesus and her counterpart in 12:41-44 have great significance for the interpretation of Mark 13. They form a kind of Markan intercalation. Both of the women exemplify the truth that faithfulness to the gospel often is most clearly shown in the midst of adversity and great unfaithfulness. Theirs are stories of women who lived faithfully in a society where others (notably the scribes and Judas) acted treacherously. In one instance we are told that wherever the gospel is preached throughout the world the story of one of these women will be told (14:9). This proclamation to the world (nations) is precisely the activity that Mark places at the centerpiece of activities that Jesus announces will take place in the eschatological era before the end (13:10). In a time characterized by great treachery the disciples, as they carry out the proclamation of the gospel, are not to fall asleep but are to remain faithful to the end (13:9-13, 33-37). To see this is to see the kingdom.

This theme underscores the whole context of Jesus' Last Discourse. With respect to the future, ultimately the Son of Man will come (13:24-27). But before that, even before the first generation has run its course, there will appear false messiahs (13:5-6, 21-23); wars, earthquakes, and famines (13:7-8); persecution of believers as they go about mission (13:9-13); and a terrible act of religious profanation in Judea (13:14-20). In response to these horrors, the disciples are to maintain their loyalty and vigilance to the way of the cross; and in spite of these massive distractions, and their constant lure to give up following Jesus and do something else, the disciples must persist until the end (cf. 13:33-37).

Thus, our analysis of the scope and setting of Mark 13 has yielded important results. Mark has carefully intercalated his version of Jesus' Last Discourse with two accounts of women who acted faithfully in a situation where great unfaithfulness was taking place. Between these two models of ideal discipleship exhibited under stressful conditions, Mark situates his version of Jesus' Last Discourse. It functions as a call to the believing community to exercise patient and faithful discipleship, both in the first generation of horrors, and later, before the end.

The Sources and Structure of Mark 13

Sources

In keeping with the Two Gospel hypothesis, Mark has utilized two major sources in the composition of his version of Jesus' Discourse in 13:5-37. They are the two earlier Eschatological Discourses of Matthew (24:4–25:46) and Luke (21:8-36). In addition, our analysis will indicate that Mark, for the composition of 13:9-13, used a major source found in Matthew 10:17-22, and for the composition of 13:33-37, Mark also echoes material found in Luke 12:35-44.

Procedurally, Mark follows several important compositional principles with reference to the selection and use of these source traditions. First, observation of Mark's compositional procedure throughout the Second Gospel indicates that the writer tends to abbreviate units of discourse which he finds in his sources. In fact, the only other Markan unit of discourse of any substantial length, with the possible exception of 9:30-50, is found in 4:1-34. Mark carries out this abbreviation by frequent omissions from his sources. Thus, it is no surprise to find omitted in Mark 13, nearly all of Matthew 24:37–25:46, and some of Luke 21.

Second, specifically Mark 13 follows closely the wording of Matthew 24:1-36; indeed, all of Luke 21:8-36, which was not found in the parallel pericopes in Matthew, was omitted (Lk 21:12a, 16b, 18, 21b-22, 23b-24, 25b-26a, 28). This indicates that Mark not only followed closely the wording of Matthew 24:1-36 but, as much as possible, was desirous of maintaining the common text of Matthew and Luke.

Third, in line with this, only a small amount of material found in Matthew 24, that had no parallels in Luke 21, was also omitted by Mark (Matt 24:10-12, 26-28, 30a). These omissions may not merely be just for the sake of lack of concurrent testimony or for brevity; this material may not have been viewed by Mark as being fully compatible with his intended compositional purposes.

What this indicates is that Mark had deep respect for the Matthean version of the common account of the Discourse shared by both Matthew and Luke.[20] In line with this, Mark included several segments of Matthean material which do not occur in Luke (Mk 13:19b-23 || Matthew 24:21b-25; Mk 13:27 || Matt 24:31; Mk 13:32 || Matt 24:36). As far as the actual composition is concerned, Mark followed the identical order of the joint pericopes which he found in the two major sources (Matt 24:1-36; Lk 21:5-36) as the basis for the composition of his version of Jesus' Last Discourse.[21] As noted, generally, Mark preferred to use the

---

[20]Farmer, *Jesus and the Gospel*, 132-34.

[21]C. S. Mann, *Mark: A New Translation with Introduction and Commentary*, AB 27 (Garden City NY: Doubleday, 1986) 508. Mann states that the composition of Matthew 24:1-36 and Luke 21:5-36 poses major problems for the Two Source Theory. As has often been noted, Matt 24:1-7 and 30-35 has significant minor agreements against the text of Mark (both positive and negative) with Lk 21:5-10 and 29-33. On the Two Source Theory these minor agreements can be explained as Mark-Q overlaps. Mark has simply followed Q. But if one goes that route, as Mann notes, why does Mark omit from Q the exact pericopes that Luke does not have in parallel with Matt 24, but places in two separate segments in his Travel Narrative: the "pure Q material" of Matt 24:26-28 || Lk 17:23-24, 37b; Matt 24:37-41 || Lk 17:26-27, 34-35; Matt 24:43-51 || Lk 12:39-46? On the one hand, there are Markan overlaps with Q when Matthew 24 and Luke 21 parallel one another; but, on the other hand, as soon as the text of Luke 21 diverges from Matthew 24

wording of the text of Matthew; but by the use of conflation and other similar literary techniques, Mark incorporated certain terminology from Luke into his version of the Discourse. He depends upon the authority of the two sources; but they are blended into an entirely different literary work that has its own integrity independent of Matthew and Luke. This will be demonstrated in the compositional discussion below.

Structural Features

Structurally, after the initial preface on the saying about the end of the temple, the question of the disciples, and the answer of Jesus (13:1-5), Jesus' speech divides into four major units (13:5b-23, 24-27, 28-31, 32-37).

The initial unit (13:5b-23) begins with a statement to watch out for deceivers (13:5b-6) and ends with a similar refrain in 13:21-23. Strategically placed throughout the unit are a series of calls to pay heed and give attention; they are not only to beware of the deceivers (13:6), but to watch out for wars and famines (13:7-8), persecutions (13:9-13), and the Horrible Desecration (13:14-20). Indeed, an inclusio, βλέπετε μή τις ὑμᾶς πλανήσῃ ("be aware lest anyone deceive you") in 13:5 and ὑμεῖς δὲ βλέπετε ("you must be aware") in 13:23, encompasses the warnings.

Yet, it is important to notice that these events are to be distinguished clearly from those things that take place at the end of the age. This is so because of the important transitional phrase ἀλλὰ ἐν ἐκείναις ταῖς ἡμέραις μετὰ τὴν θλῖψιν ἐκείνην ("but in those days after that distress") in 13:24a. This phraseology leads into a coherent picture of events that will take place at the coming of the Son of Man (13:24-27). For the author of Mark this is in the future.

The third major unit is 13:28-31. This unit constitutes a retrospective review of the course of the eschatological events narrated in 13:5-23. The course of these eschatological events is evoked by the image of a fig tree budding in the spring and quickly moving to the time of summer harvest.[22]

Finally, in the last unit, 13:32-37, there is set forth the general exhortation to watch expectantly for the coming of the Lord. This unit concludes in 13:37 with the expansive statement ὃ δὲ ὑμῖν λέγω πᾶσιν λέγω ("but what I say to you I say to all"). This is the end to another major inclusio which had its beginning in 13:4 when, after the saying against the temple, the four disciples

---

(Lk 12 and 17) the overlaps in Mark cease. Given the presupposition of the Two Source Theory, that Mark could not have known the compositional procedure of Matthew and Luke, is this a mere coincidence? Or is the theory unable to account for the literary facts?

[22]McNicol, "The Lesson of the Fig Tree in Mark 13:28-32," 201.

responded with εἶπον ἡμῖν ("say to us . . . "). What is said immediately to the four disciples is also a word for the whole church. Thus, the whole Discourse in Mark 13:5-37 may be viewed in outline form.

A. The Coming Crisis and Persecution of Believers
   1. The Beginning of the Time of Horrors (13:5-8)
   2. Persecution in Mission (13:9-13)
   3. The Coming of the Horrible Desecration (13:14-20)
   4. A Repeated Warning on the Coming Horrors (13:21-23)
B. The Coming of the Son of Man (13:24-27)
A'. The Resolution of the Crisis of This Generation Is Sure (13:28-31)
B'. A Call for Faithfulness in Watching for the Coming of the Lord (13:32-37)

Mark 13:1-4
The Destruction of the Temple and Call for an Explanation: Mark's Setting for the Eschatological Discourse

Context

Before we give an analysis of the discourse itself we must say something more about Mark 13:1-4. In Mark 12:41-44, following Luke 21:1-4, Mark has given the account of the woman who, through her gift to the temple treasury, showed great faithfulness amidst the treachery and perfidity of the temple leaders. For the next unit, Mark has Jesus give a word of doom against the temple itself (13:2). This word against the temple invokes an immediate response from an intimate group of four disciples (13:3). They ask when the destruction of the temple will take place (13:4a); and what will be the sign or indicator (σημεῖον) when all of these things are about to be fulfilled? (13:4b). These questions provide the context for Jesus' response that will come in 13:5-37.

An immediate issue is raised with respect to the connection between the immediate Markan setting in 13:1-4 and the Discourse itself in 13:5-37. Specifically, in the setting, Jesus has stated that the temple will be destroyed and the disciples have asked when that will be? But, in the Discourse itself, there is no direct reference to the temple or the destruction of Jerusalem. Is the Discourse a nonresponse to the question?

As we have noted in the previous chapters, both Matthew and Luke deal with the end of the temple in their own particular ways. Matthew presumes that the end of the temple will be coterminous with the end of the age. Luke, in 21:20-26, subsumes the end of the temple under the account of the destruction of Jerusalem in 70 CE. But, our analysis will indicate that, in Mark, the fulfillment of the prediction of the destruction of the temple will be even more subtly subsumed within the account of the emergence of the Horrible Desecration and the consequences which flow in its wake. In other words, Mark's interest will be not in narrating the actual destruction of the Temple (it is presumed that the reader knows that), but in the eschatological implications of that event.

Synopsis

Matthew 24:1-3	Mark 13:1-4	Luke 21:5-7

¹Καὶ ἐξελθὼν ὁ Ἰησοῦς
ἀπὸ <u>τοῦ ἱεροῦ</u>
ἐπορεύετο, καὶ προσῆλθον
οἱ μαθηταὶ <u>αὐτοῦ</u>.

ἐπιδεῖξαι αὐτῷ τὰς
<u>οἰκοδομὰς</u> τοῦ ἱεροῦ.

²<u>ὁ</u> δὲ ἀποκριθεὶς
<u>εἶπεν</u> <u>αὐτοῖς</u>, Οὐ
<u>βλέπετε</u> <u>ταῦτα</u> πάντα;

ἀμὴν λέγω ὑμῖν,
<u>οὐ μὴ ἀφεθῇ ὧδε</u>
<u>λίθος ἐπὶ λίθον</u>
<u>ὃς οὐ καταλυθήσεται</u>.
³<u>Καθημένου</u> δὲ <u>αὐτοῦ</u>
ἐπὶ <u>τοῦ Ὄρους</u>
<u>τῶν Ελαιῶν</u>

προσῆλθον αὐτῷ
οἱ μαθηταὶ <u>κατ' ἰδίαν</u>

<u>λέγοντες</u>,

Εἰπε <u>ἡμῖν</u> πότε ταῦτα
<u>ἔσται</u> <u>καὶ τί τὸ σημεῖον</u>
τῆς σῆς παρουσίας καὶ
<u>συντελείας</u> τοῦ αἰῶνος;

¹<u>Καὶ</u> <u>ἐκπορευομένου</u>
αὐτοῦ ἐκ <u>τοῦ ἱεροῦ</u>
<u>λέγει</u> αὐτῷ <u>εἷς</u>
<u>τῶν μαθητῶν</u> <u>αὐτοῦ</u>,
Διδάσκαλε, ἴδε

ποταποὶ <u>λίθοι</u> καὶ
ποταπαὶ <u>οἰκοδομαί</u>.
²καὶ <u>ὁ</u> Ἰησοῦς
<u>εἶπεν</u> <u>αὐτῷ</u>,
Βλέπεις ταύτας
τὰς μεγάλας οἰκοδομάς;

<u>οὐ μὴ ἀφεθῇ ὧδε</u>
<u>λίθος ἐπὶ λίθον</u>
<u>ὃς οὐ</u> μὴ <u>καταλυθῇ</u>.
³<u>Καὶ</u> <u>καθημένου</u> <u>αὐτοῦ</u>
εἰς <u>τὸ Ὄρος</u> <u>τῶν Ελαιῶν</u>
κατέναντι τοῦ ἱεροῦ
<u>ἐπηρώτα</u> <u>αὐτὸν</u>

<u>κατ' ἰδίαν</u>
Πέτρος καὶ Ἰάκωβος καὶ
Ἰωάννης καὶ Ἀνδρέας,

⁴<u>Εἰπὸν</u> <u>ἡμῖν</u> πότε
<u>ταῦτα ἔσται</u> <u>καὶ τί τὸ</u>
<u>σημεῖον</u> <u>ὅταν μέλλη</u>
<u>ταῦτα</u> <u>συντελεῖσθαι</u> πάντα;

⁵<u>Καὶ</u>

τινων <u>λεγόντων</u>

περὶ <u>τοῦ ἱεροῦ</u>
ὅτι <u>λίθοις</u> καλοῖς καὶ
ἀναθήμασιν κεκόσμηται

<u>εἶπεν</u>,
⁶<u>Ταῦτα</u> ἃ <u>θεωρεῖτε</u>,

ἐλεύσονται ἡμέραι
ἐν αἷς
<u>οὐκ ἀφεθήσεται</u>
<u>λίθος ἐπὶ λίθῳ</u>
<u>ὃς οὐ καταλυθήσεται</u>.

⁷<u>Ἐπηρώτησαν</u> δὲ <u>αὐτὸν</u>

<u>λέγοντες</u>,
Διδάσκαλε,
πότε οὖν <u>ταῦτα ἔσται</u>
<u>καὶ τί τὸ σημεῖον</u>
<u>ὅταν μέλλη ταῦτα</u>
γίνεσθαι;

Analysis

Procedurally, we will now turn to an analysis of Mark 13:1-4. The unit in 13:1-2 takes the form of a chreia consisting of both an observation made by a disciple and the response of the teacher. This is followed by a further response from several of Jesus' disciples which functions to provide the immediate setting for the Discourse.

Commencing in 11:27, after Jesus had come into Jerusalem, he walked around in the temple area engaging the religious leadership in debate. Now, in 13:1, after the debate is over, he leaves the temple area. Earlier, in both 10:17 and 10:46 Mark uses the same genitive absolute construction καὶ ἐκπορευο- μένοι αὐτοῦ ("while he was going away") as here in 13:1 to introduce a pericope. This would indicate that the use of this phraseology in the genitive absolute construction is Markan composition.

Practically all of the rest of this transitional verse in 13:1 reflects characteristic usage of recurrent Markan phraseology. Thus, Mark's use of the singular εἷς τῶν μαθητῶν ("one of the disciples") is striking since, both Matthew (24:1) and Luke (21:5), have more than one disciple formulating the observation about the splendor of the temple. However, the formulation of εἷς plus the partitive genitive is recurrent Markan terminology.[23] Thus, this construction represents Mark's compositional style. The address of Jesus as teacher may reflect Mark's dependence on Luke 21:7; but it is also characteristic of Mark.[24] Similarly, the use of ἴδε ("see"), used to introduce an independent clause, is characteristic of Mark's composition.[25] Also in this verse, Mark uses ποταποὶ λίθοι καὶ ποτα- ποὶ οἰκοδομαί ("what great stones and wonderful buildings") to describe vividly the reaction of the disciples to the temple. The dependence on Matthew is indicated by Mark's use of τὰς οἰκοδομάς (Matthew 24:1); and dependence on Luke is indicated by the use of λίθοις (Luke 21:5). Thus Mark has conflated. In accomplishing this task Mark has used the adjective ποταπός in synonomous expression. This is yet another one of his known literary usages.[26] Thus Mark 13:1 represents the strong hand of the author of the second Gospel.

After hearing the observation of the disciple about the marvelous structure of the temple Jesus responds (13:2). By the use of ταύτας τὰς μεγάλας οἰκοδομάς ("these great buildings"), Mark makes it clearer than the wording of the Matthean source tradition that the statement is against the temple. And, finally, the use of οὐ μή ("under no circumstances") twice not only indicates another use of synonymous expression,[27] but also has Jesus state in his most emphatic way that the end of the temple has come.

---

[23]Peabody, *Mark as Composer*, 82.
[24]Ibid., 78.
[25]Ibid., 63.
[26]F. Neirynck, *Duality in Mark: Contributions to the Study of Markan Redaction*, BETL 31 (Leuven: Leuven University Press, 1972) 105.
[27]Ibid.

Having stated strongly that the temple era had ended, Mark now moves into the process of making the transition to Jesus' speech about the future. In 13:3 Mark follows closely the Matthean source (24:3) and the scene shifts to the Mount of Olives. But even here there emerges certain Markan compositional features. Mark uses the phrase κατέναντι τοῦ ἱεροῦ ("opposite the Temple") not only to emphasize Jesus' separation from the temple, but also because it is a linguistic expression he prefers to use (12:41; cf. 11:2).[28]

Mark has four disciples (Peter, James, John, and Andrew) put the question about the future to Jesus.[29] In the synoptics, the four different references to Andrew are all in Mark (1:16, 29; 3:17; 13:3). This appears to be a technical expression for the truly dedicated inner core of Jesus' followers and thus anticipates the widening application of Jesus' speech set forth in the major inclusio to follow (13:5, 37).

The critical formation of the query about the future is set forth in 13:4. Compositionally, Mark maintains the twofold form of the query in the sources in Luke and Matthew and appears to conflate ὅταν μέλλῃ ταῦτα ("when will these things come to pass") in Luke 21:7 and συντελείας ("end") in Matthew 24:3.

It is difficult to determine what Mark had in mind in formulating this particular construction. The commentaries regularly note that the terminology is unclear, and controversy in interpretation goes back to the time of patristic exegesis.[30] Is the question about the end of the temple, the end of the age, or a combination of both? We may say that through conflation Mark gives a mediated rendering of the common text of Matthew and Luke. But to understand Mark 13:4 more precisely we must view carefully a particular aspect of the terminology of this verse.

In this connection we draw attention to the function of σημεῖον ("sign" or "omen") both in Mark in general and in this verse in particular. Upon hearing that the temple will be destroyed, the disciples ask when will this be? This is the most obvious meaning of πότε οὖν ταῦτα ἔσται ("when will these things be?") in 13:4a. Now the reader of Mark knows that the Temple is in ruins. After a narration of certain events reviewed in 13:5-23 the reader receives an answer to the question and knows that the prophecy of Jesus stated in 13:2 has been fulfilled. What is demanded of the reader is an appropriate discernment of the

---

[28]Peabody, *Mark as Composer*, 110.

[29]Sanders, *Tendencies of the Synoptic Tradition*, 275, claims that the addition of proper names is "strong" evidence for an editorial tendency of a later Gospel writer.

[30]Taylor, *Gospel of Mark*, 502; cf. J. Lambrecht, *Die Redaktion der Markus-Apokalypse: Literarische Analyse und Strukturuntersuchung*, An Bib 28 (Rome: Papstliches Bibelinstitut, 1967) 86-88; Pesch, *Naherwartungen*, 101.

implications of this event! This brings us to a consideration of 13:4b. By use of conjunctive καί ("and, in addition") Mark tells us that the disciples ask for a sign when all these things are about to be completed? This is the puzzling aspect of the disciples' request?

A clue to Mark's use of σημεῖον in 13:4 may be found by examining its use in Mark 8:11-13. In this latter pericope the Pharisees, who had already attributed the power of Jesus' ministry to Beelzebub, ask that Jesus produce some authenticating indicator (a sign from heaven) to put the question of his true affiliation at rest.[31] Jesus unequivocally rejects the request.[32] The basis for this rejection is that it is impossible for him to agree to produce a sign on demand. This would amount to Jesus releasing his hearers from the need to exercise faith and discernment.[33] Already the amazing feeding incidents had taken place (6:30-44; 8:1-10). What other signs or indicators were needed?[34] What is demanded is faith and discernment of the significance of what is taking place. Subsequently, the disciples in 8:14-21 are urged not to repeat this mistake.

Similarly, in Mark 13, the request of the disciples for a sign of the end is misguided. There needs to be no more talk about signs *of the end*. Mark will clearly delineate events in the first generation from what takes place at the end of time. That is enough for those who can perceive the events of the first generation through the eyes of faith. The references to signs in the heavens at the coming of the great events of the future in Mark's source tradition (Matt 24:30; Lk 21:11, 25) are omitted. The only ones who give signs of the end are false teachers.[35] What is needed is discernment about the events of the first generation narrated in 13:5b-23. The unfolding of these events, culminating in the emergence of the Horrible Desecration, for those who have the capacity for discernment, will be a sufficient answer to the question of the four disciples (cf. 13:4). The Son of Man will come and have universal impact without a sign.

---

[31]R. Gray, *Prophetic Figures in Late Second Temple Jewish Palestine: The Evidence from Josephus* (New York: Oxford University Press, 1993) 125-30, gives abundant evidence from Josephus to indicate that σημεῖον can refer to a certain type of miracle that a prophet performs to authenticate his work. This seems to be what the Pharisees have in mind with respect to their request of Jesus.

[32]Geddert, *Watchwords*, 32-33, rightly notes five reasons why, according to the Markan story line, such a request would be rejected.

[33]Ibid.

[34]It is noteworthy, on the Two Gospel Hypothesis, that Mark omits both the references to "the sign of Jonah," (Matt 12:39 ‖ 16:4 ‖ Lk 11:29) and "discerning the times" (Matt 16:2b-3 ‖ Lk 12:54-56) which Mark had in his source tradition.

[35]Again throughout Mark (8:11, 12, 13:4, 22) the request for signs are always treated negatively. They reveal lack of faith and discernment of God's true purposes.

The Coming Crisis and Persecution of Believers

Our preliminary analysis in this chapter indicated that the Passion Narrative in Mark 11-16 was dominated by two major concerns: (1) the end of the old order of leadership in Jerusalem and its replacement by a new community of faith; (2) and the call for that community (under the transparency of the disciples) to be faithful through a coming crisis which will produce both apostasy within the community and persecution without.

This is the backdrop to Mark 13:5-23. There, carefully, Mark has Jesus unfold the occurrences, which step by step lead up to the apex of a terrible crisis—the appearance of the Horrible Desecration. In the following analysis, we will highlight the function of the unfolding of these occurrences in this word Jesus is delivering about the future.

The Beginning of the Time of Horrors (Mark 13:5-8)

Matthew 24:4-8	Mark 13:5-8	Luke 21:8-11
⁴καὶ ἀποκριθεὶς ὁ Ἰησοῦς εἶπεν αὐτοῖς, Βλέπετε μή τις ὑμᾶς πλανήσῃ ⁵Πολλοὶ γάρ ἐλεύσονται ἐπὶ τῷ ὀνόματί μου λέγοντες, Ἐγώ εἰμι ὁ Χριστός καὶ	⁵ὁ δὲ Ἰησοῦς ἤρξατο λέγειν αὐτοῖς, Βλέπετε μή τις ὑμᾶς πλανήσῃ· ⁶πολλοὶ ελεύσονται ἐπὶ τῷ ὀνόματί μου λέγοντες ὅτι Ἐγώ εἰμι, καὶ	⁸ὁ δὲ εἶπεν, βλέπετε μή πλανηθῆτε· ⁸ˣπολλοὶ γάρ ἐλεύσονται ἐπὶ τῷ ὀνόματί μου λέγοντες, Ἐγώ εἰμι, καί Ὁ καιρὸς ἤγγικεν. μὴ πορευθῆτε ὀπίσω αὐτῶν.
πολλούς πλανήσουσιν. ⁶μελλήσετε δε ἀκούειν πολέμους καὶ ἀκοὰς πολέμων· ὁρᾶτε μὴ θροεῖσθε· δεῖ γὰρ γενέσθαι,	πολλοὺς πλανήσουσιν. ⁷ὅταν δὲ ἀκούσητε πολέμους καὶ ἀκοὰς πολέμων· μὴ θροεῖσθε· δεῖ γενέσθαι,	⁹ὅταν δὲ ἀκούσητε πολέμους καὶ ἀκαταστασίας, μὴ πτοηθῆτε· δεῖ γὰρ ταῦτα γενέσθαι πρῶτον,
ἀλλ' οὔπω ἐστὶν τὸ τέλος.	ἀλλ' οὔπω τὸ τέλος.	ἀλλ' οὐκ εὐθέως τὸ τέλος. ¹⁰Τότε ἔλεγεν αὐτοῖς· Ἐγερθήσεται
⁷ἐγερθήσεται γὰρ ἔθνος ἐπὶ ἔθνος καὶ βασιλεία ἐπὶ βασιλείαν καὶ ἔσονται λιμοὶ καὶ σεισμοὶ κατὰ τόπους·	⁸ἐγερθήσεται γὰρ ἔθνος ἐπ' ἔθνος καὶ βασιλεία ἐπὶ βασιλείαν, ἔσονται σεισμοὶ κατὰ τόπους, ἔσονται λιμοί·	ἔθνος ἐπ' ἔθνος καὶ βασιλεία ἐπὶ βασιλείαν. ¹¹σεισμοί τε μεγάλοι καὶ κατὰ τόπους λιμοὶ καὶ λοιμοὶ ἔσονται, φόβητρά τε καὶ ἀπ' οὐρανοῦ σημεῖα μεγάλα ἔσται.
⁸πάντα δε ταῦτα ἀρχὴ ὠδίνων.	ἀρχὴ ὠδίνων ταῦτα.	

In this pericope Jesus commences his speech to the inner circle of his followers. The pericope has two distinct parts. First, there is the warning against false messianic pretenders (13:5-6). This warning is repeated in 13:21-23. Second, there are the warnings about future wars, turmoils, earthquakes, and famines (13:7-8). The net effect is that a solemn announcement is given that grave disturbances loom in the near future. Yet these specific happenings, in and of themselves, do not constitute the end (13:7).

Compositionally, Mark has kept close to the wording of the text of Matthew with some occasional conflation with Luke.

The use of ἄρχομαι with the aorist ("he began") plus the infinitive (26 times in Mark), opens the long Discourse. It is a linguistic preference of Mark.[36] Its use creates a minor agreement in omission of something present in Mark but absent in both Matthew and Luke.

Mark's use of βλέπετε in 13:5b, which the author uses to start and finish the inclusio (cf. 13:23b), is dependent on his sources (Matt 24:4 || Luke 21:8). But, in its own right, this imperative is important for Mark. Primarily, here it means "take heed." It is used in the sense that one should appropriately discern the real meaning of what is taking place so she or he is not led astray by false pretenders to messiahship.[37]

These false pretenders are described in 13:6. Here, Mark follows the common form of his sources (Matt 24:5 || Lk 21:8) very closely. The ones who come ἐπὶ τῷ ὀνόματί μου ("in my name") will attempt to ursurp the legitimate role of Jesus.[38] The suggestion has been made that these "false pretenders" were aspirants to messiahship in the Jewish community who appeared in various cities of the empire in the first century, and especially in Jerusalem at the time of revolt in 66 CE.[39] If this is the case, this may be the first hint that what bothered Mark with the Jewish revolt was not the destruction of the temple; rather it was the emergence of various figures throughout the Greco-Roman world who gained followers and credibility with their claims to speak on behalf of divine powers during these turbulent times. As such they constitute a potential alternative to lead the faithful in the church away from their loyalty to Jesus.

At any rate, after giving a warning against the false deceivers, Mark opens 13:7 with the use of the Lukan ὅταν δὲ ἀκούσητε ("whenever you hear") drawn from Luke 21:9. However, the use of Matthew is reflected immediately

---

[36]Peabody, *Mark as Composer*, 54.

[37]Egon Brandenburger, *Markus 13 und die Apokalyptik*, FRLANT 134 (Göttingen: Vandenhoeck und Ruprecht, 1984) 157-59.

[38]Cf. ὁ Χριστός in Matt 24:5.

[39]Morna Hooker, "Trial and Tribulation in Mark XIII," *Bulletin of the John Rylands Library* 65 (1982): 85-86. This position is more plausible than the view that Mark is worrying about false pretenders of Christ appearing in the Christian community.

by καὶ ἀκοὰς πολέμων ("and rumors of wars") drawn from Matthew 24:6.[40] More than likely, as Mark follows closely his sources, at this point, he is reflecting knowledge of the turbulent conditions in the empire in the era culminating with the Rule of Nero. From the Markan perspective, in and of itself, this terrible time was past history. It was necessary to come to pass; but it was not the end (13:7b).

Besides the wars and rumors of wars of 13:7, specific turbulences and conflicts between nations and kingdoms are mentioned along with the appearance of earthquakes and famines (13:8). In the Markan context this reference can be interpreted as refering to civil conflicts within the Roman Empire. Specifically, this seems to have reference to the memory of the turbulent period of transition of power to the Flavian dynasty after the death of Nero.[41] Again, Mark wishes to stress the point that, as difficult as those events were, they did not constitute the end of history. They were only the first birthpangs of a new situation.

On this interpretation the meaning of ἀρχή ὠδίνων ταῦτα ("these are the first of the birth pangs") in 13:8 becomes crucial. For Matthew, these events were perceived as the actual birth pangs of the end of the age. But was this the case for Mark? The phraseology is the same as Matthew. But as our analysis unfolds, we believe it can be shown that it is more precise to say that Mark views the image of the birth pangs as being part and parcel of the inauguration of the eschatological crisis emerging in Nero's last days and which culminates in the time of the Horrible Desecration (Mk 13:14). This will be the true time of culmination of the horrors that the community will have to undergo.

Persecution in Mission before the End (Mark 13:9-13)

Matthew 10:17-19	Matthew 24:9, 14b, 14a	Mark 13:9-11b	Luke 21:12-14
			[12]πρὸ δὲ τούτων πάντων ἐπιβαλοῦσιν ἐφ' ὑμᾶς
		[9]βλέπετε δὲ	τὰς χεῖρας αὐτῶν
[17]προσέχετε δὲ ἀπὸ	[9]τότε παραδώσουσιν	ὑμεῖς ἑαυτούς·	καὶ διώξουσιν,
τῶν ἀνθρώπων·	ὑμᾶς	παραδώσουσιν	παραδιδόντες
παραδώσουσιν	εἰς θλῖψιν . . .	ὑμᾶς	
γὰρ ὑμᾶς		εἰς συνέδρια	
εἰς συνέδρια		καὶ εἰς	εἰς τὰς συναγωγὰς
καὶ ἐν ταῖς		συναγωγὰς	
συναγωγαῖς αὐτῶν			

---

[40]Note also the omission of ἀκαταστασίας which is found in Lk 21:9. By this omission Mark has maintained the precise text of the common account of Matthew and Luke on the issue of political conflicts.

[41]Hengel, *Studies in Mark*, 22.

μαστιγώσουσιν ὑμᾶς·

δαρήσεσθε

καὶ φυλακάς,
ἀπαγομένους
ἐπὶ βασιλεῖς

¹⁸καὶ ἐπὶ ἡγεμόνας
δὲ καὶ βασιλεῖς
ἀχθήσεσθε
ἕνεκεν ἐμοῦ

καὶ ἐπὶ ἡγεμόνων
καὶ βασιλέων
σταθήσεσθε
ἕνεκεν ἐμου

καὶ ἡγεμόνας

ἕνεκεν τοῦ
ὀνόματός

¹⁴³. . . ἐν ὅλῃ τῇ
οἰκουμένῃ

¹³ἀποβήσεται ὑμῖν

εἰς μαρτύριον
αὐτοῖς
καὶ τοῖς ἔθνεσιν.

εἰς μαρτύριον

πᾶσιν τοῖς ἔθνεσιν . . .
¹⁴ᵃκαὶ κηρυχθήσεται

εἰς μαρτύριον
αὐτοῖς.
¹⁰καὶ εἰς πάντα
τὰ ἔθνη
πρῶτον δεῖ κηρυχθῆναι
τὸ εὐαγγέλιον.

εἰς μαρτύριον.

τοῦτο τὸ εὐαγγέλιον
τῆς βασιλείας . . .
¹⁵ᵃ"Οταν οὖν . . .

¹⁹ὅταν δὲ
παραδῶσιν ὑμᾶς,

¹¹καὶ ὅταν ἄγωσιν
ὑμᾶς παραδιδόντες,

¹⁴θέτε οὖν ἐν
ταῖς καρδίαις ὑμων

μὴ μεριμνήσητε
πῶς ἢ τί λαλήσητε·

μὴ προμεριμνᾶτε
τί λαλήσητε,

μὴ προμελετᾶν
ἀπολογηθῆναι·

Matthew 10:19c-22	Matthew 24:9-12	Mark 13:11c-13a	Luke 21:15-17

¹⁹ˣδοθήσεται
γὰρ ὑμῖν

¹¹ˣἀλλ' ὃ ἐὰν
δοθῇ ὑμῖν

¹⁵ἐγὼ
γὰρ δώσω ὑμῖν
στόμα καὶ σοφίαν

ἐν ἐκείνῃ τῇ ὥρᾳ
τί λαλήσητε·

ἐν ἐκείνῃ τῇ ὥρᾳ
τοῦτο λαλεῖτε·

ᾗ οὐ δυνήσονται
ἀντιστῆναι ἢ ἀντει-
πεῖν ἅπαντες οἱ
ἀντικείμενοι ὑμῖν.

²⁰οὐ γὰρ ὑμεῖς ἐστε
οἱ λαλοῦντες
ἀλλὰ τὸ πνεῦμα
τοῦ πατρὸς ὑμῶν
τὸ λαλοῦν ἐν ὑμῖν.
²¹παραδώσει δὲ
ἀδελφὸς ἀδελφὸν
εἰς θάνατον
καὶ πατὴρ τέκνον,
καὶ ἐπαναστήσονται
τέκνα ἐπὶ γονεῖς

οὐ γὰρ ἐστε ὑμεῖς
οἱ λαλοῦντες
ἀλλὰ τὸ πνεῦμα
τὸ ἅγιον.

¹²καὶ παραδώσει
ἀδελφὸς ἀδελφὸν
εἰς θάνατον
καὶ πατὴρ τέκνον,
καὶ ἐπαναστήσονται
τέκνα ἐπὶ γονεῖς

¹⁶παραδοθήσεσθε δὲ

καὶ ὑπὸ γονέων
καὶ ἀδελφῶν καὶ
συγγενῶν καὶ φίλων

καὶ θανατώσουσιν αὐτούς.	⁹³καὶ ἀποκτενοῦσιν ὑμᾶς,	καὶ θανατώσουσιν αὐτούς·	καὶ θανατώσουσιν ἐξ ὑμῶν
²²καὶ ἔσεσθε μισούμενοι ὑπὸ πάντων	καὶ ἔσεσθε μισούμενοι ὑπὸ πάντων τῶν ἐθνῶν	¹³καὶ ἔσεσθε μισούμενοι ὑπὸ πάντων	¹⁷καὶ ἔσεσθε μισούμενοι ὑπὸ πάντων
διὰ τὸ ὄνομά μου·	¹⁰διὰ τὸ ὄνομά μου. καὶ τότε σκανδαλισ- θήσονται πολλοὶ καὶ ἀλλήλους παραδώσου- σιν καὶ μισήσουσιν ἀλλήλους· ¹¹καὶ πολλοὶ ψευδο- προφῆται ἐγερθή- σονται καὶ πλανή- σουσιν πολλούς· ¹²καὶ διὰ τὸ πληθυν- θῆναι τὴν ἀνομί- αν ψυγήσεται ἡ ἀγάπη τῶν πολλῶν.	διὰ τὸ ὄνομά μου.	διὰ τὸ ὄνομά μου.

Matthew 10:22b-23a	Matthew 24:13-15a	Mark 13:13b-14a	Luke 21:18-20a
			¹⁸καὶ θρὶξ ἐκ τῆς κεφαλῆς ὑμῶν οὐ μὴ ἀπόληται.
²²ὁ δὲ ὑπομείνας εἰς τέλος οὗτος σωθήσεται.	¹³ὁ δὲ ὑπομείνας εἰς τέλος οὗτος σωθήσεται. ¹⁴καὶ κηρυχθήσεται τοῦτο τὸ εὐαγγέλιον τῆς βασιλείας ἐν ὅλῃ τῇ οἰκουμένῃ εἰς μαρτύριον πᾶσιν τοῖς ἔθνεσιν, καὶ τότε ἥξει τὸ τέλος.	¹³ᵇὁ δὲ ὑπομείνας εἰς τέλος οὗτος σωθήσεται.	¹⁹ἐν τῇ ὑπομονῇ ὑμῶν κτήσασθε τὰς ψυχὰς ὑμῶν.
²³ᵃὍταν δέ	¹⁵ᵃὍταν οὖν	¹⁴ᵃὍταν δέ	²⁰ᵃὍταν δέ

Up until this point the focus of Jesus' speech has been on the turbulence of the period leading up to the inauguration of a terrible period of eschatological horrors that were about to come upon the whole world. Now the focus shifts to a description of the hardship that the group of disciples (the transparencies of the church) would shortly undergo as they went about the task of mission. They would be prosecuted in both Jewish and Gentile courts. The Holy Spirit would be their only defense (13:9, 11). They would be betrayed by family and hated by all (13:12-13a). But while this was happening, an unceasing mission to the Gentiles would continue (13:10). Here the overall theme of the speech is set forth strongly: in the face of the various forms of apostasy and treachery faithful discipleship must continue until the end.

Compositionally, this passage presents special difficulties for those who follow the Two Source Hypothesis. For if Mark were the earliest Gospel and was used independently by Matthew and Luke, why do Matthew and Luke diverge both in sequence and content at Mark 13:9 and come back together following the same sequence of pericopes at 13:14?[42]

The explanation of Two Source theorists are complicated and involve the postulations of other sources and some extraordinary redactional procedures. These have been exhaustively critiqued and found to be very problematic.[43]

On the other hand, on the Two Gospel Hypothesis, Mark's use of source tradition is readily explainable. On this hypothesis, Mark has three accounts of the persecution of the disciples that have close literary connections (Matt 24:9-14 || Lk 21:12-19 || Matt 10:17-22). Mark is aware that Luke 21:12-19 and Matthew 10:17-22 have close verbal affinities and are by far the two closest literary parallels. (Mark may even have been aware that Luke [21:12-19] used Matthew 10:17-22 as the basis for his composition.) Mark simply uses these two units as the basic source tradition for the composition of 13:9-13. Mark composes in keeping with his own style and will at times conflate with Matthew 24:9-14.

Thus, after an initial call to discernment in 13:9 βλέπετε δὲ ὑμεῖς ἑαυτούς ("you yourselves take heed"),[44] by the use of the repeated word παρα-διδόναι ("to hand over"), Mark moves from following the major Matthean source at Matthew 24:9 to the closer parallel of Matthew 10:17-22 and Luke 21:12b-19 as the major source of the composition (cf. Matt 10:17 || Luke 21:12).

First, Mark indicates that the persecution will come through being handed over to Jewish judicial authorities as the συνέδρια ("high council") and συν-αγωγάς ("synagogues"). This reflects a similar pattern which Jesus himself will follow (Mk 14:53-65).[45]

---

[42]Bo Reicke, "A Test of Synoptic Relationships: Matthew 10:17-23 and 24:9-14 with Parallels," in *New Synoptic Studies: The Cambridge Gospel Conference and Beyond*, ed. William R. Farmer (Macon GA: Mercer University Press, 1983) 209-22; McNicol, "Composition of the Synoptic Eschatological Discourse," 188-93. Both articles elaborate extensively on this point. The response on behalf of the Two Source theory can be found in Tuckett, *Revival of the Griesbach Hypothesis*, 167-168; idem, "Response to the Two Gospel Hypothesis: The Eschatological Discourse," 73-75; Beasley-Murray, *Jesus and the Last Days*, 231-32.

[43]Reicke, "Test of Synoptic Relationships," 209-29.

[44]Geddert, *Watchwords*, 86.

[45]Since μαστιγώσουσιν (Matt 10:17) and ἀπαγομένους (Lk 21:12) do not agree, Mark uses δέρειν (cf. Lk 12:47, 48) to describe the future punishment of the disciples in the synagogue.

Then, continuing to follow his two sources (Matthew 10:18 ‖ Luke 21:12) Mark notes, that just as Jesus, the disciples will suffer at the hands of the Gentiles (13:9b). Their persecution entails being brought to account before both the provincial ruler and the highest authorities. The call is to maintain one's committment to make a faithful testimony before them.

At the end of Mark 13:9, Mark encounters a doublet between Matthew 10:18 and 24:14b. This doublet included the statement, "to (all) the Gentiles." Having followed the order of Matthew 10:18 to this point, Mark conflated this text with Matthew 24:14b, *and then incorporated Matthew 24:14a into the account to compose 13:10.* Almost universally, commentators have noted the secondary nature of Mark 13:10, and puzzled over it.[46] But, on the basis of the Two Gospel Hypothesis, Mark's point is clear. In the midst of an era of hostility and persecution, the proclamation of the gospel will continue.

What is particularly noticeable is that Mark omits the wording of Matthew 24:14b: καὶ τότε ἥξει τὸ τέλος ("and then the end will come"). For Mark the reality of universal persecution both during the time of Nero and the period of turbulence after his death is not in and of itself the sure sign of the end of history. Thus, in place of this Matthean phraseology, Mark places the ambiguous πρῶτον δεῖ ("first it is necessary") in 13:10. This makes 13:10 a statement, to the effect, that it is a matter of divine necessity that the Gentile mission be maintained during the time of harrassment and persecution. Mission and faithfulness in persecution must go hand in hand! This was so from the time of Jesus' death and will continue to the end (13:13).

Having made this aside, Mark now resumes the discussion on the persecution of the disciples in 13:11-13. Procedurally, Mark picks up a clause introduced by ὅταν ("whenever") from Matthew 10:19 to continue the discussion on persecution (13:11). After he concludes this discussion Mark again picks up ὅταν from source material (Matthew 10:23 ‖ Luke 21:20; cf. Matthew 24:15) to introduce the next pericope in 13:14. In the verses between, Mark (11:11-13) carefully follows the source tradition of Matthew 10:19-22 ‖ Luke 21:14b-17. In the call not to be anxious we meet the odd word προμεριμνᾶν ("to worry beforehand"). It appears to be a conflation of μεριμνᾶν (Matthew 10:19) and προμελετᾶν (Luke 21:14). This is further evidence that Mark used both Matthew and Luke as sources.

The account of the persecutions are carefully narrated in Mark 13:11b-13. Persecution will come and will constitute a major test of faithfulness to the believing community. Betrayal will take place from within and without the

---

[46]Pesch, *Naherwartungen*, 129-31; J. Gnilka, *Das Evangelium nach Markus, Mark 8:27-16:20*, EKKNT 2, 2 vols. (Zurich: Neukirchen-Vluyn, 1979) 189; Taylor, *Mark*, 507; Jeremias, *Promise to the Nations*, 23.

community. Yet, in the midst of this persecution the community will be sustained by the Holy Spirit.[47] This seems to be a very nuanced description of the Neronian period and its immediate aftermath.

At 13:9, signified by the first segment of an inclusio 13:9a/23a, Mark commences his description of the beginning of a great crisis. It describes a situation of incredible treachery and unfaithfulness. Yet just as the poor widow (12:41-44) and the anonymous woman who anointed Jesus had shown incredible faithfulness (14:3-9), now in this time, the disciples are called upon to do the same. Those who continue to do such will be saved (13:13).

The Coming of the Horrible Desecration (Mark 13:14-23)

Matthew 24:15-25	Mark 13:14-23	Luke 21:20-24
<u>¹⁵ὅταν</u> οὖν <u>ἴδητε</u>	¹⁴<u>ὅταν</u> δὲ <u>ἴδητε</u>	²⁰<u>ὅταν</u> δὲ <u>ἴδητε</u> κυκλουμέ-νην ὑπὸ στρατοπέδων Ἰερουσαλήμ, τότε γνῶτε ὅτι ἤγγικεν
<u>τὸ βδέλυγμα</u> <u>τῆς ἐρημώσεως</u> τὸ ῥηθὲν διὰ Δανιὴλ τοῦ προφήτου <u>ἑστὸς ἐν</u> τόπῳ ἁγίῳ, <u>ὁ ἀναγινώσκων νοείτω.</u>	<u>τὸ βδέλυγμα</u> <u>τῆς ἐρημώσεως</u> <u>ἑστηκότα</u> ὅπου οὐ δεῖ, <u>ὁ ἀναγινώσκων νοείτω,</u>	<u>ἡ ἐρήμωσις</u> αὐτῆς.
¹⁶<u>τότε οἱ ἐν</u> <u>τῇ Ἰουδαίᾳ</u> <u>φευγέτωσαν εἰς τὰ ὄρη,</u>	<u>τότε οἱ ἐν</u> <u>τῇ Ἰουδαίᾳ</u> <u>φευγέτωσαν εἰς τὰ ὄρη.</u>	²¹<u>τότε οἱ ἐν</u> <u>τῇ Ἰουδαίᾳ</u> <u>φευγέτωσαν εἰς τὰ ὄρη</u> καὶ οἱ ἐν μέσῳ αὐτῆς ἐκχωρείτωσαν καὶ οἱ ἐν ταῖς χώραις
₁₇<u>ὁ ἐπὶ τοῦ δώματος</u> <u>μὴ καταβάτω</u> <u>ἆραι</u> τὰ <u>ἐκ τῆς</u> <u>οἰκίας αὐτου,</u> ¹⁸<u>καὶ ὁ ἐν τῷ ἀγρῷ</u> <u>μὴ ἐπιστρεψάτω</u> <u>ὀπίσω ἆραι τὸ</u> <u>ἱμάτιον αὐτου.</u>	¹⁵<u>ὁ</u> δὲ <u>ἐπὶ τοῦ δώματος</u> <u>μὴ καταβάτω</u> <u>μηδὲ εἰσελθάτω</u> <u>ἆραί</u> τι <u>ἐκ τῆς</u> <u>οἰκιάς αὐτου,</u> ¹⁶<u>καὶ ὁ εἰς τὸν ἀγρὸν</u> <u>μὴ ἐπιστρεψάτω</u> <u>εἰς τὰ ὀπίσω ἆραι τὸ</u> <u>ἱμάτιον αὐτου,</u>	<u>μὴ εἰσερχέσθωσαν</u> εἰς αὐτήν,
		²²ὅτι ἡμέραι ἐκδικήσεως αὐταί εἰσιν τοῦ πλησθῆ-ναι πάντα τὰ γεγραμμένα.

---

[47]Peabody, *Mark as Composer*, 35, identifies Holy Spirit (πνεῦμα + ἅγιον) as recurrent Markan phraseology.

¹⁹οὐαὶ δὲ ταῖς ἐν γαστρὶ
ἐχούσαις καὶ ταῖς θηλα-
ζούσαις ἐν ἐκείναις
ταῖς ἡμέραις.
²⁰προσεύχεσθε δὲ ἵνα μὴ
γένηται ἡ φυγὴ ὑμῶν
χειμῶνος μηδὲ σαββάτῳ.
²¹ἔσται γὰρ τότε

θλῖψις μεγάλη

οἷα οὐ γέγονεν
ἀπ' ἀρχῆς κόσμου

ἕως τοῦ νῦν
οὐδ' οὐ μὴ γένηται.
²²καὶ εἰ μὴ
ἐκολοβώθησαν
αἱ ἡμέραι ἐκεῖναι,
οὐκ ἂν ἐσώθη
πᾶσα σάρξ·
διὰ δε
τοὺς ἐκλεκτοὺς

κολοβωθήσονται
αἱ ἡμέραι ἐκεῖναι.
²³τότε ἐάν
τις ὑμῖν εἴπῃ,
Ἰδοὺ ὧδε ὁ Χριστός,
ἤ, Ὧδε,
μὴ πιστεύσητε·
²⁴ἐγερθήσονται γὰρ
ψευδόχριστοι
καὶ ψευδοπροφῆται
καὶ δώσουσιν σημεῖα
μεγάλα καὶ τέρατα
ὥστε πλανῆσαι,
εἰ δυνατόν,
καὶ τοὺς ἐκλεκτούς.

²⁵ἰδοὺ προείρηκα ὑμῖν.

---

¹⁷οὐαὶ δὲ ταῖς ἐν γαστρὶ
ἐχούσαις καὶ ταῖς θηλα-
ζούσαις ἐν ἐκείναις
ταῖς ἡμέραις.
¹⁸προσεύχεσθε δὲ ἵνα μὴ
γένηται
χειμῶνος·
¹⁹ἔσονται γὰρ
αἱ ἡμέραι ἐκεῖναι
θλῖψις

οἷα οὐ γέγονεν τοιαύτη
ἀπ' ἀρχῆς κτίσεως
ἣν ἔκτισεν ὁ θεὸς
ἕως τοῦ νῦν
καὶ οὐ μὴ γένηται.
²⁰καὶ εἰ μὴ
ἐκολόβωσεν κύριος
τὰς ἡμέρας,
οὐκ ἂν ἐσώθη
πᾶσα σάρξ·
ἀλλὰ διὰ
τοὺς ἐκλεκτοὺς
οὓς ἐξελέξατο
ἐκολόβωσεν
τὰς ἡμέρας.
²¹καὶ τότε ἐάν
τις ὑμῖν εἴπῃ,
Ἴδε ὧδε ὁ Χριστός,
Ἴδε ἐκεῖ,
μὴ πιστεύετε·
²²ἐγερθήσονται γὰρ
ψευδόχριστοι
καὶ ψευδοπροφῆται
καὶ δώσουσιν σημεῖα
καὶ τέρατα
πρὸς τὸ ἀποπλανᾶν,
εἰ δυνατόν,
τοὺς ἐκλεκτούς.
²³ὑμεῖς δὲ βλέπετε·
προείρηκα ὑμῖν πάντα.

---

²³οὐαὶ ταῖς ἐν γαστρὶ
ἐχούσαις καὶ ταῖς θηλα-
ζούσαις ἐν ἐκείναις
ταῖς ἡμέραις·

ἔσται γὰρ

ἀνάγκη μεγάλη ἐπὶ
τῆς γῆς καὶ ὀργὴ τῶ
λαῷ τούτῳ,
²⁴καὶ πεσοῦνται στόματι
μαχαίρης καὶ αἰχμαλωτισ-
θήσονται εἰς τὰ ἔθνη
πάντα, καὶ Ἰερουσαλὴμ
ἔσται πατουμένη ὑπὸ
ἐθνῶν, . . .

Mark 13:14-23 narrates a terrible crisis. Enveloped in this account is a description of an occurrence that, for those who have the capacity to discern, constitutes the climax of the series of eschatological events that were to take place in the generation after Jesus. With the appearance of the Βδέλυγμα τῆς ἐρημώσεως ("Horrible Desecration"), the terrible crisis has arrived (13:14). In keeping with our analysis of 13:2-4, the appearance of the Horrible Desecration, implies a connection with the destruction of the temple, but also entails familiarity with the emergence of a historical situation that for the Christian community transcends that event. Specifically, the appearance of the Horrible Desecration constitutes the climax of a series of horrors in the first Christian generation and brings one to the horizon of the coming of the Son of Man.[48] To indicate that the final crisis has arrived, compositionally, Mark commences the construction of 13:14 by use of the phraseology ὅταν δὲ ἴδητε ("whenever you see") drawn from Matthew 24:15. Mark may also have chosen to use ὅταν δέ because it appears in two major sources which he has been following (Matt 10:23 ‖ Lk 21:20). Mark has now returned from following the order of Matthew 10:17-22 to pick up the sequence of pericopes commencing at Matthew 24:15 ‖ Luke 21:20. According to our source hypothesis, Mark follows Matthew 24:15-25 with only very minor conflation with Luke 21:20-24. However, what is most striking, is Mark's decision to omit Lukan materials not paralleled in Matthew (Luke 21:20b; 21:21b-22; 23b-24). It is noticeable that these omissions from Luke are part of the vivid descriptions of the siege and fall of Jerusalem. Here we have a clear compositional indicator that Mark was not interested in giving those details. After all, the end of the temple had already been prefigured (Mk 11:12-25 cf. 15:58). Rather than give a vivid description of the fall of Jerusalem (something that was well known as old news throughout the Empire anyway, and hardly relevant to his readers in Rome), Mark ultimately placed an emphasis on the ability of the believers to discern the significance of what was happening with such an event (13:23). And what was to be discerned? Apparently what is really significant is the emergence of a dramatic new reality: the appearance of the Horrible Desecration.

This is so, because in describing this event, Mark makes some major compositional changes with respect to the source tradition. As with Luke 21:20, at least according to most of the major Egyptian manuscripts,[49] Mark omits the Matthean

---

[48]W. A. Such, "The Significance of TO SEMEION in Mark 13:4," *Irish Biblical Studies* 13 (1991): 142.

[49]The text of Nestle[26]-Aland[3] does not have the reference to Daniel in Mk 13:14 that is found in Matt 24:15. The editors of Nestle-Aland apparently were following the concurrent testimony of Sinaiticus and Vaticanus which does not have the reference to Daniel. However, it is found in Codices Alexandrinus, Koridethianus, and Petropolitanus and had

reference to Daniel. In place of saying, as Matthew 24:15, that the Desecration appears in the holy place of the temple, Mark apparently uses the masculine participle ἑστηκότα ("standing") with a neuter noun, which is different in form from the Matthean neuter participle for "standing" ἐστός.[50] He then follows with the ambiguous statement ὅπου οὐ δεῖ ("where it is not necessary") which is not in the source material. The phrase is very general and can only make sense in terms of a wider exegetical framework. Finally, given the impact of these Markan redactional changes, one must now ask what Mark means both by the use of the Matthean phrase ὁ ἀναγινώσκων νοείτω ("let the one reading understand"), and the call to the people of Judea to head for the hills. Thus it is necessary to examine this verse somewhat more closely.

In so doing, first one should note the problem with the text of Mark 13:14. Apparently most standard editions of the Greek text treat the variant readings as assimilations of the Markan text to Matthew. But, as David Wenham notes, the current text of Mark is definitely an oddity.[51] Thus, one must at least wonder whether something has happened here in the transmission of the text. Given this reality, it would be unwise to use the present text of Mark 13:14 as *the* key for unlocking the meaning of this whole unit.

Nevertheless, assuming the present form of the text to be correct, we will make several comments with reference to the interpretation of Mark 13:14. On the Two Gospel Hypothesis, the most obvious observation one can make about this text is that Mark appears deliberately to have obscured the references to Jerusalem (Luke) and the temple (Matthew).[52] As opposed to the Matthean source, the Horrible Desecration is no longer an object of veneration in the temple, but has taken on the trappings of an appalling personal demonic power. This compositional shift thus gives us a clue for understanding the Markan account of the Horrible Desecration.

---

the support of the Textus Receptus. Similar attestation can be found in favor of the Matthean ἐστός as being the reading in Mk13:14 in place of ἑστηκότα.

[50]In form ἑστηκότα would be either a masculine singular or neuter plural participle. Most commentators take it to be a masculine singular; but it is not at all clear that it should be read this way. It may be that Mark is being read too closely in connection with 2 Thessalonians 2:3-4.

[51]Wenham, *Rediscovery of Jesus' Eschatological Discourse*, 193.

[52]Cf. S. G. F. Brandon, *Jesus and the Zealots: A Study of the Political Factor in Primitive Christianity* (New York: Charles Scribners' Sons, 1967) 231. Although there is much in Brandon's views of the gospels with which we do not concur, his analysis of the Josephus account (Josephus, *Jewish War* 6.260ff.) of what happened both upon the fall of the temple in Jerusalem and subsequently in Rome is still worthy of note. Cf. Brandon, *The Trial of Jesus of Nazareth* (New York: Stein and Day, 1979; orig. 1968) 43-46; 71-73.

For Mark, the focus of the βδέλυγμα τῆς ἐρημώσεως is not the destruction of the temple. But the reference to the Horrible Desecration with the masculine participle seems to involve a reference to the work of a person (the Roman emperor Titus?). Mark seems to interpret the events of 70 CE in terms of the implementation of a policy of widespread idolatrous reverence of the emperor commencing in Jerusalem.

Indeed, for someone writing in Rome (the traditional site where Mark was composed) in the post-70 years, there was plenty of evidence to constitute a firm basis for this belief. First, there was the turbulence of the Neronian period in the sixties culminating in the martyrdom of Peter and Paul. Second, there were the violent civil wars of 68–69 CE preceding the coming to power of the Flavian dynasty when even the powerful citizens, not to mention the marginalized Christians, were unsafe in their communities. Then in 70 CE, Titus, a Roman general and a later emperor, profaned the temple by entering the innermost sacred precincts of the Jews, thus making a claim to veneration for his family equal or above that of the one worshipped as ultimate by the people of God. This was later followed by the erecting of the Roman standards at the eastern gate and the salutation of Titus as Imperator while the temple was still smoldering.[53]

In our judgment, for Mark, this action of Titus which subsequently was followed by the triumphant procession and exhibition of the fruits of victory in Rome, constituted the apex of a series of horrors of the past generation. It is noticeable that at roughly the same time in Asia a similar fear of the imposition of emperor worship was exhibited by the author of the Apocalypse (cf. Rev 13:1-18). Mark exhibits no great love or concern for the Jerusalem temple; but the demonic personalized power inherent in the emergence of the Flavian dynasty, which followed in the wake of the temple's destruction, was something else.

Given this interpretation of recent history, Mark 13:14b-23 makes admirable sense. The reader is urged to perceive the deeper meaning of the present reality (ὁ ἀναγινώσκων νοείτω). The narrative has presented Jesus as telling his disciples that a series of horrors will take place which will culminate in a terrible event in Judea. Anyone who had the misfortune to be there at this time (or metaphorically in other cities of the empire) should head for the hills (Mk 13:14b). The discerning reader, living a decade or so after the tumultuous declaration of Titus as Imperator, would understand this as an eschatological time of unparalleled treachery and adversity for the people of God. Thus Mark 13:14b-23 fittingly describes this time—the impact of which lasted to the very day of Markan composition.

In the call to flee Judea (13:14b-18) Mark has followed fairly closely the Matthean source (Matt 24:16-20). Nevertheless, there are several indicators of

---

[53]Josephus, *Jewish War* 6.316.

Markan composition in Mark 13:14b-18. The use of the imperatives (13:15) μὴ καταβάτω ("do not come down") and μηδὲ εἰσελθάτω ("do not enter") constitute another instance of Mark's preference for the use of synonymous expression. There is also evidence of conflation in 13:15 with the use of εἰσερ-χέσθωσαν (Lk 21:21), and καταβάτω (Matt 24:17). In 13:17, when the two sources are in close agreement, Mark copies closely. The omission of the call to flee on the Sabbath, found in the Matthean source (21:20), being not appropriate to the Gentile readers, is omitted.[54]

With the composition of 13:19-22 (based on Matthew 24:21-24), Mark brings the discussion about this period of crisis to a close. As the climactic expression of evils, these are terrible days (13:19-20). They have no precedent. One can only take comfort in the promise that for the elect these days were shortened.

In the meanwhile, the signs and treachery of false prophets and messiahs will continue to pervade the empire (13:21-22). This is part and parcel of the impact of this terrible unfaithfulness unleashed by this time of tribulation. Such a situation which was present from the beginning (13:5-6) will remain to the end (13:21-22).

In finishing out this first section of the Discourse in 13:19-23, Mark makes several compositional changes of note from the major source in Matthew 24:21-25. The reference to the plural αἱ ἡμέραι ἐκεῖναι ("those days") in Matthew 24:22 is used by Mark, at 13:19, to create a plural form of the verb to be, and thus a minor agreement in the text of Matthew (24:21) and Luke (21:23b) against Mark was created. In 13:19 τοιοῦτος ("such a kind") is a Markan linguistic preference. It is used six times by Mark without parallels in Matthew and Luke.[55] The synonymous expression of ἀπ' ἀρχῆς κτίσεως ("from the beginning of creation") and ἔκτισεν ὁ θεός ("God created") in 13:19 is Markan.[56] A synonymous, theological expression is created with the use of ὁ θεός (13:19) and κύριος (13:20). And, finally, in his modification of the Matthean τοὺς ἐκλεκτούς ("the elect"), Mark uses the characteristic language of (1) a verb + a relative pronoun/a cognate accusative; and (2) creates a duality or synonymous expression in his composition τοὺς ἐκλεκτοὺς οὓς ἐξελέ-ξατο ("the elect whom he chose").[57]

Thus Mark has carefully composed his description of terrible crises that came to a climax with the events in Judea in 70 CE. With the end of the inclusio

---

[54]Since Lk 17:31 || Matt 24:17-18 form a parallel this may have constituted another reason why Mark (13:15-16) may have been disposed to including these sayings since they have double attestation in the Jesus tradition.

[55]McNicol, "Composition of the Synoptic Eschatological Discourse," 194.

[56]Neirynck, *Duality in Mark*, 105.

[57]Peabody, *Mark as Composer*, 103; Neirynck, *Duality in Mark*, 46, 105.

ὑμεῖς δὲ βλέπετε ("take heed") in 13:23 (cf. 13:5,9) Mark has interpreted for his reader the horrors of the last generation.

The Coming of the Son of Man (Mark 13:24-27)

Matthew 24:29-31	Mark 13:24-27	Luke 21:25-28
²⁹Εὐθέως δὲ μετὰ τὴν θλῖψιν τῶν ἡμερῶν ἐκείνων	²⁴Ἀλλὰ ἐν ἐκείναις ταῖς ἡμέραις μετὰ τὴν θλῖψιν ἐκείνην	²⁵Καὶ ἔσονται σημεῖα ἐν ἡλίῳ καὶ σελήνῃ
ὁ ἥλιος σκοτισθήσεται, καὶ ἡ σελήνη οὐ δώσει τὸ φέγγος αὐτῆς, καὶ οἱ ἀστέρες πεσοῦνται ἀπὸ τοῦ οὐρανοῦ,	ὁ ἥλιος σκοτισθήσεται, καὶ ἡ σελήνη οὐ δώσει τὸ φέγγος αὐτῆς, ²⁵καὶ οἱ ἀστέρες ἔσονται ἐκ τοῦ οὐρανοῦ πίπτοντες	καὶ ἄστροις,
		καὶ ἐπὶ τῆς γῆς συνοχὴ ἐθνῶν ἐν ἀπορίᾳ ἤχους θαλάσσης καὶ σάλου, ²⁶ἀποψυχόντων ἀνθρώπων ἀπὸ φόβου καὶ προσδοκίας τῶν ἐπερχομένων τῇ οἰκουμένῃ.
καὶ αἱ δυνάμεις τῶν οὐρανῶν σαλευθήσονται. ³⁰καὶ τότε φανήσεται τὸ σημεῖον τοῦ υἱοῦ τοῦ ἀνθρώπου ἐν οὐρανῷ, καὶ τότε κόψονται πᾶσαι αἱ φυλαὶ τῆς γῆς καὶ ὄψονται	καὶ αἱ δυνάμεις αἱ ἐν τοῖς οὐρανοῖς σαλευθήσονται. ²⁶καὶ τότε ὄψονται	αἱ γὰρ δυνάμεις τῶν οὐρανῶν σαλευθήσονται. ²⁷καὶ τότε ὄψονται
τὸν υἱὸν τοῦ ἀνθρώπου ἐρχόμενον ἐπὶ τῶν νεφελῶν τοῦ οὐρανοῦ μετὰ δυνάμεως καὶ δόξης πολλῆς· ³¹καὶ ἀποστελεῖ τοὺς ἀγγέλους αὐτοῦ μετὰ σάλπιγγος μεγάλης, καὶ ἐπισυνάξουσιν τοὺς ἐκλεκτοὺς αὐτοῦ ἐκ τῶν τεσσάρων ἀνέμων	τὸν υἱὸν τοῦ ἀνθρώπου ἐρχόμενον ἐν νεφέλαις μετὰ δυνάμεως πολλῆς καὶ δόξης. ²⁷καὶ τότε ἀποστελεῖ τοὺς ἀγγέλους καὶ ἐπισυνάξει τοὺς ἐκλεκτοὺς αὐτου ἐκ τῶν τεσσάρων ἀνέμων	τὸν υἱὸν τοῦ ἀνθρώπου ἐρχόμενον ἐν νεφέλῃ μετὰ δυνάμεως καὶ δόξης πολλῆς.

ἀπ' ἄκρων οὐρανῶν   ἀπ' ἄκρου γῆς
ἕως [τῶν] ἄκων αὐτῶν.   ἕως ἄκρου οὐρανου.   [28]ἀρχομένων δὲ τούτων
                                      γίνεσθαι ἀνακύψατε καὶ
                                      ἐπάρατε τὰς κεφαλὰς
                                      ὑμῶν, διότι ἐγγίζει
                                      ἡ ἀπολύτρωσις ὑμῶν.

Mark is now ready to give his version of the coming of the Son of Man which he perceives as taking place some time after the terrible crisis of the first generation.

Mark has continued to follow the common source tradition of Matthew and Luke. Matthew 24:26-28 has no parallel in Luke 21. Mark omits. When Matthew 24 and Luke 21 again conjoin in the same order, Mark immediately continues the account (Matt 24:29 ‖ Lk 21:25 ‖ Mk 13:24); also, for compositional reasons, Mark omitted Matthew 24:26-28 because the source tradition of Matt 24:29-31 provided the basis for a clear and uncomplicated account of the coming of the Son of Man as the next great eschatological event that follows the Horrible Desecration. The intervention of the source material in Matthew 24:26-28 would only complicate the transition between the two units (i.e., Matthew 24:14-25 and 24:29-31). Thus, Mark 13:24-27 is parallel to Matthew 24:29-31 and Luke 21:25-27 and, assuming the Two Gospel Hypothesis, dependent thereupon.

At Mark 13:24, Mark has made a major compositional change in the use of source tradition. Mark omits the Matthean εὐθέως ("immediately") of Matthew 24:29, and he omits the Lukan reference to signs (21:25). The net impact of these omissions is very telling. After the terrible events of the Horrible Desecration will come the Son of Man. It is during this time in history before the coming of the Son of Man that the Gospel of Mark is written. There is no sign between the final crisis and the coming of the Son of Man. But Mark is wary about stating the exact time of the coming of the Son of Man. The Fall of Jerusalem has come and gone. It was contemporaneous with the time of horrors. Mark anticipates this interlude between the Horrible Desecration and coming of the Son of Man will not be long; but he does not know the precise length of time. Thus, Mark omits εὐθέως from Matthew.

Compositionally, in the construction of 13:24, Mark develops another duality or synonymous expression through the use of the demonstrative pronoun ("that") ἐκεῖνος (13:24) in a double statement.[58] Thus the composition of Mark 13:24a is a matter of the linguistic style of the author rather than a deliberate editorial

---

[58]Neirynck, *Duality in Mark*, 95.

melding together of earlier sources.[59] Mark is simply stressing that after the final crisis will come the Son of Man.

Then, in 13:24b-25, Mark follows Matthew closely in the description of the cosmic events of the end. In 13:25a, Mark takes ἔσονται ("will be") from the text of Luke (21:25a) and appears to conflate it with a form of πίπτειν ("to fall") from Matthew 24:29b to describe the falling of the stars. This conclusion is consonant with the view that Mark was blending the two source traditions.

Several omissions from the source tradition are significant (cf. Matthew 24:30a and Luke 25b-26a). A lack of concurrent source tradition seems to be a major factor; but it is most likely that Mark omits Matthew 24:30a because it has a reference to the sign of the Son of Man. Mark is not interested in signs in the heavens at all. The same holds true for Mark's use of Luke with respect to the reference to signs in Luke 21:25.[60]

The description of the coming of the Son of Man in Mark 13:27 follows the Matthean source closely. An omission from the earlier apocalyptic source tradition of the detail we found behind 1 Thessalonians 4:16, on the trumpet sound (1 Thess 4:16 ‖ Matt 24:31), and a slight variation of the Matthean source tradition on the cosmological description of the end can be seen as compositional preferences. Theologically, Mark has affirmed that although the distress of the cosmos will herald the coming of the Son of Man, and his enemies (cf. 13:22, 26) will see him, the chief point of his coming is to save the elect. The tribulation was shortened for the sake of the elect (13:20,22). Now he will gather the elect.

But Mark was very careful to delineate that these cosmic happenings set apart the end of time from the penultimate events that were carefully set forth in 13:5-23. The penultimate eschatological events are now in the past. All is ready for the coming of the Son of Man. In this interim period the community must continue to live by faith. The danger is that treachery and attendant dangers will cause them to grow weary and quit (cf. 13:33-37).

---

[59]Contra Beasley-Murray, *Jesus and the Last Days*, 422.

[60]Notice that with Matt 24:31, where there is no parallel material in Luke, Mark (13:27) continues to follow Matthew. Matt 24:31 has no reference to signs. Mark may also have used Matt 24:31 to bring completion to the thought on the events that would ensue with the coming of the Son of Man. Also noteworthy in this unit is a significant minor agreement of Matthew and Luke against Mark. See αἱ ἐν τοῖς οὐρανοῖς in Mk 13:25 for τῶν οὐρανῶν in Matt 24:29 and Lk 21:26. This agreement of Matthew and Luke against Mark is a problem on the view that Matthew and Luke independently copied Mark. Due to the authorial freedom of Mark these minor agreements are readily explained on the Two Gospel Hypothesis.

The Parable of the Fig Tree (Mark 13:28-31)

Matthew 24:32-36	Mark 13:28-31	Luke 21:29-33
³²Ἀπὸ δὲ τῆς συκῆς μάθετε τὴν παραβολήν·	²⁸Ἀπὸ δὲ τῆς συκῆς μάθετε τὴν παραβολήν·	²⁹Καὶ εἶπεν παραβολὴν αὐτοῖς· Ἴδετε τὴν συκῆν καὶ πάντα τὰ δένδρα·
ὅταν ἤδη ὁ κλάδος αὐτῆς γένηται ἁπαλὸς καὶ τὰ φύλλα ἐκφύῃ,	ὅταν ἤδη ὁ κλάδος αὐτῆς ἁπαλὸς γένηται καὶ ἐκφύῃ τὰ φύλλα,	³⁰ὅταν προβάλωσιν ἤδη,
		βλέποντες ἀφ' ἑαυτῶν
γινώσκετε ὅτι ἐγγὺς τὸ θέρος· ³³οὕτως καὶ ὑμεῖς, ὅταν ἴδητε πάντα ταῦτα	γινώσκετε ὅτι ἐγγὺς τὸ θέρος ἐστίν· ²⁹οὕτως καὶ ὑμεῖς, ὅταν ἴδητε ταῦτα γινόμενα,	γινώσκετε ὅτι ἤδη ἐγγὺς τὸ θέρος ἐστίν· οὕτως καὶ ὑμεῖς, ³¹ὅταν ἴδητε ταῦτα γινόμενα,
γινώσκετε ὅτι ἐγγύς ἐστιν ἐπὶ θύραις. ³⁴ἀμὴν λέγω ὑμῖν ὅτι οὐ μὴ παρέλθῃ ἡ γενεὰ αὕτη ἕως ἂν πάντα ταῦτα γένηται. ³⁵ὁ οὐρανὸς καὶ ἡ γῆ παρελεύσεται, οἱ δὲ λόγοι μου οὐ μὴ παρέλθωσιν.	γινώσκετε ὅτι ἐγγύς ἐστιν ἐπὶ θύραις. ³⁰ἀμὴν λέγω ὑμῖν ὅτι οὐ μὴ παρέλθῃ ἡ γενεὰ αὕτη μέχρις οὗ πάντα γένηται. ³¹ὁ οὐρανὸς καὶ ἡ γῆ παρελεύσονται, οἱ δὲ λόγοι μου οὐ μὴ παρελεύσονται.	γινώσκετε ὅτι ἐγγύς ἐστιν ἡ βασιλεία τοῦ θεοῦ. ³²ἀμὴν λέγω ὑμῖν ὅτι οὐ μὴ παρέλθῃ ἡ γενεὰ αὕτη ἕως ἂν πάντα γένηται ³³ὁ οὐρανὸς καὶ ἡ γῆ παρελεύσονται, οἱ δὲ λόγοι μου οὐ μὴ παρελεύσονται

Given the clear distinction between the time of the first generation (13:5-23), and the return of the Son of Man (13:24a), Mark now sets forth how these two critical eschatological realities are connected and how the disciples should relate to them. Thus, the Markan Jesus recapitulates with these connections in mind. The recapitulation is arranged compositionally into the last two pericopes of the Discourse (13:28-31, 32-37).

The first pericope features the parable of the fig tree. Earlier, the cursing of the fig tree (11:12-14, 20-25) functioned as a metaphor for the end of the temple and the forfeiture of leadership of the people of God by these authorities. Now, upon the destruction of the temple, the metaphor of the fig tree reemerges to give an eschatological lesson with respect to the certainty of Jesus' predictions for the first generation (13:28-31). In the second pericope, in 13:32-37, the focus shifts to the end of the age. Here, a second set of lessons, again utilizing parabolic language, encourages the disciples to wait patiently for the appearance of the Son of Man.

Compositionally, after the omission of Luke 21:28 (no parallel in Matthew), in 13:28-29, Mark show his preference for the use of cognates by using several cognate verbs in rapid succession.[61] Mark both conflates and uses concurrent testimony from Matthew and Luke to accomplish this purpose.

Matt 24:32 ‖ Mark 13:28	→	γένηται	
		γινόμενα	← Mark 13:29 ‖ Luke 21:31
Matt 24:34 ‖ Mark 13:30	→	γένηται	← Mark 13:30 ‖ Luke 21:32

Again, Mark's compositional activity leaves a significant minor agreement between Matthew and Luke in its wake (ἕως ἄν Matthew 24:34 ‖ Luke 21:32 as opposed to μέχρις οὗ in Mark 13:30).[62]

But what is most significant in this pericope is Mark's subtle theological point about the fig tree. Mark had intercalated the visit of Jesus to the temple (11:15-19) with the cursing and description of the withered fig tree (11:12-14, 20-21). In short, his point was that the leadership of the temple had outlived its usefulness. It had withered and died. Now, again, Mark following the sequence of his source tradition, will again present a lesson learned from a fig tree. Only this time it does not wither and die. Instead it sprouts, develops leaves, and comes to harvest in a predictable cycle of time. The interpretive issue is to ask how Mark understood this similitude.

The whole point of Mark 13:28-29 is to say that just as the season of the fig tree runs its cycle, so the time of horrors will also run its course—within a generation (13:30). In short, for Mark, the predictable cycle of the fig tree is a metaphor for the truth about the unfolding of the prophecies in 13:5-23. Thus the references to "these things" (13:29) and "all these things" (13:30) refers to the inauguration of the Horrible Desecration. The major alternative view that this is a reference to the coming of the Son of Man (13:24-27) is extremely difficult to hold because, by definition, the coming of the Son of Man marks the end of ordinary time, not something to be observed prior to it.

Matthew's version of the parable (24:32-33) featured the budding of the tree as an indicator that the eschatological events narrated throughout the Discourse will culminate quickly in the end of the age. Luke considered that the destruction of Jerusalem was the sign, par excellence, that the time of final redemption was

---

[61]Neirynck, *Duality in Mark*, 80.

[62]Cf. David Peabody, "A Pre-Markan Prophetic Sayings Tradition and the Synoptic Problem," *Journal of Biblical Literature* 97 (1978): 391-409.

near. Mark highlights the similitude on the fig tree to refer to the rapid happening of certain events culminating in the emergence of the Horrible Desecration.

Finally, even though the great crisis is supposed to take place within a generation, a certain ambiguity about the precise timing of the coming of the Son of Man has emerged (cf. 13:33). It is noticeable that Mark does not utilize the Lukan reference to the nearness of the kingdom of God (Luke 21:31), and omits the Lukan ἤδη ("already") of 21:30b.[63]

The Call to Vigilance (Mark 13:32-37)

Matt 24:36; 25:13-15; 24:42-43; 25:5, 12-13	Mark 13:32-37	Luke 21:34-36; 12:37a, 38a, 41, 44
^{24.36}Περὶ δὲ τῆς ἡμέρας ἐκείνης καὶ ὥρας οὐδεὶς οἶδεν, οὐδὲ οἱ ἄγγελοι τῶν οὐρανῶν οὐδὲ ὁ υἱός, εἰ μὴ ὁ πατὴρ μόνος.	³²Περὶ δὲ ἡμέρας ἐκείνης ἢ τῆς ὥρας οὐδεὶς οἶδεν, οὐδὲ οἱ ἄγγελοι ἐν οὐρανῷ οὐδὲ ὁ υἱός, εἰ μὴ ὁ πατήρ. ³³βλέπετε, ἀγρυπνεῖτε· [καὶ προσεύχεσθε]	³⁴Προσέχετε δὲ ἑαυτοῖς μήποτε βαρηθῶσιν ὑμῶν αἱ καρδίαι ἐν κραιπάλῃ καὶ μέθῃ καὶ μερίμναις βιωτικαῖς καὶ ἐπιστῇ ἐφ' ὑμᾶς αἰφνίδιος ἡ ἡμέρα ἐκείνη ³⁵ὡς παγὶς· ἐπεισελεύσεται γὰρ ἐπὶ πάντας τοὺς καθημένους ἐπὶ πρόσωπον πάσης τῆς γῆς. ³⁶ἀγρυπνεῖτε δὲ
^{25.13}Γρηγορεῖτε οὖν, ὅτι οὐκ οἴδατε τὴν ἡμέραν οὐδὲ τὴν ὥραν.	οὐκ οἴδατε γὰρ πότε ὁ καιρός ἐστιν.	ἐν παντὶ καιρῷ δεόμενοι ἵνα κατισχύσητε ἐκφυ- γεῖν ταῦτα πάντα τὰ μέλλοντα γίνεσθαι καὶ σταθῆναι ἔμπροσθεν

---

[63]Of course, on the Two Gospel Hypothesis, this may be another case of the demonstrable feature of this chapter of Mark's preference for Matthean wording. Nevertheless, as one can see that from 13:32-37 there is a certain ambiguity in Mark about the precise time of the end.

[14]Ὥσπερ γὰρ <u>ἄνθρωπος</u> <u>ἀποδημῶν</u>

ἐκάλεσεν

<u>τοὺς</u> ἰδίους <u>δούλους</u> <u>καὶ</u> <u>παρέδωκεν</u> αὐτοῖς τὰ ὑπάρχοντα αὐτοῦ, [15]καὶ ᾧ μὲν ἔδωκεν πέντε τάλαντα, ᾧ δὲ δύο, ᾧ δὲ ἕν, <u>ἑκάστω</u> κατὰ τὴν ἰδίαν δύναμιν, καὶ ἀπεδήμησεν.

[24.42]<u>γρηγορεῖτε οὖν</u> ὅτι <u>οὐκ οἴδατε</u> ποίᾳ ἡμέρα <u>ὁ κύριος</u> ὑμῶν <u>ἔρχεται</u> [43]ἐκεῖνο δὲ γινώσκετε ὅτι εἰ ἤδει ὁ οἰκοδεσπότης ποίᾳ φυλακῇ . . .

[25.5] . . . καὶ <u>ἐκάθευδον</u>.
[25.12]<u>λέγω ὑμῖν</u> οὐκ οἶδα ὑμᾶς.
[25.13]<u>γρηγορεῖτε</u>

---

[34]<u>ὡς ἄνθρωπος</u> <u>ἀπόδημος</u> ἀφεὶς τὴν οἰκίαν αὐτοῦ

<u>καὶ δοὺς</u> <u>τοῖς δούλοις</u> αὐτοῦ

τὴν ἐξουσίαν

<u>ἑκάστω</u> τὸ ἔργον αὐτοῦ καὶ τῷ θυρωρῷ ἐνετείλατο ἵνα γρηγορῇ. [35]<u>γρηγορεῖτε οὖν·</u> <u>οὐκ οἴδατε</u> γὰρ πότε <u>ὁ κύριος</u> τῆς οἰκίας <u>ἔρχεται</u>.

ἢ ὀψὲ ἢ μεσονύκτιον ἢ ἀλεκτοροφωνίας ἢ πρωί, [36]<u>μὴ ἐλθὼν</u> ἐξαίφνης <u>εὕρῃ</u> ὑμᾶς <u>καθεύδοντας</u>. [37]ὅ <u>δὲ ὑμῖν λέγω</u> <u>πᾶσιν</u> λέγω, <u>γρηγορεῖτε</u>.

τοῦ υἱοῦ τοῦ <u>ἀνθρώπου</u>.

[12.37]μαχάριοι οἱ <u>δοῦλοι</u> ἐκεῖνοι,

οὓς <u>ἐλθὼν ὁ κύριος</u> εὑρήσει <u>γρηγοροῦντας·</u>

[38]κἂν ἐν τῇ δευτέρᾳ κἂν ἐν τῇ τρίτῃ φυλακῇ <u>ἔλθῃ</u> καὶ <u>εὕρῃ</u> οὕτως, . . .

[41]Εἶπεν <u>δὲ</u> ὁ Πέτρος, Κύριε, πρὸς <u>ἡμᾶς</u> τὴν παραβολὴν ταύτην <u>λέγεις</u> ἢ καὶ πρὸς <u>πάντας;</u>

[44]ἀληθῶς <u>λέγω ὑμῖν</u> ὅτι ἐπὶ <u>πᾶσιν</u> τοῖς ὑπάρχουσιν αὐτοῦ καταστήσει αὐτόν.

We come now to the final section of Mark's account of the Discourse. Here, the focus clearly shifts to an emphasis on preparations for the coming of the Son of Man. As in other key places in the Gospel (3:7-8; 4:33-35; 6:6; 9:49-50), Mark ends a major unit with a summary. The summary consists primarily of two strong warnings to be vigilant in light of the unexpectedness of the end.

Structurally, the two strong warnings (13:33-34, 35-37) both begin and end with imperatives highlighting the call "to take careful notice" (βλέπετε ἀγρυπνεῖτε = 13:33) and "to be watching always" (γρηγορεῖτε = 13:35, 37) for the coming of the Lord. The warnings are preceded by a transitional logion that sets forth the basis for this advice (13:32). One is always to be ready for the coming of the Son because no one knows the day or the hour when he will arrive. This unknown time of coming contrasts with the Horrible Desecration which definitely takes place in a generation (13:30). Mark uses Matthew 24:36, with few changes, as the major source for this verse.

Another important structural feature for the understanding of the whole of the Discourse is also very noticeable in this unit. The Discourse is preceded by the question of the disciples (13:4). The question is formulated by the construction εἰπὸν ἡμῖν ("say to us"). After Jesus' Discourse the unit finishes with the expansive call to the disciples ὃ δὲ ὑμῖν λέγω, πᾶσιν λέγω ("what I say to you I say to all") in 13:37. The disciples in 13:4 have become transparencies for the whole of the church. As noted earlier, the whole of the Discourse is thus placed within this major inclusio.

Although the structural features of 13:33-37 are readily understandable, the nature of the sources utilized by Mark is another matter. Most exegetes would agree with Tuckett's comment that this pericope is secondary.[64] But secondary to what? This pericope presents some difficulty to those who use the Two Source Theory to explain its compositional history. This is so because, after Matthew and Luke have maintained the Markan order so closely throughout this chapter, pericope after pericope (with the exception of Mark 13:9-13 where they *both* diverged), now again they *both* move away drastically from the text of Mark. On this source theory, this seems very odd—if not inexplicable! This problem for Markan priority is only partially resolved by a very complicated hypothesis about Markan overlaps.[65]

Our position is much more straightforward. On the Two Gospel hypothesis, Mark had before him two source traditions on Jesus' Last Discourse (Lk 21:34-36; Matt 24:36–25:46). These sources diverge widely. Mark, who wished to con-

---

[64]Tuckett, *Greisbach Hypothesis*, 182.

[65]McNicol, "Composition of the Synoptic Eschatological Discourse," 199, has reviewed various explanations given by advocates of the Two Source Theory to explain the composition of Matthew, Mark, and Luke at this point. The most frequent way of explanation is to point to a Mark-Q overlap or the use of parallel material Mark found in his Sondergut. But, even granted the existence of Q and its availibility to Mark, why did Mark consistently omit from Q those passages where Q is supposed to be the source of Matthew 24 and Luke 17 and 12 (see n. 21, above) and then utilize Q piecemeal in 13:37 for "The Parable of the Doorkeeper" which is not in Matthew or Luke? For a response to our earlier analysis of this unit in McNicol, "Composition of the Synoptic Eschatological Discourse," 197-200, see Tuckett, "Response to the Two Gospel Hypothesis: The Eschatological Discourse," in *The Interrelations of the Gospels*, BETL 95, ed. David L. Dungan (Leuven: Leuven University Press and Peeters; Macon GA: Mercer University Press, 1990) 75-76; and F. Neirynck, "Response to the Two Gospel Hypothesis: Note on the Eschatological Discourse," ibid., 77-80; and G. Beasley-Murray, *Jesus and the Last Days*, 232-33.

tinue to stress communal readiness for the coming of Christ, and also was preparing to make a transition into the Passion narrative, now was ready for closure.
As in other units of his composition (cf. 4:21-25; 9:49-50), Mark implemented
closure through a brief summary. In perfect consistency with his compositional
procedure he did the same thing in this unit.

Before we give an analysis of how Mark gave an abbreviated summary,
there is one other very important piece of evidence to take into consideration.
Examination of our synopsis appears to indicate that Mark echoes the wording,
not only of Luke 21:34-36, and Matthew 24-25, but perhaps also of certain phraseology found in Luke 12:37-44. Is this a rare case where Mark reaches back
into Luke's Travel Narrative and incorporates material therefrom into his summary? Or, is it the case that Mark had independent access to certain source material that we have shown was probably utilized variously by Paul (1Thess 5:3) and
Luke (21:34-36; cf. 12:37-44) in their respective compositions? As we trace the
Markan compositional activity we will argue that it is probably the former.

Compositionally, Mark 13:32-37 represents a classic case of the Markan zigzag pattern within pericopes.[66] Mark was following closely Matthew 24:36 to
form 13:32. There he stated the basis for preparing for the unexpected coming
of the final hour.

At this point, Mark gives attention to the source material available in this
area. Two sources stand out: (1) Matthew 24:42–25:46; (2) Luke 21:34-36 and
very similar thematic material to Luke 21:34-36 found in Luke 12:37-44.

First, Mark turns to the Lukan source and uses the Lukan watchwords. Since
προσέχετε ("give heed") in Luke 21:34, was the original watchword in his
Lukan source, Mark redacts with the use of his characteristic βλέπετε ("take
heed") in 13:33. Mark then takes ἀγρυπνεῖτε ("watch") directly from his
Lukan source (Luke 21:36). The additional reference on the call to pray, if the
text can be substantiated, could also well have been taken from δεόμενοι in
Luke 21:36.[67] This forms Mark 13:33a. Mark now is ready to make a transition
back to the Matthean source material.

As part of this process of composition, Mark appears to have blended
καίρῳ ("in season") in Luke 21:36[68] with the repeated wording of Matthew
24:42 and 25:13 οὐκ οἴδατε ("you do not know") to form Mark 13:33b. Mark
may have been interested in the wording of Matthew 25:13 because it marks the

---

[66]T. R. W. Longstaff, *Evidence of Conflation in Mark? A study in the Synoptic
Problem*, SBLDS 28 (Missoula MT: Scholars Press, 1977) 128-201.

[67]There is good textual support from most of the major text types for the longer
reading καὶ προσεύχεσθε in Mk 13:33. We favor its inclusion in the basic Greek text.

[68]Note also that ἐν καιρῷ also appears in Matt 24:45. Thus we have another case
of Mark's use of the concurrent testimony of Matthew and Luke.

transition between the two great parables of Matthew 25 on watching (25:1-13, 14-30) and thus evokes considerable reinforcement to his theme of "watching" with a reader who was familiar with Matthew. Having made the transition from following Luke to Matthew, Mark then completes the first warning of watching by paraphrasing Matthew 25:14-15a to form 13:34. Thus, this verse (13:34) is not an echo of a fragmentary parable (often called the Parable of the Doorkeeper) drawn from source tradition, but Markan composition. It is carefully phrased in light of the Passion narrative.

The only significant wording in 13:34, which is not easily explainable, is the phrase καὶ τῷ θυρωρῷ ἐνετείλατο ("and he ordered his doorkeeper"). As most commentators note, this is odd because the plural reference to servants earlier in the verse has now shifted focus to the singular "doorkeeper" in the latter part of the verse. What has precipitated this change? Perhaps, Mark has moved to the singular because, for him, the reference to the charge to the doorkeeper is an anticipation of the conduct of Jesus in the Passion narrative.[69] He will keep his commitment. More likely, the doorkeeper represents the ideal disciple who will remain faithful through the coming hour of trial (cf. 13:9-13). On the other hand, the reference to the servants (13:34a) could then be a transparency of the Twelve for later church leaders—indeed many in the church in Mark's time were listless because of persecution and apostasy (cf. 13:35, 37). We know that in the end, both at Gethsemane and upon his arrest, the disciples abandoned Jesus;[70] but Jesus—the faithful one—remained steady under the most terrible duress and thus sets the model for future discipleship. Mark's readers are being urged to exert a similar kind of endurance to that shown by Jesus before and during his trial as they await the coming of the Lord.

This brings us to the second and final warning of 13:35-37. Here again Mark makes an interesting zigzag which incorporates a similar literary pattern to that found in 13:33-34. Mark starts out in 13:35 by utilizing Matthew 24:42. This is the same verse that Mark echoed in commencing the First Warning in 13:33b. Mark had used Matthew 24:36 earlier in the composition (Mk 13:32). In sequence, there is no parallel to Matthew 24:37-41 in Luke 21. So, Mark omits because there is not concurrent testimony and because he is creating a summary. This takes Mark to Matthew 24:42 which opens with the watchword γρηγορεῖτε οὖν ("therefore watch"). Mark utilizes this phraseology as the opening part

---

[69]Geddert, *Watchwords*, 99-100.

[70]Note the threefold call to watch (Mk 13:34, 35, 37) in this pericope and its analogue (14:34, 37, 38) in Gethsemane. This has been noted by Geddert, ibid. Geddert acknowledges his indebtedness to the earlier work of R. H. Lightfoot, *The Gospel Message of St. Mark* (Oxford: Clarendon Press, 1950) 48-59, who saw a number of connections between Mark 13 and the Passion narrative. In our view these could be developed further.

of 13:35. This brings us to a very important literary move made by Mark. Earlier in this chapter, in discussing the composition of Mark 13:9-13, we observed that, on our hypothesis, there were linguistic indicators that led us to conclude that Mark may have been aware of Luke's pattern of composition when Luke moved back to the Mission Discourse and utilized Matthew 10:17-22 for the composition of Luke 21:12-19. Now at this point, a similar phenomenon seems to have occurred. On the Two Gospel Hypothesis Luke utilized special material on "slaves waiting for the coming of the master" for the composition of Luke 12:36-37a, and "on girding the loins" for the composition of Luke 12:35a and 37b-38.[71] Luke also appears to have utilized some eschatological terminology on a similar theme drawn from Matthew's version of the Eschatological Discourse (Matt 25:1-13) in the composition of Luke 12:35-38.[72] And Luke clearly used Matthew 24:43-44 for the composition of Luke 12:39-40. Mark, working in the same unit of Matthew, observes these compositional moves by Luke and moves back to Luke 12:37-44 (especially 12:37-38) where Mark finds material on the watches of the night. This rather radical transition to Luke 12:37-38 serves Markan compositional concerns. Mark 13:35b refers to the fourfold watch. Mark is preparing the way for his account of the four segments of the coming night that precedes the Passion.[73] The change from the reference to the three-part watch in Luke to the four-part watch in Mark is generally considered as an accomodation to the Markan proclivity to state customs in Roman terms. But since it also functions as an anticipation of the night before the Passion, Mark's redaction of Luke 12:37f. is understandable. Jesus would move faithfully through the four watches of the Passion night and not quit in his committment to God. The first disciples were less successful. The reader of Mark is exhorted to make his or her choice about discipleship.

Finally, Mark composes 13:36-37. The Markan ἐξαίφνη ("unexpectedly") in 13:36 probably reflects the Lukan source (cf. αἰφνιδιός ["sudden"] in Luke 21:34). In the same verse the reference to ὑμᾶς καθευδόντας ("you sleeping") is possibly an allusion to the Matthean parable of the virgins (Matthew 25:5). Again, a major concern of Mark is to prepare for the events of the night of testing. The disciples are being urged to watch and not fall asleep (13:35, 36). Later, in Gethsemene, three times they fail to watch and fall asleep (14:32-42).

---

[71]McNicol, "Composition of the Synoptic Eschatological Discourse," 164.

[72]McNicol, "Composition of the Synoptic Eschatological Discourse," 164; L. Cope et al., "Narrative Outline of the Composition of Luke," SBLSP 33, ed. Eugene H. Lovering, Jr. (Atlanta: Scholars Press, 1994) 544. Note especially the common terminology between Lk 12:35-37 and Matthew 25:1-3 on the subject of "lamps," "marriage feasts," and such terminology as γρηγορεῖν (Matt 25:13 ‖ Lk 12:37) and ἀνοίγειν (Matt 25:11 ‖ Lk 12:36).

[73]Mark 14:17, 41, 42; 15:1; cf. Gaston, *No Stone on Another*, 479.

Thus, Mark ends his account of the Discourse with a great crescendo. The wording of Mark 13:37, perhaps drawing on Luke 12:41, ends the great inclusio starting in Mark 13:4. The disciples' mistaken question about the need for a future sign (13:4) has been clarified. Now the readers of Mark, "I say to all" (πᾶσιν λέγω) unmistakably are addressed in 13:37, as well as the disciples, in 13:32-37. The precise time of the coming is unclear. There is a tendency to be slack in discipleship. One must always be prepared. Given all the difficulties that the church has endured since Jesus left, it would be tragic if believers were not ready for an unexpected appearance of the Lord.

Summary and Conclusion

Mark 13 must be understood within the wider framework of the total message of the second Gospel. On the Two Gospel Hypothesis, Mark was written some years after the Fall of Jerusalem—probably in Rome. It was written to a community that had already experienced persecution and martyrdom (cf. 10:30, 35-45). It had lived through the experience of the idolatrous pretensions of the post-Neronian period. This was the great Crisis that is dramatically set forth in 13:14-23.

For the author of Mark, the disciples were transparencies of the church. In Mark 13:9-13, the disciples were warned about the persecutions they would face in the course of mission. Only those who endured to the end would be saved (13:13). In a time of great treachery and betrayal, they were called to be faithful; in imitation of what happened at Jesus' Passion, when the crisis came suddenly, they were called to keep faith through the watches of the night (13:35). Initially they failed. Likewise, the believers to whom Mark was writing must keep their committments in their time. It appears that, as the disciples, some of their leaders had succumbed to treachery and betrayed Christ. Yet the church must keep watch for the final resolution of all things with the Coming of the Lord (13:35). It should not escape notice that immediately preceding and following the Markan version of the Last Eschatological Discourse were model accounts for discipleship in the narration of how two faithful women showed great faith in the midst of treachery (12:38-44; 14:1-11).

Compositionally, the Discourse itself has been created primarily on the basis of the concurrent testimony shown from the common material of the Matthean and Lukan versions of the Eschatological Discourse (Matthew 24:1-42; Luke 21:5-36). Even when Mark chose to leave Matthew 24–25 and Luke 21, at Mark 13:9-13 and 33-37, Mark mainly uses concurrent verbal or thematic testimony (cf. Matt 10:17-22 || Lk 21:12-19 at Mk 13:9-13; and Lk 21:34-36 and Lk 12:37-44 at Mk 13:33-37).

In Mark 13:4, Jesus was asked by an inner circle of disciples when would the temple be destroyed and what will be the sign with respect to the events of the end? In response, the Markan Jesus does not mention the temple in his reply. Rather, he sketches the coming of a series of eschatological horrors that will occur in the coming generation (13:5-23). The perceptive reader in the post-70 CE era knows that these horrors culminated in the blasphemous actions of Titus during or immediately following the destruction of Jerusalem (13:15 cf. 13:16-23). To those with "eyes to see" and "ears to hear" Jesus had not only answered the question put to him 13:4, but had given an interpretation of how the Kingship of God emerged despite the horrors of the first generation (cf. Mk 9:1).

But after those horrors of the first generation, unexpectedly, at an unknown time, the Son of Man will appear (13:21-26; 32-37). The Markan church was demoralized. It was in danger of forgetting this reality. Thus the Markan church was urged not to be self-absorbed with its own internal difficulties, but to look and see how the Kingdom had already dawned even with persecutions. The Kingdom was present for those who could see, and would come in its entirety at the arrival of the Son of Man.

Epilogue.
The Abiding Value
of Jesus' Last Eschatological Discourse

At the outset we stated that the purpose of this monograph is to give an explanation of how the earliest collections of sayings of Jesus, and interpretations of biblical texts on eschatological matters attributed to him, were used by Paul and the Synoptic writers to construct a coherent theological vision of the future. In the interest of making this a manageable project, we have confined our analysis to the Thessalonian letters (Paul), specifically the connection between material on eschatological concerns echoed there, and the Synoptic Gospel accounts of Jesus' Last Eschatological Discourse. At the end of most chapters of this work we presented certain tentative conclusions. We are now in a position to set forth the entire results in this epilogue.

In the first chapter we argued that, given the present state of our knowledge concerning the transmission of the sayings of Jesus, there are sufficient grounds to assert that, in principle, a number of those sayings in the area of eschatology were taught to Paul and that he in turn transmitted these as part of basic Christian teaching to the mission churches he founded. Textual evidence from the Thessalonian letters, in our view, confirms this hypothesis. Paul presumes the Thessalonians had a knowledge of eschatological teachings that came from Jesus. In his letters, in a number of places, Paul echoed these sayings and drew doctrinal conclusions from them.

As noted in our second chapter, specifically with respect to 1 Thessalonians, Paul did this on several occasions. In 1 Thessalonians 5:2 he echoed the parable of the Thief in the Night while giving parenesis about appropriate conduct for Christians as they await the coming of the Day of the Lord. This parable also appears in Matthew 24:42-43. (The Lukan version [12:39] was probably drawn from Matthew.) Second, in 1 Thessalonians 5:3, Paul uses a tradition of interpretation of Scripture on preparing for the *Sudden Calamity of the End*. Our analysis of Luke 21:34-36 found this same tradition embedded in this text. We gave evidence that Luke utilized a version of this tradition for the composition of Luke 21:34-36. Third, 1 Thessalonians 4:16a appears to be a direct echo of material found in Matthew 24:30b-31. In this case, Paul has taken a saying of Jesus and used it as the basic authority for making a doctrinal statement as to what will happen to believers, both dead and alive, at the coming of the Lord. Thus, there is good evidence from 1 Thessalonians that Paul knew eschatological sayings attributed to Jesus. They may well have been part of a collection; but it is not apparent that these sayings came from a structured collection that is at all analogous to the Last Eschatological Discourse in the synoptic gospels.

The use of Jesus Tradition in 2 Thessalonians 2:1-12 was the subject of chapter 3. There we found considerable evidence that the writer echoed a tradition that was remarkably similar to a source that was determined (chapter 4) to be behind much of Matthew 24:3b-31. The grounds for this conclusion were twofold. First, we identified three strong sets of linguistic parallels (2 Thess 2:1 ‖ Matt 24:3b, 31; 2 Thess 2:2a, 3, (11) ‖ Matt 24:4b, 6b; 2 Thess 3b-4 ‖ Matt 24:11-12, 15) which led us to suggest that Matthew and the author of 2 Thessalonians, most likely, drew upon a common source. Second, the fact that this tradition was marked by a similar specific threefold scenario about the future: (1) perception of a present era of trouble; (2) to be followed by a time of treachery and apostasy culminating in the appearance of the Horrible Desecration in the Temple; and (3) only to be resolved with the parousia of Jesus, could be used as strong confirmatory evidence for the conclusion we drew from the linguistic data. We concluded that the author(s) of 2 Thessalonians and Matthew used this source tradition, partly involving an interpretation of the Horrible Desecration passages in Daniel, for their own theological purposes. For 2 Thessalonians, the fact that the scenario described in the source had not yet taken place provided proof that the Day of the Lord had not come. Likewise, for Matthew, this scenario was to be an integral part of the eschatological occurrences at the end of the age which he expected soon. Although it is very difficult on internal grounds to resolve the issue of the precise authorship of 2 Thessalonians, and circumstances of its composition, we concluded that there was a strong possiblity that both 2 Thessalonians and Matthew were written in the mid to very late 60s of the first century of our era.

Indeed, the source and redaction analysis of Matthew 24–25 in chapter 4 served to confirm this conclusion. For Matthew, the leadership of Israel had been invalidated by a series of withering indictments by Jesus, and this leadership had passed to the disciples (transparencies for leaders in the church). Now, although this new leadership was instrumental in bringing Gentiles into the people of God, *the temple still was operative* and before its impending destruction it would play a role in being the locale of the appearance of the Horrible Desecration—another crucial event at the end of the age.

Associated with this crucial event at the end was the continued proliferation of pseudo-messiahs and false prophets with their claims that great signs and wonders portend the culmination of all things. In contrast to the various figures who claim to have knowledge and signs that the end had come, Matthew uses the same major source as the author of 2 Thessalonians to claim that the only heavenly sign of the end that will be given will be the Son of Man himself—in his parousia. By using this source, which we have designated the *Final Crisis of the Era*, Matthew has made a three-stage scenario of the end (present crisis, appearance of the Horrible Desecration, parousia of Christ) serve as the basic structure of his version of a Discourse on eschatological matters given by Jesus on the Mount of Olives. To fill out the composition of the full body of the Discourse, Matthew adds additional material on *The Coming of the Son of Man* (24:27, 37-39, 44) several parables, some known also to Paul, and Sondergut.

At the heart of the Matthean version of the Discourse is the expectation that upon the appearance of the Horrible Desecration in the temple, immediately thereafter ($\epsilon\dot{\upsilon}\theta\acute{\epsilon}\omega\varsigma$ = Mt 24:29) will come the parousia of the Son and the end of the age. As the Matthean community awaits faithfully for this latter event to come, it must continue the mission to the nations (both Jews and Gentiles); for at the end not only will the Christian community be judged for their level of persistence in mission—but the nations will be called to account before the Son of Man to give an account of how they welcomed this message (25:31-46).

With the composition of Matthew 24–25 the definitive ingredients of mainstream Christian views about the future emerge in narrative form. These views consist of a perception of instability in the present time, the expectation of an unstable future marked by treachery and apostasy, culminating in some great crisis, and the final vindication of the elect in the presence of the Messiah. Such a view has had enormous significance in shaping Christian views of history. Apocalyptic versions of history continue to resurface in one form or another in Christianity because such notions are embedded in a foundational document: the first gospel. The Lukan and Markan versions of the Discourse are only variations on the theme.

For Luke, a central reality for his version of the Discourse was that Jerusalem now lay in ruins. Therefore, the Matthean connection between the Horrible Desecration in the Temple and the coming of the Son of Man immediately (Matt 24:15-29a) needed clarification. Luke provides the clarification by referring the Horrible Desecration to the destruction of Jerusalem (Lk 21:20-26) and by putting this whole event into a history of salvation framework.

Already twice, in 12:35-48 and 17:20-37, Luke had used Matthew 24–25 as a source to give teachings on preparation for the coming of the Son of Man; in Luke 21:5-36 he fits the destruction of Jerusalem into this synthesis. This account of the destruction of the holy city is framed within a distinct unit of 19:28–21:38. There, Luke highlights the coming of Jesus the prophet/king to claim his city and receive his kingship (cf. 19:11-27). The king is rejected (19:39-40). A dialogue between Jesus and various representatives of the leaders of the city, as with Matthew, ends with a rejection of the leadership which is contrasted with those of true piety (20:45–21:4). Then comes the Lukan account of Jesus' Last Eschatological Discourse which, essentially, is a prophetic speech announcing the destruction of the temple/city, presumably for its perfidity. For the composition of his account, Luke has used elements of Matthew 24:3-36, which were not used in the composition of 12:35-48 and 17:20-37. Luke had noticed that Matthew 24:9-14 echoed certain features of Matthew 10:17-22 and thus turns to this source to do the same in the composition of 21:12-19. As noted above, in Luke 21:34-36, Luke appears to have used the same source on the *Sudden Calamity of the End*, as was utilized by Paul in 1 Thess 5:3.

The net result is that the Lukan account of the Last Discourse has a somewhat different focus than that of Matthew. At the very center of the Lukan account, six graphic verses portray the siege and final devastation of the city (21:20-26). Much of the terminology is Lukan composition drawn from the Greek Bible; Jesus is pictured as the fulfillment of the biblical prophetic witness against the sins of the city (cf. 19:41-44; 21:6). To the post-70 CE reader of Luke there was no question that these prophecies had been fulfilled. This was Luke's point. Since the destruction of the holy city vindicated Jesus as prophet, one must now listen to his announcement that, since the end of Jerusalem was the culmination of the eschatological signs (cf. 21:7, 11, 20-26 [especially 25-26]), all things are now in place for the arrival of the kingdom of God (21:28, 31).

The Lukan community is to wait patiently for the coming of the kingdom (21:34-36). That it is coming is already hinted at in the restoration of Israel through the acceptance of the messiahship of Jesus among Jew and Gentile all the way to Rome (Acts 1–28). Given this view of salvation history one should not grow weary because God's purposes will eventually be fulfilled.

Finally, in our last chapter, we turned to an analysis of the Markan account of the Discourse (13:1-37). On our source hypothesis, Mark's account was created primarily from the concurrent testimony drawn from the material common to Matthew and Luke in Matthew 24:1–25:30 and Luke 21:5-36. Exceptions to this rule may be Mark 13:9-13 and 13:33-37. In the former, the principle of the use of concurrent testimony still may be seen as evident—albeit in a more nuanced manner. This is so because Mark had observed that Luke, at 21:12-19, had utilized Matthew 10:17-22 as the basis for his composition. Mark, at 13:9-13, has several parallels (Matt 24:9-14; 10:17-22; Lk 21;12-19; and perhaps even Lk 12:11-12) before him. On the basis of the closest parallel (Matt 10:17-22 ‖ Lk 21:12-19), Mark composes from the concurrent testimony of these two units. And, with respect to the composition of Mark 13:33-37, Mark both abbreviates the endings of Matthew and Luke (Matt 24:42–25:30; Lk 21:34-36), and in a similar compositional procedure to that shown in 13:9-13, having observed that Luke both used terminology drawn from Matthew 25:1-13 in the composition of Luke 12:35-38 and used Matthew 24:43-44 for the composition of Luke 12:39-40, in turn utilizes terminology drawn from Luke 12:37-44 to fill out his composition.

In our estimation, the Gospel of Mark, like that of Luke, was written after the Fall of Jerusalelm—more specifically during the middle to later part of the Flavian period. The venue of composition probably was Rome. Commentators have long noticed that Mark was written to a community that had an experience with persecution (cf. Mk 10:30). The description of the horrors in 13:5b-23 could accurately depict, from the point of view of a believer in the church at Rome post-70 CE, the first generation of the church until the early Flavian period. The community still faces the threat of treachery and betrayal and the tremendous demoralization that followed in the wake of the late Neronian and early Flavian period. Now in a brief interlude before the end, the community waits for the coming of the Son at an unspecified time (cf. Mk. 13:24,32). In the meanwhile it must deal with demoralization by reclaiming its faith that in the gospel the kingship of God has already come for those who have eyes to see and ears to hear.

As the years have gone by since the first century, the specific contexts which produced both the Pauline expressions about the future in Thessalonians and the various versions of the Synoptic Eschatological Discourse have passed into ancient history. Since the conversion of Constantine, Christians in the West have had little to fear about living in a culture where they may face such terrors as the enforcement of emperor worship. Nevertheless, these ancient accounts became part of the canonical scriptures of the church and, particularly in the Markan version, continue to have tremendous impact upon the contemporary church. In a world where Christianity no longer stands in a privileged position these texts may be claimed anew as valuable resources by contemporary theologians for building a Christian doctrine of the future.

By studying the compositional history of the emergence of this Discourse we believe we have detected the essence of its theological vision which constitutes its abiding worth. For, in the time before the return of the Messiah to complete the final act of the drama of the history of salvation, this Discourse projects a very realistic view of reality; in the presence of a rebellious world the people of God must continue to be on guard with respect to the subtle claims and power of contemporary idolatries. Operating from a base of functional atheism, and demanding ultimate allegiance in terms of time and resources, these idolatries pose an ever-present danger. In the face of delay of the coming of the kingdom, and widespread disaffection and treachery, the words of Mark 13:37 continue to ring in the ears of contemporary disciples.

And what I say to you
I say to all:
Watch!

Bibliography

Aejmelaeus, Lars. *Wachen vor dem Ende: Die Traditionsgeschichtlichen Wurzeln von 1. Thess 5:1-11 und Luk 21:34-36.* SFEG 44. Helsinki: Finnische Exegische Gesellschaft, 1985.

Agbanou, V. K. *Le Discours Eschatologique de Matthieu 24–25: Tradition et Rédaction.* Paris: J. Gabalda, 1983.

Aland, Kurt, ed. *Synopsis Quattuor Evangeliorum. Locis parallelis evangeliorum apocryphorum et patrum adhibitis edidit Kurt Aland.* Editio tertia decima et recognita ad textum editionum ²⁶Nestle-Aland et ³Greek New Testament aptata [13th edition revised]. Stuttgart: Deutsche Bibelgesellschaft, 1984.

Allison, Dale. "The Pauline Epistles and the Synoptic Gospels: The Pattern of the Parallels." *New Testament Studies* 28 (1982): 1-32.

Anderson, H. *The Gospel of Mark.* NCB. Greenwood SC: Attic Press, 1976.

Aune, David E. *The New Testament in Its Literary Environment.* LEC 8, ed. Wayne Meeks. Philadelphia: Westminster Press, 1987.

Aus, R. "God's Plan and God's Power: Isaiah 66 and the Restraining Factors of 2 Thess 2:6-7." *Journal of Biblical Literature* 96 (1977): 537-53.

Bacon, Benjamin W. "The 'Five Books' of Matthew against the Jews." *The Expositor* 15 (1918): 56-66.

Barrett, C. K. *A Commentary on the First Epistle to the Corinthians.* HNTC. New York: Harper & Row, 1968.

Bauckham, Richard. *The Climax of Prophecy: Studies on the Book of Revelation.* Edinburgh: T. & T. Clark, 1993.

Bauer, D. *The Structure of Matthew's Gospel: A Study in Literary Design.* JSNTSS 31. Sheffield: Almond Press, 1988.

Beare, Frank. "The Synoptic Apocalypse: Matthean Version." In *Understanding the Sacred Text: Essays in Honor of Morton S. Enslin on the Hebrew and Christian Beginnings.* Ed. John Reumann. Valley Forge: Judson, 1972: 115-34.

Beasley-Murray, G. R. *Jesus and the Future: An Examination of the Criticism of the Eschatological Discourse, Mark 13, with Special Reference to the Little Apocalypse Theory.* London: Macmillan, 1954.

_____. "Second Thoughts on the Composition of Mark 13," *New Testament Studies* 29 (1983): 414-20.

_____. *Jesus and the Kingdom of God.* Grand Rapids: Eerdmans, 1986.

_____. "The Vision on the Mount: The Eschatological Discourse of Mark 13," *Ex Auditu* 6 (1990): 39-52.

_____. *Jesus and the Last Days: The Interpretation of the Olivet Discourse.* Peabody MA: Hendrickson, 1993.

Best, E. *A Commentary on the First and Second Epistles to the Thessalonians.* HNTC. New York: Harper & Row, 1972.

Betz, O. "Jesus' Gospel of the Kingdom." In *The Gospel and the Gospels*, ed. P. Stuhlmacher, 53-74. Grand Rapids: Eerdmans, 1991.

Boers, H. "The Form-Critical Study of Paul's Letters: 1 Thessalonians as a Case Study." *New Testament Studies* 22 (1976): 140-58.

Boismard, M.-É. "Résponse aux deux autres hypothèses." In *The Interrelations of the Gospels*, BETL 95, ed. David L. Dungan, 259-88. Leuven: Leuven University Press/Peeters; Macon GA: Mercer University Press, 1990.

_____, and A. Lamouille. *Synopsis Graeca Quattuor Evangeliorum*. Leuven: Peeters, 1986.

Brandenburger, E. *Markus 13 und die Apokalyptik*. FRLANT 134. Göttingen: Vandenhoeck und Ruprecht, 1984.

Brandon, S. G. F. *Jesus and the Zealots: A Study of the Political Factor in Primitive Christianity*. New York: Charles Scribner's Sons, 1967.

_____. *The Trial of Jesus of Nazareth*. Repr. New York: Stein & Day. 1979 = 1968.

Brown, S. "The Matthean Apocalypse." *Journal for the Study of the New Testament* 4 (1979): 2-27.

Bruce, F. F. *Tradition Old and New*. Grand Rapids: Zondervan, 1970.

_____. *1 and 2 Corinthians*. NCB. Greenwood SC: Attic Press, 1976.

_____. *1 and 2 Thessalonians*. WBC 45. Waco TX: Word Books, 1982.

Burkitt, F. "The Use of Mark in the Gospel according to Luke." In *The Beginnings of Christianity*, part 1, vol. 2, ed. F. J. Foakes Jackson and Kirsopp Lake, 106-20. London: Macmillan, 1922.

Burnett, Fred W. *The Testament of Jesus-Sophia: A Redaction-Critical Study of the Eschatological Discourse in Matthew*. Lanham MD: University Press of America, 1981.

Burridge, Richard A. *What Are the Gospels? A Comparison with Graeco-Roman Biography*. Cambridge: Cambridge University Press, 1992.

Chance, J. B. *Jerusalem, The Temple, and the New Age in Luke-Acts*. Macon GA: Mercer University Press; Leuven: Peeters, 1988.

Collins, R. *Studies on the First Letter to the Thessalonians*. BETL 66. Leuven: Leuven University Press/Peeters, 1984.

Collison, F. J. G. "Linguistic Usages in the Gospel of Luke." Diss., Southern Methodist University, 1977 (Ann Arbor MI: University Microfilms, on demand).

Cope, O. Lamar. "Matthew XXV:31-46 'The Sheep and the Goats' Reinterpreted." *Novum Testamentum* 11 (1969) 32-44.

_____ et al. "Narrative Outline of the Composition of Luke," SBLSP 33, ed. Eugene H. Lovering, Jr., 516-73. Atlanta: Scholars Press, 1994.

Dahl, N. *Jesus in the Memory of the Early Church*. Minneapolis: Augsburg Publishing House, 1976.

Davies, W. D. "Reflection on a Scandanavian Approach to the Gospel Tradition." In *Neotestamentica et Patristica: Eine Freundesgabe Oscar Cullmann*, ed. W. C. Van Unnik, 14-34. Leiden: Brill, 1962.

Dibelius, M. *From Tradition to Gospel*. Trans. B. L. Woolf. New York: Charles Scribner's Sons, 1935.

Dihle, A. *Studies zur griechischen Biographie*. Göttingen: Vandenhoeck und Ruprecht, 1956.

Dodd, C. H. "Matthew and Paul." *Expository Times* 58 (1946–1947): 293-98.

_____. *The Apostolic Preaching and its Developments: Three Lectures with an Appendix on Eschatology and History*. Repr. New York: Harper & Bros., 1964; =1936.

_____. *More New Testament Studies*. Grand Rapids: Eerdmans, 1968.

Donaldson, T. *Jesus on the Mountain: A Study in Matthean Theology*. JSNTSS 8. Sheffield: JSOT Press, 1985.

Doyle, B. Rod. "Matthew's Intention as Discerned by His Structure." *Revue Biblique* 95 (1988) 34-54.

Donfried, K. "The Cult of Thessalonica and the Thessalonian Correspondence." *New Testament Studies* 31 (1985): 336-56.

_____. "2 Thessalonians and the Church of Thessalonica." In *Origins and Method towards a New Understanding of Judaism and Christianity: Essays in Honour of J. C. Hurd*, JSNTSS 86, ed. B. H. McLean, 128-44. Sheffield: JSOT Press, 1993.

Dungan, D. L. *The Sayings of Jesus in the Churches of Paul: The Use of the Synoptic Tradition in the Regulation of Early Church Life*. Philadelphia: Fortress Press, 1971.

_____. "Two-Gospel Hypothesis." In *Anchor Bible Dictionary*, ed. D. N. Freedman et al., 6:671-79. New York: Doubleday, 1992.

Dunn, J. D. G. "The Relationship Between Paul and Jerusalem according to Galatians 1 and 2." *New Testament Studies* 28 (1982): 461-78.

Dupont, J. *Les Trois Apocalypses Synoptiques Marc 13; Matthieu 24–25; Luc 21*. Lectio Divina 121. Paris: Cerf, 1985.

Ellis, E. E. "The Silenced Wives of Corinth (1 Cor 14:34-35)." In *New Testament Textual Criticism, Its Significance for Exegesis. Essays in Honour of Bruce M. Metzger*, ed. E. J. Epp and G. D. Fee, 213-20. Oxford: Clarendon Press, 1981.

Farmer, W. R. *The Synoptic Problem: A Critical Analysis*. Corr. repr. Dillsboro NC: Western North Carolina Press; Macon GA: Mercer University Press, 1976.

_____. *Jesus and the Gospel: Tradition, Scripture, and Canon*. Philadelphia: Fortress Press, 1982.

_____. "Peter and Paul and the Tradition Concerning the Lord's Supper in 1 Cor 11:23-26." *Criswell Theological Review* 2/1 (1987): 119-40. This essay appears in a revised form as "Peter and Paul, and the Tradition concerning 'The Lord's Supper,' in 1 Cor 11:23-26." In *One Loaf, One Cup: Ecumenical Studies of 1 Cor 11 and Other Eucharistic Texts*, NGS 6, ed. Ben F. Meyer, 35-55. Macon GA: Mercer University Press; Leuven: Peeters, 1993.

Fitzmyer, Joseph A. *The Gospel according to Luke (X–XXIV). Introduction, Translation, and Notes*. AB 28A. Garden City, New York: Doubleday, 1985.

France, R. T. *The Gospel according to Matthew*. Grand Rapids: Eerdmans, 1985.

Furnish, V. P. "The Jesus-Paul Debate: From Baur to Bultmann." *Bulletin of the John Rylands Library* 47 (1965): 342-81.

Gaston, L. *No Stone on Another: Studies in the Significance of the Fall of Jerusalem in the Synoptic Gospels*. NovTSup 23. Leiden: Brill, 1970.

Geddert, T. *Watchwords: Mark 13 in Markan Eschatology*. JSNTSS 26. Sheffield: JSOT Press, 1989.

Gerhardsson, B. *Memory and Manuscript: Oral Tradition and Written Transmission in Rabbinic Judaism and Early Christianity*. ASNU 22. Lund: C. W. K. Gleerup, 1961.

_____. *Tradition and Transmission in Early Christianity*. CN 20 Lund: C. W. K. Gleerup, 1964.

_____. *The Origins of the Gospel Tradition*. Philadelphia: Fortress Press, 1979.

_____. "The Gospel Tradition." In *The Interrelations of the Gospels*, BETL 95, ed. D. Dungan, 497-545. Leuven: Leuven University Press/Peeters; Macon GA: Mercer University Press, 1990.

Geiger, R. *Die Lukanische Endzeitreden: Studien zur Eschatologie des Lukas-Evangeliums*. Bern: Herbert Lang, 1973.

Giblin, C. H. *The Threat to Faith: An Exegetical and Theological Re-Examination of 2 Thessalonians 2*. An Bib 31. Rome: Pontifical Biblical Institute, 1967.

_____. "2 Thessalonians 2 Re-Read as Pseudepigraphal: A Revised Reaffirmation of the Threat to Faith." In *The Thessalonian Correspondence*, BETL 87, ed. R. F. Collins, 459-69. Leuven: Leuven University Press/Peeters, 1990.

Gnilka, J. *Das Evangelium nach Markus, 8:27–16:20*. EKKNT 2. Zürich: Neukirchen-Vluyn, 1979.

Goulder, M. *Midrash and Lection in Matthew*. London: SPCK, 1974.

———. *Luke: A New Paradigm*. 2 vols. JSNTSS 20. Sheffield: JSOT Press, 1989.

Grayston, K. "The Study of Mark XIII." *Bulletin of the John Rylands Library* 56 (1974): 371-87.

Guelich, R. *Mark 1–8:26*. WBC 342. Dallas: Word Books, 1989.

———. "The Gospel Genre." In *The Gospel and the Gospels*, ed. P. Stuhlmacher, 173-210. Grand Rapids: Eerdmans, 1991.

Gundry, R. "The Hellenization of Dominical Tradition and Christianization of Jewish Tradition in the Eschatology of 1–2 Thessalonians." *New Testament Studies* 33 (1987): 161-78.

Hahn, F. "Die Rede von der Parusie des Menschensohnes Markus 13." In *Jesus und der Menschensohn für A. Vögtle*, 240-60. Freiburg: Herder, 1975.

Hartman, L. *Prophecy Interpreted: The Formation of Some Jewish Apocalyptic Texts and of the Eschatological Discourse, Mark 13 Par*. Con BNT 1. Lund: C. W. K. Gleerup, 1979.

———. "The Eschatology of 2 Thessalonians as included in a Communication." In *The Thessalonian Correspondence*, BETL 87, ed. R. F. Collins, 470-85. Leuven: Leuven University Press/Peeters, 1990.

Hawkins, J. C. *Horae Synopticae: Contributions to the Study of the Synoptic Problem*. Second edition, revised and supplemented. Oxford: Clarendon Press, 1909.

Hengel, M. *Studies in the Gospel of Mark*. Trans. John Bowden. Philadelphia: Fortress Press, 1985.

Hofius, O. "Gal 1:18: ἱστορῆσαι Κηφᾶν." *Zeitschrift für die neutestamentliche Wissenschaft* 78 (1984): 73-85.

———. "Unknown Sayings of Jesus." In *The Gospel and the Gospels*, ed. P. Stuhlmacher, 336-60. Grand Rapids: Eerdmans, 1991.

Holland, G. S. *The Tradition That You Received from Us: 2 Thessalonians in the Pauline Tradition*. HUT 24. Tübingen: J. C. B. Mohr (Siebeck), 1988.

Holtz, T. *Der Erste Brief an die Thessalonicher*. EKKNT 13. Zürich: Neukirchen-Vluyn, 1986.

Hooker, M. "Trial and Tribulation in Mark XIII." *Bulletin of the John Rylands Library* 65 (1982): 78-99.

Jeremias, J. *Unknown Sayings of Jesus*. London: SPCK, 1958.

———. *The Parables of Jesus*. Second revised edition. Trans. S. H. Hooke. Repr. New York: Scribner's Sons, 1972; ET 1955; orig. ²1952.

———. *Jesus' Promise to the Nations*. Trans. S. H. Hooke. Repr. Philadelphia: Fortress Press, 1982 =1958; orig. 1956.

Jervell, J. *Luke and the People of God: A New Look at Luke-Acts*. Minneapolis: Augsburg, 1972.

Jewett, R. *The Thessalonian Correspondence: Pauline Rhetoric and Millenarian Piety*. Philadelphia: Fortress Press, 1986.

Johanson, B. *To All the Brethren: A Text Linguistic and Rhetorical Approach to 1 Thessalonians*. ConBNT 16. Stockholm: Almquist and Wiksell International, 1987.

Kingsbury, J. *Matthew: Structure, Christology, Kingdom*. Philadelphia: Fortress Press, 1975.

———. "The Figure of Jesus in Matthew's Story: A Literary-Critical Probe." *Journal for the Study of the New Testament* 21 (1984): 3-36.

_____. "The Figure of Jesus in Matthew's Story: A Rejoinder to David Hill." *Journal for the Study of the New Testament* 25 (1985): 61-81

Kittel, G., and G. Friedrich, et al., eds. *Theological Dictionary of the New Testament*. Ten volumes. Trans. and ed. G. W. Bromiley. Grand Rapids: Eerdmans, 1963–1976; orig. 1933–1976.

Kline, M. "The Old Testament Origins of the Gospel Genre." *Westminster Theological Journal* 38 (1975): 1-27.

Kloppenborg, J. S. "Didache 16,6-8 and Special Matthaean Tradition." *Zeitschrift für die neutestamentliche Wissenschaft* 70 (1979): 54-67.

_____. *The Foundation of Q: Trajectories in Ancient Wisdom Collections*. Philadelphia: Fortress Press, 1987.

Koester, H. "1 Thessalonians—Experiment in Christian Writing." In *Continuity and Discontinuity in Church History: Essays presented to G. H. Williams*, SHT 19, ed. F. F. Church and T. George. Leiden: Brill, 1979.

_____. "From Paul's Eschatology to the Apocalyptic Schemata of 2 Thessalonians." In *The Thessalonian Correspondence*, BETL 87, ed. R. F. Collins, 441-58. Leuven: Leuven University Press, 1990.

Lambrecht, J. "Die Logia—Quellen von Markus 13." *Biblica* 47 (1966): 321-60.

_____. *Die Redaktion der Markus-Apokalypse: Literarische Analyse und Strukturuntersuchung*. An Bib 28. Rome: Papstliche Bibelinstitut, 1967.

_____. "The Parousia Discourse: Composition and Content in Matthew, XXIV–XXV." In *L'Évangile selon Matthieu: Rédaction et Theologie*, BETL 29, ed. M. Didier, 309-41. Gembloux: Ducolot, 1972.

Lightfoot, R. H. *The Gospel Message of St. Mark*. Oxford: Clarendon Press, 1950.

Lindars, Barnabas. *New Testament Apologetic: The Doctrinal Significance of the Old Testament Quotations*. London: SCM Press, 1961.

Lohr, C. H. "Oral Techniques in the Gospel of Matthew." *Catholic Biblical Quarterly* 23 (1961): 403-35.

Longstaff, T. R. W. *Evidence of Conflation in Mark? A Study in the Synoptic Problem*. SBLDS 28. Missoula MT: Scholars Press, 1977.

Lövestam, E. *Spiritual Wakefulness in the New Testament*. Lund: C. W. K. Gleerup, 1963.

Lüdemann, G. *Paul Apostle to the Gentiles: Studies in Chronology*. Trans. F. S. Jones. Philadelphia: Fortress Press, 1984.

Luz, U. *Matthew 1–7. A Commentary*. Trans. W. C. Linss (*Das Evangelium nach Mattäus, 1. Teilband, Mt 1–7*). EKKNT. Minneapolis: Augsburg/Fortress, 1989.

Maddox, R. *The Purpose of Luke-Acts: Studies of the New Testament and its World*. Ed. John Riches. Edinburgh: T. & T. Clark, 1982.

Malherbe, A. "'Gentle as a Nurse': The Cynic Background to 1 Thess 2." *Novum Testamentum* 12 (1970): 203-17.

_____. "Exhortation in First Thessalonians." *Novum Testamentum* 25 (1983): 238-56.

_____. *Paul and the Thessalonians, The Philosophic Tradition of Pastoral Care*. Philadelphia: Fortress Press, 1987.

Mann, C. S. *Mark. A New Translation with Introduction and Commentary*. AB 27. Garden City NY: Doubleday, 1986.

Manson, T. W. *The Sayings of Jesus as Recorded in the Gospels according to St. Matthew and St. Luke Arranged with Introduction and Commentary*. Repr. of part 2 of *The Mission and Message of Jesus* (1937). London: SCM Press, 1971.

Marshall, I. H. *The Gospel of Luke. A Commentary on the Greek Text*. NIGTC. Grand Rapids: Eerdmans, 1978.

_____. *1 and 2 Thessalonians*. NCB. Grand Rapids: Eerdmans, 1983.

Marxsen, W. *Mark the Evangelist: Studies on the Redaction History of the Gospel.* Trans. James Boyce et al., with Roy Harrisville. Nashville: Abingdon Press, 1969.

Mattill, A. J., Jr. *Luke and the Last Things: A Perspective for the Understanding of Lukan Thought.* Dillsboro NC: Western North Carolina Press; Macon GA: Mercer University Press, 1979.

Meier, John P. *The Vision of Matthew: Christ, Church, and Morality in the First Gospel.* New York: Paulist, 1978.

Metzger, Burce M., ed. *A Textual Commentary on the Greek New Testament. A Companion Volume to the United Bible Societies' Greek New Testament (third edition).* London/New York: United Bible Societies, 1971.

McNicol, A. J. "The Lesson of the Fig Tree in Mark 13:28-31." *Restoration Quarterly* 27 (1984): 193-207.

_____. "Discipleship as Mission: A Missing Dimension in Contemporary Discussion on Matt 28:18-20." *Christian Studies* 10 (1989): 27-47.

_____ et al. "The Two Gospel Hypothesis Textual Discussion: The Composition of the Synoptic Eschatological Discourse." In *The Interrelations of the Gospels*, BETL 95, ed. David L. Dungan, 157-200. Leuven: Leuven University Press/Peeters; Macon GA: Mercer University Press, 1990.

Momigliano, A. *The Development of Greek Biography.* Cambridge: Harvard University Press, 1971.

Moule, C. F. D. *An Idiom Book of New Testament Greek.* Second edition. Cambridge: Cambrige University Press, 1959.

Munck, J. *Paul and the Salvation of Mankind.* Richmond: John Knox Press, 1959.

Neirynck, F. "Le Discours Anti-Apocalyptique de Mc. XIII." *Ephemerides Theologicae lovanienses* 45 (1969): 154-64.

_____. *Duality in Mark: Contributions to the Study of Markan Redaction.* BETL 31. Leuven: Leuven University Press, 1972.

_____. "Marc 13. Examen Critique de l' interprétation de R. Pesch." In *Evangelica. Gospel Studies: Collected Essays*, BETL 60, ed. F. Van Segbroeck, 565-97. Leuven: Leuven University Press/Peeters, 1982.

_____. "Paul and the Sayings of Jesus." In *L'Apôtre Paul. Personnalité, style et conception du ministère*, BETL 73, ed. A. Vanhoye, 265-321. Leuven: Leuven University Press/Peeters, 1986.

_____. "Response to the Multiple-Stage Hypothesis: The Eschatological Discourse" and "Note on the Eschatological Discourse." In *The Interrelations of the Gospels*, BETL 95, ed. David L. Dungan, 108-24 and 77-80. Leuven: Leuven University Press/Peeters; Macon GA: Mercer University Press, 1990.

Orchard, J. Bernard. "Thessalonians and the Synoptic Gospels." *Biblica* 19 (1938): 19-42.

_____, and Harold Riley. *The Order of the Synoptics: Why Three Synoptic Gospels?* Macon GA: Mercer University Press; Leuven: Peeters, 1987.

Peabody, David. "A Pro-Markan Prophetic Sayings Tradition and the Synoptic Problem." *Journal of Biblical Literature* 97 (1978): 391-409.

_____. *Mark as Composer.* NGS 1. Macon GA: Mercer University Press, 1987.

Pesch, R. *Naherwartungen: Tradition und Redaktion in Mk 13.* Düsseldorf: Patmos, 1968.

_____. "Markus 13." In *L'Apocalypse johannique et l'apocalyptique dans le Nouveau Testament*, BETL 53, ed. J. Lambrecht, 355-68. Leuven: Leuven University Press, 1980.

Plevnik, J. "I Thess 5, 1-11: Its Authenticity, Intention, and Message." *Biblica* 60 (1979): 71-90.

Reicke, B. "Synoptic Prophecies on The Destruction of Jerusalem." In *Studies in New Testament and Early Christian Literature. Essays in Honour of Allen P. Wikgren*, NovTSup 33, ed. D. E. Aune, 121-34. Leiden: Brill, 1972.

_____. "A Test of Synoptic Relationships—Matthew 10:17-23 and 24:9-14 with Parallels." In *New Synoptic Studies: The Cambridge Gospel Conference and Beyond.* ed. W. R. Farmer, 209-29. Macon, Georgia: Mercer University Press, 1983.

Riesenfeld, H. *The Gospel Tradition: Essays.* Philadelphia: Fortress Press, 1970.

Riesner R. "Der Ursprung der Jesus-Überlieferung." *Theologische Zeitschrift* 38 (1982): 493-513.

_____. *Jesus als Lehrer: Eine Untersuchung zum Ursprung der Evangelien-Überlieferung.* WUNT 2/7. Tübingen: J. C. B. Mohr (Siebeck), 1984.

Rigaux, B. *Saint Paul: Les E;pitres aux Thessaloniciens.* Paris: Gabalda, 1956.

Robinson, J. A. T. *Jesus and His Coming.* Philadelphia: Westminster, 1979.

Rolland, P. "From the Genesis to the End of the World: The Plan of Matthew's Gospel." *Biblical Theology Bulletin* 2 (1972): 155-76.

Sanders, E. P. *The Tendencies of the Synoptic Tradition.* SNTMS 9. London: Cambridge University Press, 1969.

_____. *Paul, the Law, and the Jewish People.* Philadelphia: Fortress Press, 1989.

Schippers, R. "The Pre-Synoptic Tradition in 1 Thessalonians II 13-16." *Novum Testamentum* 8 (1966): 223-34.

Schubert, P. "The Structure and Significnace of Luke 24." In *Neutestamentliche Studien für Rudolf Bultmann*, BZNW 21, ed. W. Eltester. Berlin: Alfred Töpelmann, 1954.

_____. "The Final Cycle of Speeches in the Book of Acts." *Journal of Biblical Literature* 87 (1968): 1-16.

Schürmann, H. *Traditionsgeschichtliche Untersuchungen zu den Synoptischen Evangelien.* Düsseldorf: Patmos, 1968.

Shuler, P. *A Genre for the Gospels: The Biographical Character of Matthew.* Philadelphia: Fortress Press, 1982.

_____. "The Genre of the Gospels and the Two Gospel Hypothesis." In *Jesus, the Gospels, and the Church. Essays in Honor of William R. Farmer*, ed. E. P. Sanders, 69-88. Macon GA: Mercer University Press, 1987.

_____. "The Genre(s) of the Gospels." In *The Interrelations of the Gospels*, BETL 95, ed. David L. Dungan, 459-83. Leuven: Leuven University Press/Peeters; Macon GA: Mercer University Press, 1990.

Sterling, G. E. *Historiography and Self-Definition: Josephas, Luke-Acts and Apologetic Historiography.* NovTSup 64. Leiden: Brill, 1992.

Streeter, B. H. *The Four Gospels. A Study in Origins, Treating of the Manuscript Tradition, Sources, Authorship, and Dates.* London: MacMillan, ¹1924.

Stuhlmacher, P. "The Theme: The Gospel and the Gospels." In *The Gospel and the Gospels*, ed. P. Stuhlmacher, 1-25. ET Grand Rapids: Eerdmans, 1991; orig. 1983.

Such, W. A. "The Significance of TO SEMEION in Mark 13:4." *Irish Biblical Studies* 13:134-54.

Swanson, Reuben J. *The Horizontal Line Synopsis of the Gospels. Greek Edition.* Volume 1. *The Gospel of Matthew.* Dillsboro NC: Western North Carolina Press; Macon GA: Mercer University Press, 1982.

Talbert, C. H. *Literary Patterns, Theological Themes and the Genre of Luke-Acts.* SBLMS 20. Missoula MT: Scholars Press, 1974.

_____. *What Is a Gospel? The Genre of the Canonical Gospels.* Philadelphia: Fortress Press, 1977; repr. ROSE 9, Macon GA: Mercer University Press, 1985.

_____. *Reading Luke: A Literary and Theological Commentary on the Third Gospel.* New York: Crossroad Publishing Company, 1982.

_____. "Seminar on Gospel Genre: Introduction." In *A Colloquy on New Testament Studies: A Time for Reappraisal and Fresh Approaches*, ed. Bruce Corley, 197-202. Macon GA: Mercer University Press, 1983.

_____. "Ancient Biography," *Anchor Bible Dictionary*, ed. D. N. Freedman et al., 1:745-49. New York: Doubleday, 1992.

Taylor, J. "'The Love of Many Will Grow Cold': Matt 24:9-13 and the Neronian Persecution." *Revue Biblique* 96 (1989): 352-57.

Taylor, V. "A Cry From the Siege: A Suggestion Regarding a Non-Marcan Oracle Embedded in Lk 21:20-36." *Journal of Theological Studies* 26 (1925): 136-44.

_____. *Behind the Third Gospel: A Study of the Proto-Luke Hypothesis.* Oxford: Clarendon Press, 1926.

_____. *The Gospel according to St. Mark: The Greek Text With Introduction, Notes, and Indexes.* London: Macmillan, 1966.

Tannehill, R. *Dying and Rising with Christ: A Study in Pauline Theology.* BZNW 32. Berlin: Alfred Töpelmann, 1967.

Telford, W. R. *The Barren Temple and the Withered Fig Tree: A Redaction-Critical Analysis of the Cursing of the Fig Tree Pericope in Mark's Gospel and Its Relation to the Cleansing of the Temple Tradition.* JSNTSS 1. Sheffield: JSOT Press, 1980.

Tevis, D. G. "An Analysis of Words and Phrases Characteristic of the Gospel of Matthew." Diss., 1983. (Ann Arbor MI: University Microfilms, on demand.)

Tiede, D. *Prophecy and History in Luke-Acts.* Philadelphia: Fortress Press, 1980.

Theissen, G. *The Gospels in Context: Social and Political History in the Synoptic Tradition.* Trans. Linda M. Maloney. Minneapolis: Fortress Press, 1991.

Thompson, W. G. "A Historical Perspective on the Gospel of Matthew." *Journal of Biblical Literature* 93 (1974): 243-62.

Trilling, W. *Untersuchungen zum zweiten Thessalonicherbrief.* ETS 27. Leipzig: Benno, 1972.

_____. *Der zweite Brief an die Thessalonischer.* EKKNT 14. Zürich: Neukirchen, Benziger, 1980.

_____. "Literarische Paulusimitation im 2. Thessalonicherbrief." In *Paulus in den neutestamentlichen Spätschriften: Zur Paulusrezeption im Neuen Testament*, ed. K. Kertledge, 146-56. Freiburg: Herder, 1981.

Tuckett, C. M. *The Revival of the Griesbach Hypothesis: An Analysis and Appraisal.* SNTSMS 44. Cambridge: Cambridge University Press, 1983.

_____. "Synoptic Tradition in the Didache." In *The New Testament in Early Christianity*, BETL 86, ed. J.-M. Sevrin, 197-230. Leuven University Press/Peeters, 1989.

_____. "Response to the Two-Gospel Hypothesis." In *The Interelations of the Gospels*, BETL 95, ed. David L. Dungan, 47-76. Leuven: Leuven University Press/Peeters; Macon GA: Mercer University Press, 1990.

_____. "Synoptic Tradition in 1 Thessalonians?" In *The Thessalonian Correspondence*, BETL 87, ed. R. F. Collins, 160-82. Leuven: Leuven University Press/Peeters, 1990.

Tyson, Joseph B. "Source Criticism of the Gospel of Luke." In *Perspectives on Luke-Acts*, Special Studies series no. 5, ed. Charles Talbert, 24-39. Danville VA: Association of Baptist Professors of Religion; Edinburgh: T. & T. Clark, 1978.

_____. *The Death of Jesus in Luke-Acts.* Columbia: University of South Carolina Press, 1986.

Vielhauer P. *Geschichte der urchristliche Literatur.* Berlin: W. de Gruyter, 1978.

Walter, N. "Tempelstörung und Synoptische Apokalypse." *Zeitschrift für die Neutestamentliche Wissenschaft* 57 (1966): 38-49.

Wanamaker, C. A. *The Epistles to the Thessalonians: A Commentary on the Greek Text.* NIGTC. Grand Rapids: Eerdmans, 1990.

Wenham, D. "Recent Study of Mark 13." *TSF Bulletin* 71 (1975): 6-15; and 72 (1975): 1-9.

_____. "A Note on Matthew 24:10-12." *Tyndale Bulletin* 31 (1980): 155-62.

_____. "Paul and the Synoptic Apocalypse." In *Gospel Perspectives: Studies of History and Tradition in the Four Gospels*, ed. R. T. France and D. Wenham, 2:345-75. Sheffield: JSOT Press, 1981.

_____. "'This generation will not pass . . .': A Study of Jesus' Future Expectation in Mark 13." In *Christ the Lord: Studies in Christology Presented to Donald Guthrie*, ed. H. H. Rowdon. Leicester: IVP, 1982:

_____. *The Rediscovery of Jesus' Eschatological Discourse.* Volume 4 of *Gospel Perspectives.* Sheffield: JSOT Press, 1984.

_____. *Paul: Follower of Jesus or Founder of Christianity?* Grand Rapids: Eerdmans, 1995.

Wright, A. G. "The Widow's Mites: Praise or Lament?—A Matter of Context." *Catholic Biblical Quarterly* 44 (1982): 256-65.

Wright, N. T. *The Climax of the Covenant: Christ and the Law in Pauline Theology.* Minneapolis: Fortress Press, 1991.

_____. *Christian Origins and the Question of God.* Volume 1. *The New Testament and the People of God.* Minneapolis: Fortress Press, 1992.

Zmijewski, J. *Die Eschatologiereden des Lukas-Evangeliums: Eine Traditions- und Redaktionsgeschichtliche Untersuchung zu Lk 21, 5-36 und Lk 17, 20-34.* BBB 40. Bonn: Peter Hanstein, 1972.

Indexes

Author Index

Selected Scripture and Early Christian Literature
(Major textual discussions are in **bold** type.)

Old Testament

New Testament

15 . . . . 51, 52, 53, 60, 62, 80,
  101, 102, 104, 105, 107, 135,
  137, 173, 176, 177
15-16 . . . . 91, 137
15-20 128
15-21 91
15-22 . . . . . **100-103**, 107, 136
15-25 174
16 . . . . 138, 139
16-20 . . . . 102, 178
17-18 . . . . 138, 179
19-22 137
20 179
21 . . . . 78, 91, 103, 105, 141
21-22 . . . . 103, 114
21-24 . . . 76, 77, 79, 80, 89, 113
21-25 . . . . 160, 179
22 . . . . 78, 105, 141
23 104
23-24 92
23-28 . . . . **103-104**
24 . . . 4, 50, 61, 78, 104, 106, 141
24-26 55
25 104
26 . . . . 51, 104
26-27 141
26-28 . . . . 160, 181
27 . . . . . 4, 63, 76, 84, 85, 86, 87,
  88, 89, 104, 106, 113, 195
27-28 93
28 . . . . 85, 141
29 . . . . 78, 91, 92, 101, 131, 137,
  141, 144, 181, 195
29-31 . . . . 54, 67, 76, 77, 79, 80,
  89, 103, 104, **105-107**, 108, 113,
  142, 180, 181
30 . . . . . . 79, 81, 87, 92, 93, 105,
  148, 160, 166
30-31 . . . . 4, 29, 31, 34, 35, 36,
  37, 43, 54, 63, 67, 93, 141
31 . . . . . 4, 35, 49, 62, 78, 81, 83,
  106, 160, 182
32 184
32-33 . . . . 83, 144, 184
32-34 100
32-36 . . . . . . **107-109**, 143, 183
33 . . . . 74, 108
34 . . . . . 73, 74, 75, 90, 103, 105,
  108, 145, 184
34-35 145

35 108
36 . . . . 22, 75, 93, 108, 110,
  145, 160, 185
36-51 5
36-25:13 22
36-25:46 187
37 . . . . 22, 76, 84, 86, 88,
  89, 92, 111
37-38 . . . . 63, 108
37-39 . . . . . 85, 87, 88, 113, 195
37-41 . . . . 93, 110, 160
37-25:30 . . . . **109-11**
37-25:46 73
38 86
38-39 . . . . 76, 84, 86, 88, 89
39 . . . . 22, 63, 92
40 112
40-41 88
42 . . . . . . 22, 108, 110, 113, 145,
  147, 188, 189
42-43 . . . . 4, 19, 20, 23, 37, 42,
  43, 67, 85, 88, 89, 185, 193
42-44 . . . . 21, 22
43 . . . . 22, 23, 108
43-51 160
44 . . . . 19, 22, 76, 84, 85, 86, 88,
  89, 108, 110, 113, 195
45 . . . . 108, 112, 147, 188
45-51 . . . . . . 22, 28, 42, 89, 110
46-47 114
47 90
49 . . . . 28, 42, 89
50 . . . . 22, 108
50-51 88
51 110
25:1-13 . . . . 110, 189
5 . . . . 42, 185
10 . . . . 110, 114
10-12 88
12-13 185
13 . . . . 22, 108, 188
13-15 185
14 111
14-30 189
19 79
28-30 88
30 . . . . 110, 111
31-32 94
31-46 . . . . 95, **111-12**, 195
32 . . . . 100, 112

216   *Jesus' Directions for the Future*

Early Christian Literature

Titles in the New Gospel Studies Series

1. David Barrett Peabody, *Mark as Composer* (1987)
2. Dennis Gordon Tevis, *Matthew as Composer* (forthcoming)
3. Franklyn J. G. Collison, *Luke as Composer* (forthcoming)
4. Thomas R. W. Longstaff and Page A. Thomas, eds., *The Synoptic Problem. A Bibliography, 1716–1988* (1988)
5/1 5/2 5/3. Édouard Massaux, *The Influence of the Gospel of Saint Matthew on Christian Literature before Saint Irenaeus* (1991, 1992, 1994)
6. Ben F. Meyer, ed., *One Loaf, One Cup. Ecumenical Studies of 1 Cor 11 and Other Eucharistic Texts* (1993)
7. David J. Neville, *Arguments from Order in Synoptic Source Criticism. A History and Critique* (1994)
8. Hajo Uden Meijboom, *A History and Critique of the Origin of the Marcan Hypothesis, 1835–1866. A Contemporary Report Rediscovered* (1993)
9. Allan J. McNicol, *Jesus' Directions for the Future. A Source and Redaction-History Study* (1996)

Related Titles from Mercer University Press

Hans-Herbert Stoldt, *History and Criticism of the Marcan Hypothesis*, trans. and ed. Donald L. Niewyk (1980)

William R. Farmer, ed., *New Synoptic Studies. The Cambridge Gospel Conference and Beyond* (1983)

Bruce C. Corley, ed., *Colloquy on New Testament Studies. A Time for Reappraisal and Fresh Approaches* (1983)

Bernard Orchard, *A Synopsis of the Four Gospels in a New Translation* (1982)

Bernard Orchard, *A Synopsis of the Four Gospels in Greek* (1983)

Bernard Orchard and Harold Riley, *The Order of the Synoptics. Why Three Synoptic Gospels?* (1987)

Ed Parish Sanders, ed., *Jesus, the Gospels, and the Church* (1987)

Harold Riley, *The Making of Mark. An Exploration* (1989)

David L. Dungan, ed., *The Interrelations of the Gospels. A Symposium* (1990)

Harold Riley, *The First Gospel* (1992)

Harold Riley, *Preface to Luke* (1993)

(d) William R. Farmer, *The Synoptic Problem. A Critical Analysis* (Corrected reprint: Western North Carolina, 1976)

(d) William O. Walker, Jr., ed., *The Relationships among the Gospels. An Interdisciplinary Dialogue* (Trinity, 1978)

(d) = distributed by Mercer University Press

Jesus' Directions for the Future:
A Source and Redaction-History Study.
  New Gospel Studies 9 (NGS-9) by Allan J. McNicol

Mercer University Press, Macon GA 31210-3960.
Isbn 0-86554-497-2. Catalog and warehouse pick number MUP/H390.
Text, interior, and cover designed, and camera-ready pages and cover
  composed by Edd Rowell on a Gateway 2000
    via WordPerfect wp/5.1 and wpwin/5.1/5.2/6.0
    and printed on a LaserMaster 1000.
Text font: TimesNewRomanPS 10/12, 10/11, and 9/10.
  Heads: TimesNewRomanPS bf 14/14. Titles: TimesNewRomanPS bf.
Printed and bound by Braun-Brumfield, Inc., Ann Arbor MI 48106.
  Printed via offset lithography on 50# Natural Smooth, 500ppi.
  Smyth sewn and cased into Arrestox C 11400 (gray) cloth,
    2 stamps on front (black panel plus foil), foil stamping on spine and c. 4,
      over standard binder's boards, with headbands and matching endleaves.
                                                              [November 1996]